P9-DDW-585

A Plain CHART of the
CASPIAN SEA,
According to the Observations of Cap.t John Elton,
Author of Elton's Quadrant &c.
Thomas Woodroofe Master of the British Ship,
Empress of Russia,
Who Navigated this SEA three Years,
Presented to Mr. Jonas Hanway of
S.t Petersburgh in 1745,
by his most Obedient Servant,
Thomas Woodroofe.

N.B. This Chart mentions the frequented
Places only, and such as are of Use
to Navigators.

Publish'd according to Act of Parliament Jan.y 1.st 1753.

J. Gibson sculp.t

The Taste of Dreams

Also by Vanora Bennett

Crying Wolf: The Return of War to Chechnya

Vanora Bennett

The Taste of Dreams

An Obsession with Russia and Caviar

review

Copyright © 2003 Vanora Bennett

The right of Vanora Bennett to be identified as the Author of
the Work has been asserted by her in accordance with
the Copyright, Designs and Patents Act 1988.

First published in 2003
by REVIEW
An imprint of Headline Book Publishing

1 3 5 7 9 10 8 6 4 2

All rights reserved. No part of this publication may be reproduced,
stored in a retrieval system, or transmitted, in any form or by any means
without the prior written permission of the publisher, nor be otherwise
circulated in any form of binding or cover other than that in which
it is published and without a similar condition being imposed
on the subsequent purchaser.

Every reasonable effort has been made to trace and contact the
copyright owner of all materials in this book. The author and publisher
will be glad to rectify or correct any omissions or mistakes on notification.

Cataloguing in Publication Data is available from the British Library

ISBN 0 7553 0063 7

Typeset in Fournier MT by Avon DataSet Ltd,
Bidford-on-Avon, Warwickshire

Printed and bound in Great Britain by
Mackays of Chatham PLC, Chatham, Kent

Designed by Peter Ward

HEADLINE BOOK PUBLISHING
A division of Hodder Headline Ltd
338 Euston Road
London NW1 3BH

www.reviewbooks.co.uk
www.hodderheadline.com

In memory of Larissa Deville

Contents

ACKNOWLEDGEMENTS

Many thanks to Philippe Baliakine, Michael Binyon, David Blundell, Clem Cecil, Mia Foster, Valery Karpov, Natasha Karpova, my mother Rhuna Martin and other heroic readers of early drafts. Especially heartfelt thanks to Chris McWatters, my endlessly patient husband, who not only made all the right suggestions for improving manuscripts but also, by performing a series of quiet domestic miracles, somehow made more writing time appear.

Among those whose encouragement helped to begin this book are David Goodhart, Ian Jack and Tif Loehnis. Among those who inspired me to finish it are Olya and Kolya in Moscow, whose infinite kindness kept me supplied with a variety of things Russian from bootleg computer programmes to occasional tastes of caviar; and of course my wonderful editor in London, Geraldine Cooke.

CHAPTER ONE

Dreams

Lumpfish is just as good as caviar, my mother said. It was part of her birthday ritual for me: a dawn feast among sprays of roses in the garden behind our shabby and beautiful house, sparkling wine with peaches, diet crispbread, sour cream and imitation caviar. Delicious, my mother laughed in the doubtful July sunlight. Absolutely delicious, who needs the real thing?

I loved the little whiff of hedonism about that modest English ceremony. And, of course, I wanted to taste the real thing.

Caviar meant Russia to me, and Russia meant escape.

The Soviet Union still existed then, and people still talked in hushed voices and capital letters about the Evil Empire and Propaganda and the Camps.

But what I first knew of Russia came from fairy stories.

Baba Yaga the witch had iron teeth and breakfasted off little girls in a hut that hopped around on a giant chicken's foot. Little Stupid outwitted her two ugly sisters with the silver saucer and transparent apple that her merchant father brought her back from the fair. She set the apple spinning, and as she looked at the little glass mist it became, she saw the Tsar, the little father – God bless him! – sitting on his high throne. Ships sailed on the seas, their white sails swelling in the wind. There was Moscow with its white stone walls and painted churches. Why, there were the market at Nizhny Novgorod, and the Arab merchants with their camels, and the Chinese with their blue trousers and bamboo staves. And then there was the great River Volga, with men on the banks towing ships against the current. Yes, and she saw a sturgeon asleep in a deep pool. And the little pretty one went on staring into the glass whirlpool, and seeing all the world she had never seen before, floating there before her, brighter than leaves in the sunlight . . .

The fairy stories went with the émigrés from Eastern Europe who used to come to our London house when I was a small child.

They weren't all Russian, exactly. There was a Czech count, and a Polish nurse, and a Hungarian conman with a number one cut who kept changing his name to dodge the taxman. Most of the émigrés were musicians like my parents. They dropped in for five minutes, with a corked bottle or strange raisin cakes, and stayed for days. You could hear them laughing through the closed music-room door, popping another cork and cackling as the party really got going, tooting on the flute or piccolo.

My father played the flute for them, and he also played them the scratchy 78s he bought in junk shops on the wind-up gramophones he bought in junk shops. He played gypsy laments, the gopak, the sounds of the shtetl, and sentimental café music performed by infant prodigies who'd survived Cossack bloodlettings. I wanted to play it myself so much I even tried to learn the violin. The music felt as Russian to me as the battered Chagall print over the piano (a man in a tweed jacket playing the flute, a naked woman and a goat in the treetops, all dancing with happiness). It was what I hummed while the émigrés told their

Peter-and-the-Wolf stories: full of menacing forests and brushes with death, like their own lives, and always with happy endings.

My school taught Russian – émigré-speak – to fourteen-year-olds. I signed up. 'We can't afford it,' my father said grumpily. I gave up the violin so we could.

By then we had moved house, to where my grandmother had lived. The cosy old émigrés had faded away, to be replaced by glitzier, younger flute pupils from America and Japan, and my father's music parties had gone underground.

Our new house was his childhood home. It had a separate basement flat. He'd taken himself, his heaps of sheet music, his collection of gramophones and his flute-mending equipment down there. Now we could only faintly hear the parties, and the laughter, and the flute tunes, through the floorboards.

The new house felt lonely. But it had bookcases full of old Everyman books. Someone who had lived there had liked Russian novels. My mother was reading *Crime and Punishment*. I started on Pushkin, and worked down the shelves.

The stories Russian adults used to tell in the nineteenth century turned out to be all mockery, mistrust and bittersweet endings. Literature's aristocratic anti-heroes wore gloves to the opera, drank champagne called Ai, and ate caviar (at least until they were exiled for fighting duels). They won the love of beautiful women, but they never quite grew up enough to know what to do with it. They played childish, nasty tricks on their admirers instead. Fate and the spurned women usually got the last laugh.

My guide to this second Russia of cads and come-uppances was lovely, absurd Mrs Wilsdon, née Brodianskaya, daughter of Russian refugees turned secondary-school teacher in London.

Her white hair was dyed an energetic chestnut. She had a huge Orthodox cross in perpetual motion on her chest, a jacket of a thousand tiny furs clinging to her torso, little thin legs in trousers twinkling furiously down corridors, and the whiff of a cigarette just half-smoked, half-swallowed in the staff room trailing behind her. She patted and petted and stroked and hugged her pupils; she cooed at them (and at the pet pugs she cosseted at home) in a grand, if grating, English voice full of Russian endearments and diminutives. 'Oh, the *dear* little doggies,' she would cry, and her face would soften as if she was about to weep. 'Oh, you *clever* little girly.'

She talked and talked, and snuffled with puggy laughter. Between her stories, we tussled with the secretive Russian language. We fought hostile curly letters, struggled with gerundives, and limped through texts in which each word was a new battle with a dictionary. Each step forward was a torment. But we persevered; we wanted to be let in on the secret of Mrs Wilsdon's Russian soul.

Mrs Wilsdon's family memories were as sentimental, colourful, and sociable as the fairy stories I remembered. Hearty uncles hunted bears in the forests, hospitable grandmothers forced another plateful of meaty soup on their guests, sly Polish counts cheated at cards, and children picked mushrooms in the forest. That life didn't end happily. It was destroyed by the Russian Revolution in 1917, when her family moved to Paris to escape the Bolsheviks. They had hungry times there, and homeless times, but she also remembered friendships that survived every hardship, and breathless reunions, years later, between family members who'd long ago given each other up for dead.

There was a third Russia that Mrs Wilsdon hated to be reminded of. Her homeland only existed now in books and memories. She didn't want to even think about the parallel-universe country that had existed on its ruins since 1917. She thought of the Soviets as barbarians, grunting and scratching themselves in the ruins of the high civilisation they had destroyed. The Soviet Union happened to have some of Russia's geographical boundaries, but had nothing else in common with it. As far as she was concerned, everything Soviet was vulgar, brutish and wrong, whether it was socialist-realist novels called *Cement* or Solzhenitsyn. The proletarian, slogan-infested Soviet language offended her ear. Her face darkened at the very word 'Soviet'.

At home, upstairs in the kitchen, my mother turned on the radio to mask the sounds of the flute party underfoot, and opened the brown envelopes that were always arriving, and sighed. When there was a Russian music programme, she opened her beautiful eyes very wide and talked about the Soviet Union, where musicians were generously funded by the state and hero-worshipped by everyone else. 'Not that it's a good place, of course,' she'd add, recollecting herself, putting the bills down to concentrate on the dark thought she was thinking. 'They've spent so many years arresting people in the middle of the night – the Two O'Clock Knock, they call it – that life there has become pretty grey and frightening for everyone. We're better off here.'

I quietly added Soviet writing to my reading list, and found another Russia waiting, with gaunt revolutionaries stalking into bright futures, alone, with their coats flapping.

At home, the flute party went on and on in the basement. But upstairs there were only silences lasting days or weeks, or rows about wrongly spent money, wasted time and real or possible lovers.

My mother put a brave face on it, and gave me my lumpfish birthday party.

Meanwhile, like someone preparing for exile, my father took to hiding flute cases and wallets full of money in the attic and at the top of cupboards. We knew they were there. He was always tiptoeing around checking on them. No one said anything. Not saying anything became a survival tactic. It saved time and trouble to know nothing and remember nothing. The house had no central heating. Up in the attic, I turned up the radio to shut out the whiplash voices, wore a big coat all through the winter, and read.

When my parents finally separated, the house went quiet. There were no more flute parties. One November day, my father and a friend brought a van and took away everything he'd need to start a new life with one of the basement flute pupils. Most of the furniture went. The old photos went. The van went, without a forwarding address.

My mother and sister and I stayed meekly behind with the old books no one could be bothered with, and the second-best lamps and sheets, and the silence.

It was unnerving being in the house now it was so empty. I'd never asked my father much about it, and now I couldn't. I tiptoed through the rooms, full of questions now it was too late, feeling as cut off from the past as the Soviet barbarians in the ruins of Mrs Wilsdon's Russia. Who had lived and died in which rooms? Where in the garden had my father buried Jumble, his first dog? Who had been here before his grandmother retired to London and found the house? When the ancient builder remembered affectionately that his first job had been turning our kitchen into a ballet studio for Miss Barbara, I was embarrassed. I had no idea who Miss Barbara could be.

I finished school and sold my violin. I spent all the money at once on tickets to Moscow, Leningrad and the White Russian haunts of Paris. I wanted to get away from the silence, see the many Russias I'd only read about, live dangerously and eat caviar.

CHAPTER TWO

Three Tastes

Caviar comes from the Caspian Sea, situated between the south-east of the old Soviet Union and the north of Iran. There, in the river estuaries, three members of the sturgeon family live and breed.

THE SEVRUGA

with its starred body and long pointed nose measures about 1½ metres in length. Weighing about 3 to 12 kilos and yielding on average 2 kilos of roe, it is caught only in the spring. Its small grey eggs are much prized for their light, sweet taste.

THE OSIETRA

the true sturgeon, with its characteristic short, round nose, is usually about 2 metres in length. Specimens are still found in central and eastern Europe. Like the Beluga, the Osietra is also caught in the spring and autum. It weighs from 13 to 20 kilos, with a yield of 5 kilos of roe. The eggs are large and vary in colour from dark to golden brown, with a strong distinctive taste.

THE BELUGA

largest of the sturgeon family and reaching lengths of up to
4 metres, the Beluga has the greatest lifespan. Cases have been
recorded of them living past a hundred, with body weights
exceeding one ton. It is caught in the spring and autumn and
yields around 10 to 15 kilos in roe. The eggs are large and
fragile and vary in colour from light to dark grey. They
have a nutty taste that is both subtle and delicate.

Menu from Caviar Kaspia *restaurant in London*

'If it were not a pleasure, it would be an imperative duty to
eat caviar . . . It is said that when sturgeon are in season, no
less than two-thirds of the female consists of roe. It is
certainly odd to think of a female weighing perhaps 1,000
lbs being two-thirds made up of eggs . . . At such a rate of
reproduction, the world would soon become the abode of
sturgeons alone, were it not that the roe is exceedingly
good.'

E.S. DALLAS, *Kettner's Book of the Table* (1877)

I had my first taste of real caviar that summer, at the age of
eighteen, on a Russian-language course in the Soviet Union.

It was on sale in a canteen run by a soup dragon of a woman
slopping coffee from an urn into dirty glasses. The hotel was
a concrete brutality by a highway on the edge of Moscow.

There was a heatwave outside, a flypaper on the wall, and buzzing round the windows. In a glass-fronted butcher's cabinet, there were plates of open sandwiches, slices of very white bread topped with slivers of curling cheese, sausage, or caviar.

Everything but the caviar cost a few kopecks. The surly soup dragon never had change, and snapped at any customer who failed to pay her the correct midget coins. But when I bought a red salmon caviar sandwich and a black sturgeon caviar sandwich she was within her rights to give me nothing back from a tiny 10-rouble note. The sandwiches cost £10, an enormous amount of money.

So far Soviet Moscow had been a disappointment: no wolves or chandeliers or sensitive oppressed poets, just a lot of rules and a lot of ugly men in square glasses and nylon suits shepherding us around in coaches. My hotel had been thrown together in a rush for the Moscow Olympics a month before. The waiters looked the types to spit in the food. It took an hour to get to the city centre. The walk to the metro went through baked mud, unused concrete blocks, and forests of giant pipes.

I was still hoping for something more romantic. I blocked out the cabbage smells and our hosts' enthusiasm for American cars, jeans and the Beatles. Instead I communed soulfully with the cobwebby country dachas that smelled of wood and samovar steam, where you could imagine Uncle Vanya grumbling in a corner. I didn't join in when the other students interrogated our guides about the invasion of Afghanistan, making them wince politely and change the subject; I tried to see a great innocence in the dirty summer air and the bare arms of pedestrians. We walked from museum of atheism to museum of atheism, and saw churches. We puffed on murderous *papirosy* cigarettes. We hummed the Radio Moscow jingle, the chorus from a wistful song called 'Moscow suburban evenings'. We ate cucumbers.

Now I'd found caviar, a trace of the real Russia. Full of expectation, I spread out the butter and the tiny spoonful of roe. But there was nothing opulent or luxurious about what I ate. The bread was chewy, the taste greasy and vaguely salt. I didn't finish it.

My next taste of caviar was in Paris, in 1984.

It was Easter, the high feast of the Orthodox religious year. The eight tables in the refectory were groaning with food. There were platters of meat and shot glasses for vodka. There were tall *koulitch* raisin cakes and fat *paskha* cheesecakes, with the letters XB picked out in angelica, standing for the Russian words 'Christ Is Risen'. On the top table, where Sister Natalya was fussily shaking out Father Igor's napkin for him, two jars of caviar waited on white saucers.

Reverently, I slipped in and took my place at one of the tables, among men with stolid faces and long raggedy beards.

Almost a lifetime after the Russian Revolution, I'd somehow fallen into a timeless place where the Russia that might have been still existed. I was living in a mansion near Versailles, a former White Russian boarding school which had been converted into a centre for Russian studies. The priests who ran it took in students for a term at a time, for cash. We had lessons in the morning, and were on our honour to talk Russian at table; White Russians came to dinner. Here, every wrinkled lady walking in the gardens or coming out of the little onion-domed chapel might be a former princess. There were priests on every staircase. The flower-scented air was full of regrets.

The walls were still hung with faded group shots of the little blond émigré boys from Russia who used to come to school here. In those days, as Father Igor and Father Andrei liked to remind us, there had been dozens of Russian-language papers and periodicals, theatres, clubs and schools in Paris. Of the million Russians who fled the Revolution, four hundred thousand had settled here.

Now only one émigré paper still survived. It was printed in an unfamiliar, un-Soviet typeface. The back pages gave the times of funerals at the Russian cathedral.

There were old photos wherever you went in the émigré Russia of Paris.

Among them there was almost always a sepia shot of the Imperial family, who had been killed after the Russian Revolution by a Bolshevik firing squad. The mother, in proud profile, wore a dress stiff with jewels; the dapper father a neat beard and a mulish expression. The children were arranged in front of them: four dark girls in pearls and soft white lace, and a sad-eyed boy in a sailor suit.

The Tsar and his family died like that, arranged in rows, in the middle of a cellar, in the middle of Russia, in the middle of a summer night in 1918. Their executioner had tricked them into believing they were going to be photographed again.

Once he had got them into the cellar, and found chairs for the Tsarina (she had painful sciatica) and the crippled haemophiliac Tsarevich Alexei, Yakob Yurovsky, the chief executioner, spread the eleven prisoners out against the back wall. He told them that there was a rumour going about that they had escaped. The White armies of the civil war were too close for comfort. People in Red Moscow would need to see a photo.

He stood them in two lines. Nicholas was in front, flanked by his wife and son. In the second row, Yurovsky put the daughters behind the Empress, and the servants behind the Tsarevich.

But no photographer appeared. Instead, eleven men with revolvers came in through the double doors. The pretence was over. Yurovsky held up a piece of paper, and read from it: 'In view of the fact that your relatives are continuing their attacks on Soviet Russia, the Ural Executive Committee has decided to execute you.' Nicholas looked at his family and back to Yurovsky. 'What? What?' he said.

Then the shooting began. Afterwards, the bodies were hidden in the forest.

The White army moved into Yekaterinburg and found the remains. It was a temporary advance; they were soon driven back. Even before their final defeat, the Russians still pouring into Paris knew they had no home to go back to now the Tsar was dead. The photos they hung up were their icons of the past. But the White refugees who reached Paris had no time for regrets. They had no money. Many only had stateless person's passports, and no French work permits. They learned to live on their wits.

Only a few made the rest of their lives a monument to nostalgia. Colonel Boris Feodorovitch Dubentseff, the last officer to have been welcomed into his Cossack regiment by the Tsar – and to have the right to be buried in full dress uniform – was one. He was ninety-four, and as wizened as a grasshopper, when I met him in the bleak suburb of Courbevoie where he'd set up a Cossack museum in 1925. He lived surrounded by tokens of the past: the gloves of Catherine the Great, who had founded the

Cossack regiment in 1775, candlesticks, swords and double-headed eagle flags. He got together once a month with the other Cossacks who had fought the losing White fight with him, from the Don river basin to Constantinople and Serbia. They remembered their wounds, toasted the Tsar, and went to each other's funerals.

Most Russians took to their new life as chancers and underdogs with gusto. They set up yoghurt factories. They drove taxis, or worked in restaurants, where they had to watch out for other hard-up Russian aristocrats trying to cadge free meals. As they became established, they set up their own restaurants. There are dozens in Paris even today.

Prince Dmitry Obolensky got jobs as a ship's purser, an instructor at a riding school for Americans, a dealer in rabbit skins in Normandy, a guide to Paris nightlife for Americans, secretary to a 'crazy Scot' who wanted to buy the rivers of Corsica for salmon fishing, and a revolver-toting night watchman outside the Paris Opera. His brother Peter tried his hand at being a night watchman, then a taxi driver.

Old arguments inside White Russian circles didn't fade away as the newcomers learned to live in France. Quarrels from the past were exported to the new country. The French TV star Yves Mourousi remembers how his Russian grandmother always refused to shake hands with his great-uncle, Prince Yusupov. Back in Russia, Yusupov had killed Rasputin, the Tsarina's favourite, a rank-smelling, lustful holy man with hypnotic eyes. Most people were glad to see Rasputin go. Still, the old lady said, 'It isn't done to shake hands with an assassin, even if the man he killed was Rasputin,' and she kept her hands too busy to touch his.

Paris became a hotbed of Russian political plotting. Monarchists, fascists, crooks and the secret societies of the Red enemy all shared the same mean streets. A Russian lunatic called Paul Gorgulov assassinated a French president in 1932, and was guillotined. Also in the 1930s, Soviet agents snatched two White generals off the streets of Paris, in broad daylight, and spirited them away on Russian ships.

George Orwell's greatest friend while he was down and out in Paris was an eternally hopeful White Russian called Boris. When they were both down to their last twenty-eight francs, they heard through the émigré bush telegraph of a possible way to earn some money: by writing articles for a Bolshevik secret society. A hush-hush meeting above a laundry was organised. Passwords were demanded. The surly Russian under the propaganda posters was angry that the newcomers hadn't brought a bundle of laundry – cover in case the police were watching. He wanted twenty francs to let them join his group.

Once these formalities were sorted out, Orwell was engaged to write communist propaganda at 150 francs an article. 'Remember to bring a parcel of washing next time you come,' the cross comrade said in parting. Orwell and Boris were delighted, but the work, and the money, never materialised. Eventually they went back to the secret office (with laundry) – to find it had vanished after the Russian gentleman had got into trouble with the rent.

'And that was the last we ever heard of the secret society,' Orwell said. 'Who or what they really were, nobody knew. Personally I do not think they had anything to do with the Communist Party; I think they were simply swindlers, who preyed upon Russian refugees by extracting entrance fees to an imaginary society. They were clever fellows, and played their part admirably. Their office looked exactly as a secret Communist office should look, and as for that touch about bringing a parcel of washing, it was genius.'

The reality of emigration – the uncertainty, mischief, scams and subterfuges – had been forgotten decades before I went to Paris in 1984. Most of the original émigrés were dead. Their children were going grey. Their blonde grandchildren, at a White Russian ball I went to in the Paris suburbs, couldn't (or wouldn't) speak Russian.

The restaurants kept up their old photos, but their money came from peddling the dream of a lost aristocratic way of life. Only the people at the monastery still lived in a golden haze of nostalgia. Perhaps that was because most people at the monastery weren't actually Russian at all, but foreigners living the same pre-1917 fantasy as I was.

It took me a while to notice, partly because we all spoke Russian together (and my Russian wasn't good enough yet to spot other foreigners' foreign accents), but mostly because I so wanted to believe in the make-believe. But it was impossible to avoid realising forever that the relentless Sister Natalya, who patrolled the student corridors at night making sure we didn't commit any improprieties, also went by the French name of Soeur Nathalie. Father Igor, with his beard and flowing robes, turned out to be German; Father Andrei was Polish.

The men who gave us lessons in the mornings were Russian, but the other, Soviet, kind. The centre was a halfway house for anyone who had fallen out with Moscow.

One teacher was on his way to Israel. Another had been caught printing his soft porn novels on Moscow University equipment and put on a plane to the West. Uncle Kolya, with his big white walrus moustache and his big happy smile, had got out after years in Stalinist camps. The one I liked best was the small, sharp man with a knowing smile, who was killing time with us while he waited for a visa somewhere but never told us where. He smoked tiny roll-ups all through classes, and taught us Soviet school-of-life tricks – how to wash without stopping at the basin when you're late (rub spit in your eyes and run) and how to get over a vodka hangover (beer).

The priests weren't above making money out of their Russian image. As well as taking in students, they charged rich suburban French ladies in the big villas nearby huge fees to learn to paint icons. The classes, and the half-finished icons, and gold leaf, and paintbrushes, were kept in a studio we students couldn't go into. We could only peep through the window at the tormented Byzantine faces the Frenchwomen were copying from glossy French art books, and wonder why they bothered.

I thought the money-spinning schemes were endearing, though, and in the spirit of the entrepreneurial but chaotic émigrés – especially as no one could manage the money that came in. Food supplies ran out long before the end of every month. Meat and cider would give way to cheap tongue in white sauce, little meaty hills sticking out of steaming liquid like shark's fins. That was mid-month. We survived the last few days of every month on plain boiled pasta and tap water.

The Easter feast spread out in front of us now was so lavish that we would almost certainly be living on pasta and water for weeks to come. But everyone had a devil-take-tomorrow look about them. Chairs scraped; bearded faces ducked down a little faster than dignity allowed and tucked in.

The inner circle – the priests, Sister Natalya, and Uncle Kolya – had already feasted through the night. They had held Easter Mass at midnight, with candles, incense, bells and a procession around the church chanting 'Christ is risen'. The ceremony ends with kisses and a drunken breakfast of painted eggs and vodka in the small hours.

I sat next to Uncle Kolya. He looked a bit dishevelled, but he was still cheerfully spearing slices of cold beef and pickles, pies and pasties on to his heaped plate and slurping down vodka.

'There's no point in stinting yourself,' Uncle Kolya said. 'Many Russian things have to be done in threes to be worth anything, and vodka is one of them.' He poured another round and waved his glass about, slurring: 'To the troika!'

One of the young beards was at the table too. He was stocky and Soviet-born (his plastic shoes gave the game away). He had reached France two years before and was researching religion here. Had he learned much French? I asked him. 'No,' he replied scornfully. 'Why? We are not in France here.' And he raised his glass to Uncle Kolya.

Getting into the surreal spirit of the feast now, I lifted my glass to complete the troika. Mr School-of-Life sat down at the last empty seat. He was tiptoeing, and his face was lit up with mischief. There was something in a napkin in his hand.

He sat down, hid the napkin so that no one could see it from the top table, where Sister Natalya was ministering to Father Igor and his guests of honour, and opened it up. There was a big jar of caviar in it. Beard and Uncle Kolya were both staring at it and grinning hugely.

No one said anything. In silence, Mr School-of-Life fished

three teaspoons out of his pocket and gave one to Beard and one to Uncle Kolya. He looked at me, hesitated, smiled, took a small fork from the table for himself and gave me the third spoon.

'Now don't be shy and English about this,' he whispered. 'Just tuck in. But don't say a word.'

We passed the jar round on our laps, covering it with the napkin, hardly daring to breathe as we slipped one black spoonful after another into our mouths and washed them down with vodka. The vodka had gone to my head. I couldn't taste a thing, but I didn't care: it was exhilarating enough just to know that I was eating caviar with real Russian believers at their thousand-year-old Easter feast. We didn't look at the top table, but we couldn't help being aware that one of the white saucers was empty and Sister Natalya was searching for the missing luxury. We could hear the dishes being moved. We could hear her trotting to the kitchen and back. We could feel her suspicious stares raking our backs.

We must have looked guilty. None of us could stop smiling. But perhaps she just thought we were drunk. Afterwards, Uncle Kolya winked and gave me the jar to dispose of.

Sister Natalya never found it. I threw it away, after I'd slept off the lunch, in the municipal bin on my way to the station that evening (there was no telling how thoroughly Sister Natalya might search the wastepaper baskets around the Russian centre).

It was only when I took the jar out of my pocket that I read the label. 'Caviare de lompe,' it said: lumpfish again.

* * *

The caviar I tasted in Leningrad soon afterwards was real. And it was stolen. Eating it was the start of my brief career as a Russian gangster's moll.

It happened like this.

In the dining room of the hotel where my latest language course was being held, I refused whatever wolf or cat or rat meat had been served up for lunch disguised as a rissole. The strangely handsome young waiter wasn't as churlish as most of his Soviet colleagues. He edged closer, smiled enticingly, and asked in a whisper if there was anything else he could get me.

'Caviar?' I said, but I only meant it as a joke. The waiter nodded and disappeared for the rest of the meal. I wasn't surprised; I hadn't expected anything more. But he caught me in the lobby on my way out of the ornate art nouveau dining room.

'Open your bag,' he hissed, and slipped four big flat glass jars into it.

I was completely flummoxed. 'Thank you very much – *ogromnoye spasibo* – thank you,' I spluttered. He vanished.

He intercepted me again after dinner. He had another jar in his pockets. I stammered more thanks. He said something too fast for me to understand. 'What did you say?' I asked.

'When – are – we – going – to – *kiss?*' he asked, looking exasperated, and grabbed me. But I wasn't grateful enough for that. I laughed and ran away, full of heartless power. There was nothing he could do. The doorman was watching him.

'I don't know what to do with it,' I said nervously, making pyramids of the jars.

It was the middle of the night. My roommate and I were looking at the snow. It made our window ghostly white. It was nearly summer at home.

'If I put it in the fridge, the floor maids will find it,' I went on.

'And steal it,' she said.

'But if I hide it in my bag, it might go bad.'

'Or the floor maids will find it . . .'

'And steal it.'

'What if the room's bugged? And They hear us talking about it?'

'They'll send the floor maids to find it . . .'

'And steal it.'

'And eat it all themselves.'

My roommate was laughing. I was already feeling for the bottle opener on my door key, picking up the first jar, working out the best angle to stab the lid from.

'So there's nothing else for it,' I said, feeling brave. 'Let's eat it before They do!'

We only had plastic spoons. We dug in, straight from the jar. It was rich and soft.

After a few mouthfuls we remembered that the boys next door had a bottle of sweet Soviet champagne in their fridge.

I stepped outside, intending to knock very quietly on their door and see if they were still awake and wanted to share.

The floor maid on guard at the end of the corridor gave me a nasty look. 'Girl!' she said. 'It's too late to knock on men's bedroom doors. It's unseemly. Go to sleep.'

I retreated. But after a few more spoonfuls we had the idea of calling the boys on the internal phone, and waking them up even if they were asleep. They tiptoed in with the champagne. They brought two more plastic spoons.

We ate more caviar. We sawed off the champagne bottle's plastic cork with a penknife. We drank it from tooth-mugs. We ate more caviar, and stopped whispering.

There was a hiss from outside the door. 'Girls! Girls!' We pretended not to hear. The footsteps padded off, but came back five minutes later.

'Young People!' the floor maid's voice said, even more crossly. 'I can hear you! You should be asleep! You should be ashamed of yourselves! I'm going to call the Administrator!'

Most of the caviar had gone. I opened the door. It seemed stupid now to be scared.

'Sorry. We'll be very quiet. We're eating caviar. Would you like some?' I said.

Like magic, the bad temper left the floor maid's face. Her eyes widened as she looked at the jar, a bit smeary now, with three spoons standing up in the remaining caviar. My roommate had a lopsided moustache of dark fish eggs and another dollop of them on her finger: she'd got bored of using a spoon and started using her hands.

I could see the floor maid's resolve weakening, and her mouth watering. 'We've even got a spare spoon,' my roommate said, offering hers.

The floor maid made up her mind. She came in, sat down on the bed and set to work on the rest of the jar. The grin on her face got broader every second.

'In life, everything is possible,' she said, indistinctly, scraping the glass clean. The caviar had made her change sides. We were friends for life.

The next morning I hid the other jars of caviar somewhere so safe that my roommate, the boys next door and the floor maid never found them. Feeling bolder that usual, I skipped class, went to a payphone and invited myself to meet some Russians.

I hadn't dared call until now. They were friends of an older friend of mine in London. They were intellectuals. They had drop-out jobs as night watchmen to keep the authorities happy (Soviet citizens had to have jobs). They wanted to marry their way West, so half a dozen of them were instantly available to have lunch with me.

They all brought wives. They were all formally divorced, in case any of them met a Westerner who would marry them and get them a passport, but they were still very much together. Over cucumbers and very neatly sliced sausage and cheese, they explained what they were hoping for, some day. They wanted *fiktivny brak*, a fictitious marriage: a business arrangement involving a ceremony and a few hours of wrestling with bureaucracy, a small kindness by someone with the privilege of a Western passport, which would let one more Russian escape from the bondage of Communism and enter the free world.

It was all couched in very general terms. They weren't pressuring me to promise myself to any of them, exactly; but they were very interested indeed in getting to know as many Westerners as possible, to broaden their chances of getting away. They were so straightforward about what they wanted that I promised to introduce them to the other, older students in my language group. I was only eighteen; I felt privileged to be told about this unfathomable Soviet custom, but safe in the knowledge that I was too young to try it myself.

'I'm sure you'll meet people who'll want to help,' I enthused to the spotty, skeletally thin, fair-haired man who had been deputed by the group to walk me back to the metro. 'I think it would be wonderful to set someone free to live where they want.' Valera nodded equally enthusiastically, and kissed my hand before leaving.

I meant to meet the nice intellectuals again the next day. But the gangsters swaggered into the hotel bar at midnight, and changed everything.

Russians weren't allowed into hotels for foreigners unless they worked in them.

This lot were obviously Russian, and obviously didn't care about rules. The six-foot-tall woman in front, with devil cheekbones and narrow eyes, sauntered straight up to the bar, lit a fag, and blew a contemptuous cloud of smoke over the Finnish drunks passing out next to her over their vodka. The small, curvy, China-doll girl trotting along behind, with long dark curls and tarty Soviet shoes, simpered innocently at the men. Bringing up the rear was a dark man who had made himself look even more like Jean-Paul Belmondo than nature intended by kitting himself out in an expensive Italian leather jacket.

I was in a dark corner with some students. But I stared. He caught my eye. 'Finns,' he explained easily, in English, not bothering with introductions, not bothering with my friends. 'Drunks. Scum. Naturally Tanya hates them. Anyone would.'

'How did you get in past the doorman?' I asked, already most of the way to being in love.

Grisha's reply was enigmatic. 'Never meet stupidity halfway.'

They'd come to the hotel to check out the Westerners. Grisha spoke English, a bit of Italian, a bit of German, and quite a lot of Finnish (the drunken Finns from the country next door were his best customers, and his ex-wife was a hard-currency prostitute with a Finnish protector). He wanted to buy jeans and dollars; in return, he'd sell you anything from a Red Army belt to a wife to a thousand-year-old icon, as long as you made it worth his while.

Word got around in minutes. The pitch-dark bar was a good place to do business unseen. One by one, the students slipped up to try their luck. Dollars changed hands under tables, and dates were made to look at jeans. I stayed and watched. The black marketeers didn't seem to mind. They were on a roll.

Then the official singer came back, and began warbling her extra-sentimental version of 'Moscow Suburban Evenings'. We couldn't hear ourselves whisper any more. 'We could all go to my room,' I found myself saying, sitting next to Grisha, basking in his smile. Between deals, he'd been telling me stories about vodka taxis and bribing policemen. 'I've got jeans you could look at. And I've got caviar we could eat.' In a twinkling of an eye four of us were in my room.

The caviar was out, oompah music was playing on the radio, and vodka had appeared (a present to Grisha from the barman). Incredibly, the floor maid smiled and simpered as we all trooped down the corridor, in contravention of every possible hotel rule. She even said, 'Good evening,' with a reminiscent lick of her lips.

Devil-eyed Tanya had disappeared into the night. But the pretty pouting girl, Natasha, was still with us. She'd moved fast. She was already kissing an English graduate student in a plumber's boiler suit in an armchair.

I was watching Grisha as he lolloped in the other armchair, closer to the doorway, holding court, grinning like a Cheshire cat, looking at the jeans the students were bringing in to sell. They were hoping he'd pay them rouble fortunes for their tired old supermarket rags. But he wrinkled his nose, pinched the cloth, and rejected half of them. 'The English have no style,' he said fastidiously. 'If only you were Italians.'

We ate more caviar. The English graduate student, who was called Andrew, stopped kissing Natasha for long enough to say happily, 'I think I'm in love.'

We ate more caviar. Andrew said, 'I'm definitely in love.' Natasha did more pretty pouting. She didn't understand a word.

We ate more caviar. Andrew said, 'I think I'll marry her. She'd like England.'

'Ah,' said Grisha. 'We'd all like British passports.'

We ate more caviar. I didn't want to sell Grisha my jeans and tapes and Walkman any more. I gave them to him instead, and dreamed he would ask me to take him away to freedom too.

Grisha wasn't thinking about leaving Leningrad that night. But he liked me giving him Western goods as presents. 'Why would you do such a thing?' he said, shovelling my things into a bag before I changed my mind, pushing the caviar my way, shrugging his shoulders cheerfully in time to the music.

'I'll sell them, you know.'

I nodded, too lovesick to say anything back.

He shook his head, but he was smiling as he said, 'You must be the only real Communist in the Soviet Union.'

From then on, I was part of his gang.

* * *

All I'd seen in Leningrad at first was the grime and the cold, the dark alleyways, the slum courtyards, the stray cats and the giant banners reading: 'Leningrad – Hero City! Leningrad – Cradle of the Revolution!' But suddenly I noticed it was beautiful. Our hotel was old and grand, with marble floors and gilt furniture and silk cascading down the twenty-foot-high windows. The city was magical too. It had canals and drawbridges and vistas of Italianate palaces in sparkling pastel colours. Naval cadets with raw cheekbones wandered down Nevsky Prospekt, the shabby main avenue, in ankle-length greatcoats, in Dostoyevsky's footsteps. In April, the ice on the Neva was still breaking up, cracking and heaving and crashing away to the Gulf of Finland.

Other people scurried around, looking at the ground, worried about doing things wrong, worried about getting into trouble. We walked tall. Everything was possible.

We met, secretively, as night fell, in doorways along Nevsky. We ate in a sniggering group in gangster restaurants, in private rooms, where only the right knock on the door and knowing the right doorman and crossing his palm with the right kind of money got you in. The only food was *dikoe*, unspecified sorts of game bird. It was best not to be too nosy about what the brownish corpses were. It didn't matter, anyway. These were the kinds of restaurants where there were four different glasses for the drink but where you stubbed fag ends out in the food. We never paid.

Devil-eyed Tanya taught me to swear in Russian. 'Fuck your mother. Fuck your grandmother. Fuck all your ancestors!' she hissed. Her drunken husband, who was almost always too sodden with vodka to do more than smash empty shot glasses in fireplaces, like a character in a bad film, taught me jokes. 'Who fucks like a bear and winks?' he slurred. 'I don't know, who?' I said, racking my brain. He guffawed. He winked.

Andrew and Natasha were engaged. Natasha had come from the provinces to work in a Leningrad factory for a year. Now she was going to England, she was off sick all the time. She lay around in my room at the hotel all day, having hot baths, making herself up with blue eyeshadow, giggling with the floor maid, and trying on my clothes. Almost every night, she borrowed the only good thing I had left, a tight black velvet dress, to wear out to the gangster dives. 'She wants you to give it to her,' Andrew wheedled. 'It would make her so happy.'

'You've still got some of that caviar, haven't you?' Andrew asked one night. 'Bring it out with you tonight. I'm fed up with *dikoe*.' So we ate caviar again, and behaved dangerously.

We stayed out so late that the drawbridges went up, trapping us on the wrong side of town. Foreigners weren't allowed to stay out all night. The floor maid might report me. Grisha laughed, and took me to his flat.

'Shhh,' he said as we got in the taxi. 'Don't talk. Don't let the driver hear your foreign voice.' His flat was miles out of town, in a rundown concrete prefab housing estate. When we got out of the taxi, we disturbed the crows sleeping in the tree by his doorway. They rose out of the bare branches, flapping and cawing. 'Shhh,' Grisha said again. 'We don't want to wake the caretaker. She is a terrible old woman, always snooping and eavesdropping.'

There was graffiti on the stairs, and a room at the top with a bed and a lot of Italian clothes draped on the doors. There, Grisha made rather perfunctory love to me. 'I am not really interested in sex. Only in happiness,' he said grandly afterwards. 'I want life to be full of fun for me and my friends.' I was stealing glances at his profile. I didn't understand what was happening, but I wanted to make him happy. A wistful look was creeping over his face. 'You think we live like this all the time, with parties every night. But we don't. The truth is that there aren't so many good times.'

Dawn was golden the next morning. Wild and free and self-willed, we went shopping among the palaces while good, stupid people were at work. We laughed at the empty shelves and shoddy goods of this strange economy, in which a lifetime of labour brought so little reward but just a little buying and selling of rare consumer goods from the West made you a rouble millionaire. Grisha bought me presents: a giant green lace bra, and a worker's padded jacket, just for fun. 'What do you want this rubbish for?' he asked, and kissed the top of my head, and took me out to lunch.

He waited until the ice cream (topped with chalky factory meringue, the only pudding in town that month) before getting serious.

'So you are not against fictitious marriages?' he began. He looked nervous.

'No,' I murmured, breathily encouraging, ready for anything.

'I have a friend who needs to leave the country. Will you marry him?' he went on, a bit faster.

I wasn't ready for that. Shock sent chilly tingles through me. I pushed the ice cream away. 'Er . . .' I found myself stammering. 'But don't *you* want to leave the country?'

'I want my friends to be happy. This friend's need is greater than mine. You are my friend too. Please help him.'

'. . .'

'He'd pay for you to come back to Leningrad twice and for all the paperwork.'

'. . .'

'And we could find you a beautiful sable coat.'

'. . .'

'I wouldn't ask unless I knew you were my friend.'

Thoughts were racing through my head: disappointed, crossed-in-love ones, and others. Fear of being laughed at for being naive. Fear of being too young to play the gangster game of life. I didn't want to be a sulking child; I wanted Grisha to think I was cool. I took a deep breath and rose to the challenge.

'OK, I'll do it,' I said. 'What's my fiancé's name?'

Volodya was twenty-eight, a tennis player ('the number ten seed in the Soviet Union,' Grisha said persuasively), and he needed to get to the West to reach the top in tennis. He was blond with a chipmunk face. Because he was a sports star, he was well off and had his own little car. We drove out of town for an awkward lunch in a deserted concrete restaurant for top people. He gave me a photo of himself, looking solemn on a beach in Sochi.

Somewhere in the middle of another chalky-factory-meringue pudding, Volodya lost his businesslike look. He leaned forward, held my hand, and said in English, 'You – like – me.' I interpreted this, correctly and with a sinking heart, as being a translation of the Russian phrase, 'I fancy you.' Our fictitious marriage, allegedly a purely business arrangement, already seemed to be getting out of hand. 'Ve vill meet again later,' he went on, stolidly ignoring my frown. 'Grisha organise party.'

That night was our last night in Leningrad. We were going to go out in style. I got my black velvet dress out of the cupboard. Andrew came in. 'Natasha wants you to give it to her. She looks great in it. Make her happy.' I gave the dress to Natasha, and brushed down my black jacket instead.

Devil-eyed Tanya loped into my room next. 'I want you to give me your jacket,' she said. 'I love it. I'll never see one like it again in the Soviet Union.'

'How about tomorrow, when we fly out?' I said weakly. 'It's all I've got left to wear tonight.'

She stripped off her own top. 'Here,' she said. 'Swap.' It was an order.

Grisha came in last, whistling. 'Bring some of that caviar,' he said. 'You should have dressed up. You're going to the evropeiskaya with your fiancé.' He pocketed a jar.

We dined, at a huge table, in a grand art deco hall. We had more sliced game birds, more vodka, more champagne, more meat dishes and Moscow salad, more dancing, more disrespectful fag ends in the plates. 'You look beautiful,' Volodya said, and squeezed my hand under the table. I took it away.

Grisha took Volodya and me upstairs to deliver two icons to the Western pop group staying on the fourth floor. Volodya and I stood quietly in the half-dark sitting room, looking at the jewelled metal icon covers glowing, while Grisha sorted out the money in the other room. We didn't know what to do, or say. 'Be romantic, fiancés,' Grisha said cheerfully when he came out.

As we left the restaurant, he grinned at Irka, a plump provincial miss up in town for the weekend, with frizzy blonde hair and a scantily clad barrel of a body, who had been drawn to our table. 'Come on, Irka,' he said, 'we're kidnapping you,' and she trotted along behind as we swept out.

The black marketeers' headquarters was somewhere in the middle of town, in a big solemn street off Nevsky Prospekt. Their flat was gloomy and high-ceilinged and full of antiques. A grand piano stood in a corner. Icons hung on the walls. A glass-fronted cabinet held more valuables.

Tanya's husband started throwing glasses into the fireplace before he'd even had a drink. The caviar was brought out. Irka was clearly used only to the little caviar sandwiches served in the grumpy democratic cafeterias where ordinary people went. Her eyes widened at the size of this jar. Everyone tucked in except me. My appetite had gone.

Grisha put on a record of gypsy music. Violins sobbed. Hearts broke. Volodya drew me out to the corridor. He was slurring slightly. 'How many children will we have?' he asked. I smiled awkwardly, shook my head and went back into the room.

'What beautiful music,' I said brightly. Perhaps Grisha noticed something sad in my voice. He took the record from the turntable and gave it to me. 'You have admired it and it is a gift to you,' he said, with over-elaborate courtesy. 'We are not civilised Europeans, you know. We are wild Eurasians, Scythians, Mongols. To us, hospitality is everything. If you say you like something of mine, I am obliged to give it to you.'

Trying even harder to please, he pulled another gift from a cupboard: a malachite egg pendant. 'Tomorrow we will be back on the street, buying jeans from tourists on Nevsky,' he added, and his wistful look was back. 'This is to remember us by, and remember the good times.'

Someone was playing Chopin waltzes on the piano now. Andrew and Natasha were swaying to the music. 'In my opinion, you're really in love with Andrew,' Grisha said. I laughed. He relaxed.

We stayed up all night, till it was time to go to the airport in the morning. Without caviar, time seemed to pass very slowly; I found myself sneaking looks at my watch.

As it got light, Grisha took me to the window and pointed at the tall grey building over the road.

'Look. That window there is the one they watch us from,' he said, melodramatically. 'The KGB. All this is only possible because my father's a bigshot in the KGB. So no one touches us. But they watch, all the same. Of course I must pay the price for our life. I can never leave the country. It would look too bad for my father if I did.' He knew he'd hustled too hard to get me to marry his friend. He was trying to soften the blow now with his story about being unable to leave himself, I thought sourly. But I did recognise it, grudgingly, as quite a kind thought.

We rushed back through the hotel at dawn to pack our bags. Mine was empty except for the green lace bra and worker's jacket. Volodya brought champagne. There were half a dozen people in the room, all making toasts and wild promises and crashing clumsily around, all still high on the night's craziness.

When I unpacked in London, the last jar of caviar, which I'd hidden up the sleeves of the worker's jacket, had gone. Someone must have taken it out while I wasn't looking.

Perhaps it was just as well.

* * *

Once I got back to England, I couldn't think what Russian madness had possessed me. Volodya went on sending me letters with his 'passport makings' so I could apply for the documents we'd need to get married. (So did the emaciated intellectual, Valera, from the group I'd met right at the start, who seemed to feel I had proposed to him.) I'd started university by then. I couldn't imagine what I'd do with a Soviet husband, especially one who didn't understand he was a business arrangement. It was embarrassing. I wrote saying I'd made a mistake.

I never saw Volodya again, though I heard later that he'd married another foreigner and gone to live in Sweden.

I never saw Grisha again either. He died. I found out from an Englishwoman called Mary, who phoned me one day to say she was about to marry him to get him out of the country. (I was too embarrassed to tell her the things he'd said about his father being in the KGB, and it being impossible for him to leave.) She flew to Leningrad for the wedding, but Grisha never met her at the airport. She went to his little flat, with its treeful of crows, in Volodya's car. Grisha was dead on the bed. He was thirty-one.

The cause of death was listed, blandly, as heart failure. Perhaps it was. Possibly he really did have a father in the KGB, who couldn't afford for him to leave the Soviet Union and had him bumped off. What I thought likeliest, though, was that he died of a surfeit of high living: one scam too many, one jar too many of stolen caviar.

CHAPTER THREE

What Eating Caviar Feels Like

Russians have a special word for the dangerous wildness of people like my caviar eaters, living disobediently among the timid in a giant bureaucracy, ignoring the absurdly strict rules, glimmering darkly with selfish glee. The word is *azart*.

The dictionary definition of azart is:

> **Azart**, s, m, heat; excitement; fervour; **voyti v a.**, to grow heated, excited.
> **Azartny (~en, ~na)**, adj, heated; venturesome; **~naya igra**, game of chance.

But azart means more. It's an extreme form of acute compulsion known only in Russia, where the counter-pressures of conformity are so strong. Azart is the dangerous feeling that anything is possible that gamblers get at the roulette table. It's a drug. It's a head-rush. It means taking risks, and not giving a damn about anyone or anything as long as you get what you want. And it means not being satisfied that you've got enough till you've got far too much.

Azart makes you rich. It makes you powerful. It brings you limos and lovers for every day of the week. Even saying the word out loud makes you open your eyes wide with excitement and flare your nostrils. It dazzles and fizzes and sizzles.

Most of Russian literature is a black comedy about azart. It tells the stories of the people who shock the rest, the ones who make a mad grab for something they can't realistically hope to get and that no one in their right mind would even try for. The anti-heroes strut through the pages of Pushkin, Gogol, Dostoyevsky and the rest, lit up with their crazy ideas, cruising for a bruising.

And they get it. People gifted, or afflicted, with azart may lead fantastical, golden, implausible lives for a while, but they all come to a bad end. They fly too close to the sun. They burn out. They go down. They're doomed. When they get their comeuppance, the reader – who represents everyone who doesn't dare but envies anyone who does – can be quietly pleased that they've been properly punished.

Think of Raskolnikov, the student in *Crime and Punishment*. He's half-crazed with debt and worry. He decides to kill and rob an old moneylender. But he doesn't want to think he's just a criminal. Instead he lets himself believe he's got a grander motivation. Killing will prove he's as much a superman as Napoleon, the nineteenth century's first Übermensch, who charged around Europe wiping out insignificant mortals for the greater good. It doesn't prove that. Raskolnikov ends up in prison in Siberia.

Who cares? Azart stops you fearing failure. There's always another chancer ready to try his luck.

'Money is everything!' is the gloating motto of

Dostoyevsky's Gambler, Alexei Ivanovich. He pays back the General's scheming, gambling-obsessed family for his humiliating years as a tutor by going gambling with their rich Granny. Everyone in the General's family wants to inherit Granny's money to pay their debts and fund their gaming habits, but Granny has no intention of dying. She and Alexei play roulette. They win big, fling their money about in a reckless and unseemly way, but then start to lose. They chase their losses, in a cycle of worsening desperation and exhaustion. The family's prospects are destroyed. Granny eventually burns out and returns to Moscow. Two years later, Alexei is still drifting hopelessly from casino to casino.

And then there is pale, cold, sinister Hermann, with his Napoleonic profile, another young man of modest background ready to risk everything for instant success. This creation of Alexander Pushkin hears that the old Countess knows a supernatural way to win at cards. He uses a flirtation with the Countess's pretty ward, Lizaveta Ivanovna, to get into her house and, at gunpoint, orders the old lady to reveal her gaming secret. He scares the Countess to death, and terrifies Liza. All is not lost: the Countess's ghost comes to him, and tells him that if only he marries Liza and plays the three, the seven and the ace in sequence he will win. But Hermann still brings doom on himself. He doesn't bother with the conditions. He certainly doesn't bother with Liza. He wins on the three; he wins on the seven.

On the third evening, everyone was expecting him; the generals and privy councillors left their whist to watch such extraordinary play. The young officers leapt up from their sofas and all the waiters collected in the drawing room. Everyone pressed round Hermann. The other players left off punting, impatient to see what would happen. Hermann stood at the table, prepared to play alone against Tchekalinsky, who was pale but still smiling. Each broke the seal of a pack of cards. Tchekalinsky shuffled. Hermann took a card and covered it with a pile of banknotes. It was like a duel. Deep silence reigned in the room.

Tchekalinsky began dealing; his hands trembled. A queen fell on the right, an ace on the left.

'Ace wins!' said Hermann, and showed his card.

'Your queen has lost,' said Tchekalinsky gently.

Hermann started: indeed, instead of an ace, there lay before him the queen of spades. He could not believe his eyes or think how he could have made such a mistake.

At that moment it seemed to him that the queen of spades opened and closed her eye, and mocked him with a smile. He was struck by the extraordinary resemblance.

'The old woman!' he cried in terror.

Tchekalinsky gathered up his winnings. Hermann stood rooted to the spot. When he left the table, everyone began talking at once.

'A fine game, that!' said the players.

Tchekalinsky shuffled the cards afresh and the game resumed as usual.

Hermann went out of his mind. He is now in room number 17 of the Obukhov Hospital. He returns no answer to questions put to him but mutters over and over again, with incredible rapidity: 'Three, seven, ace! Three, seven, queen!'

* * *

It might not get you anywhere in literature, but azart comes off better in real life.

Three centuries ago, for instance, Peter the Great cocked a snoot at the defeated Swedes by building a completely new city – inventing it – on the frosty marshland of the Neva estuary, within spitting distance of his old enemy. It was an impossible job, but his sheer pig-headed determination made it happen. While St Petersburg was being built, the science-mad, seven-foot-tall Tsar tried out his new tooth-extracting instruments on the housemaids.

An even bigger victory for azart belongs to a shifty bunch of bank robbers, bomb throwers, political plotters, idealists and suspected German agents from early last century. Most of them had form. They were the scuzzy type with dirty fingernails that the police would be sure to pick out and keep back for more questioning. Not so long before, their plump, bearded, purposeful little leader had scuttled out of town, wearing an absurd blonde wig, and spent a frightened night in a haystack before creeping off to safety via Finland. But he came back to the Russian capital (somehow getting through enemy German territory unharmed in the middle of the First World War) and got ludicrously lucky. He was Vladimir Ilych Lenin, and he inherited the fantastically conservative Russian empire and the revolution that had toppled the Tsar in February. The Soviet authorities later built a museum in the shape of a concrete haystack up on the Gulf of Finland, and solemnly displayed the blonde wig in Lenin's honour.

The Communists nationalised azart. In the Soviet Union, only the state was allowed to have giant, ambitious, crazy projects. The state flirted with making rivers run backwards, drying out seas, building giant canals and railways across impossible territory, destroying whole classes of people, transplanting entire nations from one end of the Soviet Union to the other, and even building a tower in Moscow that would be a few feet taller than the tallest building in the world, the Empire State Building. The Palace of Nations was to be topped with a giant representation of Lenin. Lenin's stocky body in its concrete overcoat was to be topped with a top-class restaurant, inside the leader's head. Anyone who was anyone would be able to look out at Moscow, as he ate, through Lenin's eyes.

Azart was out of reach for *homo sovieticus*. Ordinary people had to keep their heads down just to survive the mad whims of their masters. But they were supposed to raise those bowed heads from time to time, to admire their masters' genius and yell, 'Hoorah!' Azart needs to be noticed, and to make other people gasp and stretch their eyes, because it only exists as contrast. If everyone acts with azart, the result is chaos: who has time to notice someone else being flamboyant if they're busy being flamboyant themselves? A good audience is subservient, reverent and gullible. It swallows whatever nonsense it is fed without asking awkward questions – just like the cowed, naive Soviet people. Mr Average's job was to be humble before the azart of the state, and he was humble beyond humbleness. He hung his head in public before his betters. He flattered, lied and cajoled. He even invented special language to be self-effacing with.

Of all the little hand-wringing phrases and cultural cringes in Soviet Russian, the commonest is the meek prefix '*pod-*'. '*Pod*' just means 'under'. But if you put it before a verb, it adds a hint of hesitancy just right for being humble with. 'Tell me, please!' is the standard, exclamatory, way to ask for information in Russian. But 'Won't you please *pod*-tell me?' which sounds wheedling and imploring, is a commoner way of saying the same thing.

[42]

And there's more to the *pod*-verbs than grovelling. They are as double-edged as flattery. As you look down the pages of dictionary entries for *pod*, you realise that the deceitfulness lurking inside the meaning keeps coming out. *Pod*- gives many words entirely new meanings, and the new meanings are almost always about sneaking off and bending the rules to suit yourself. To *pod*-work means to moonlight, to *pod*-listen to eavesdrop, to *pod*-make to forge. This is language shifting from the passive to the active, from self-abasement to sly, knowing, winking falsehood. I'll appear to obey you, these verbs say, but when you're not looking I'll be off on the scam.

This deceptive language belonged to people who had learned to deceive to survive. Under their forelock-tugging, cap-doffing, cheering, sycophantic exteriors, most Soviet citizens were dreaming grandiose dreams: world domination, world travel, marble in the bathroom, millions in the bank. Azart might not have been very visible in the sedate, repressed Soviet Union, but it was there, holding its breath, waiting to come out.

One of the few ways in which those restrained Soviet people could let rip – and express the crazy extravagance lurking in their souls – was by eating caviar.

To a Russian, caviar is edible azart.

It looks a simple, if peculiar, food – too simple to be the stuff of anyone's dreams.

It's a dark fish roe whose English name comes from the Turkish. Its oily pearls stick together in the bowl and pop softly on the tongue. It is subtle and rich. Neither very salty nor very fishy, it still tastes mysteriously of the sea. You serve it alone, or wobbling enigmatically on pancakes or boiled egg halves.

Ordinary people, expecting ordinary nourishing food, have

not always been pleased to get caviar instead. During the First World War, British soldiers given tins of caviar by a quirk of rationing were so disgusted by what they nicknamed fish jam that they spat it out and bought sardines.

Yet caviar is prized by sophisticates all over the world. It is rare and expensive. As any coffee-table book on caviar will remind you, just being able to buy it is a sign of wealth and success and power.

Since Russian émigrés brought their local delicacy West and made it fashionable in the salons of Paris and London a century ago, salesmen and delicatessens have spun an aspirational if slightly fishy history of the stuff, designed to appeal to snobbery, insisting that really important people through the ages have never been able to do without the noble sturgeon's eggs and flesh.

The ancient Greeks paid fortunes for sturgeon flesh, says one coffee-table book, and the ancient Romans heralded its appearance at table with flowers and trumpets.

In 1240, Batu Khan, the grandson of Genghis Khan, was honoured by a feast at a monastery on the banks of the River Volga. The menu began with fish soup made from sterlet, and included a large roasted sturgeon, eel pâté, *piro\zhki* stuffed with mushrooms, followed by crystallised apples and caviar. Over the next five years, Batu Khan conquered southern Russia and all the lands around the Volga and the Black and Caspian Seas, the home of the sturgeon.

In 1554, Ivan the Terrible conquered the south, the Volga and the Caspian seashore for the Russians, taking sturgeon fishing under Russian control. By the end of the seventeenth century Russia had established a marketing monopoly on caviar.

Russian tsars and Manchurian emperors, greedily but wisely, always kept the best caviar for themselves.

The newcomer to caviar may be overwhelmed by talk of the *goût raffiné* (or in Russia the *izyskanny vkus*) that lets only the most sophisticated of palates find a dignified pleasure in these gleaming bubbles of cholesterol. But he may also think it absurd to eat fish eggs. He may uneasily recall the gullible courtiers admiring the Emperor's new clothes, and wonder: does caviar actually taste good?

That question is pointless. Your spoonful of black eggs is full of far more than salt and oil and protein. It is weighed down with symbolism, and each dream of caviar adds a new flavour to what you taste as you swallow.

Foreigners have their reasons for finding caviar delectable.

In the West, where caviar has the *cachet* of being from exotically far away, caviar tastes of vague but splendid things, most happily expressed in delicate etiquette French. It means grand, because to be offered caviar is an initiation into the secret world of old aristocracies and the rich. It means *savoir-vivre*. It means *gourmet*.

But the eggs also hold hints of regret and nostalgia.

Until modern times, there was nothing especially Russian about sturgeon. It was eaten south, east and west of Muscovy.

In the Byzantine empire, which inherited the ancient world's love of fishy tastes and had fifty everyday ways of preparing fish, the sturgeon was loved as the noblest of finny creatures. The fourteenth-century *Book of Fish* (*Opsarologos*) showed both the complex layering of Byzantine society and the prestige of the sturgeon when it portrayed different sorts of fish as protagonists in a trial for high treason. Grey mullet (kephalos), perch (labrax) and sole (psession), all excellent fish to eat, represented high functionaries. Cheaper and less tasty sardines (engraulis), scorpion fish (skorpios) and other less prestigious sea fish (smaris), were the minor dignitaries. The accused was represented as a dried mackerel. The emperor, naturally, was a sturgeon.

In the Middle Ages, the sturgeon swam in most of the rivers of Europe: the Thames, the Seine and Gironde, the Po, the Ebro, the Guadalquivir, and the upper stretches of the Danube. Wherever they appeared, sturgeon were prized: fish for kings as well as king of fish. In England, the thirteenth-century Edward II passed an edict on 'fishes royal', awarding himself the first sturgeon of any catch. Alfonso II of Aragon had done the same with fish from the Ebro in 1165. A seventeenth-century French finance minister, Jean-Baptiste Colbert, brought in special regulations to preserve the sturgeon around Paris, under which the King was given any sturgeon caught in the Seine. Louis XVI got one of the last in 1782.

But European civilisation did for the gentle and defenceless sturgeon. The cities built along the continent's great rivers grew and got too dirty for a prehistoric, boneless creature that had not evolved in 180 million years. The sturgeon turned out to be unusually vulnerable to an explosion of urban pollution. It died out across western Europe in the nineteenth century. It died out in America in the twentieth. Only in southern Russia did it go on migrating between its freshwater birthplace in the Volga and its saltwater home in the Caspian Sea. Russia hadn't developed enough to build big cities along its river banks. So the Volga stayed clean and pure, and the sturgeon stayed alive.

When Europeans and Americans eat caviar, they don't just taste a dream of grandeur. They also taste nostalgia for the

Garden of Eden they once lived in, but destroyed.

Caviar is Russia's own luxury food, so there are no regrets, and no wincing *soupçons* of foreign snobbery about the way it is appreciated in its homeland. Russians eat caviar with straightforward gusto, whenever they have a glut of money and something to celebrate. And what they taste in it is energetic and dynamic and harsh.

Russians were able to make caviar production their national speciality only because they inherited the fishing technology of the Tatars defeated by Ivan the Terrible.

The Tatars had developed unusually efficient ways of catching sturgeon, a giant fish that is difficult to land because it can weigh up to two tonnes. They built *uchugi*, log barriers with hooks, across the Volga's tributaries into the Caspian. These traps effortlessly caught the sturgeon migrating upstream to their spawning grounds, on the way to lay their eggs and die.

But then the Russians came, and the defeated Tatar town of Astrakhan became a dying place, stinking of fish and full of flies and plague and famine. The misery that defeat brought to the Tatars is described eloquently by Anthony Jenkinson, an early English traveller who went down the Volga six years after the Russian conquest.* The Astrakhan area in 1558, he said, was:

> most destitute and barren of wood and pasture, and the ground
> will bear no Corne: the Aire is there most infected, by reason

---

* Anthony Jenkinson wrote reports to the merchants of the London Muscovy Company and his travels were included in: *Richard Hakluyt: Voyages and Discoveries. The Principal Navigations, Voyages, Traffiques and Discoveries of the English Nation* (1589–90).

(as I suppose) of much fish, and specially Sturgeon, by which only the Inhabitants live, having great scarcity of flesh and bread. They hang up their fish in their streets and Houses to dry for their provision, which causeth such abundance of flyes to increase there, as the like was never seen in any Land, to their great Plague. And at my being at the said Astracan, there was a great Famine and Plague among the people, and specially among the Tartars, called Nagayans, who the same time came thither in great numbers to render themselves to the Russes their Enemies, and to seeks succour at their hands, their Countrey being destroyed. But they were but ill entertained or relieved, for there dyed a great number of them for hunger, which lay all the Island through in heapes dead, and like to beasts unburied, very pittiful to behold: many of them were also sold by the Russes, and the rest were banished from the Island. At that time it had been an easie thing to have converted that wicked Nation to the Christian Faith, if the Russes themselves had been good Christians: but how should they show compassion unto other Nations, when they are not mercifull unto their own? At my being there I could have bought many goodly Tartars children, if I would have had a thousand, of their owne Fathers and Mothers, to say, a Boy or a Wench for a Loafe of bread worth sixe pence in England, but we had more need of victuals at that time than of any such Merchandize.

Astrakhan recovered. Victorious Russians moved in. Two centuries later, when a British adventurer called Captain Jonas Hanway stopped there on his way down the Volga, it had become the biggest fishery centre in the empire. Juicy, delicious grapes grew in abundance in the town. Gardens and vineyards were watered by wheels. The well-off ate partridge and quail, or sturgeon and caviar on fish-only fasting days; the poor were paid in bread and salt. The local salt was shipped around Russia, and so was fish. Salted fish from the area's giant fisheries was traded all year. Caviar was salted in large quantities on the Volga. As soon as winter set in, frozen blocks of fresh fish and unsalted caviar were also dispatched, on sleds, on the six-hundred-league journey north to St Petersburg.

The people who fished the sturgeon were Cossacks, the odd fish of the Russian south. The Cossacks had once been bands of runaway serfs, defrocked priests, criminals and outlaws who had long ago escaped the rule of Muscovy and settled on the fringes of the empire. They were wild men in hairy hats, exempt from the serfdom to which other Russians were subjected, and they were eventually granted special privileges – the right to farm and fish in freedom – in exchange for saddling up and riding off to defend the empire whenever it was threatened. The only authority they recognised was that of their own councils, run by an elected leader called an *ataman*. William Tooke, an eighteenth-century traveller in Russia, specified that while part of the Russian shore of the Caspian was let out to Astrakhan merchants, another part belonged, 'in virtue of antient privileges, to the Uralian Kozaks, who not only claim that right on the river Ural, but also on a tract of coast extending seventy versts in length'. The Cossacks, he noted, 'are particularly famous for making excellent kaviar'.

That history gives Russians today a sense of caviar as conquest food. It's a delicacy snatched from the mouths of the defeated khans. Its taste also recalls the dashing, freebooting lifestyle of the free Cossacks, who are revered to this day for never knuckling under to the powers that be.

Among a people who might laugh under their breath at authority, but will almost always shrug and submit to it in the end, those wild, dangerous, ungovernable hints in the taste of caviar have a very special savour.

The Soviet government tried its best to make caviar eating safe, turning it into a meek, tidy, obedient business. The fisheries and factories were nationalised. The eggs were heavily pasteurised. And caviar was packed into neat, sterilised, colour-coded glass jars: blue for beluga, red for osyotr, yellow for sevruga.

It didn't make any difference. Nor did the fact that poaching, smuggling, and general light-fingeredness with caviar were dangerous games. You could get a bullet in the brain for the crime of Stealing Especially Valuable State Property. But everyone still wanted caviar.

Caviar had to be served at every wedding party and every official function – and in big, cheerful, glistening dollops, too, far bigger than you could hope to get from one mean-spirited, colour-coded little jar. If you couldn't lay on caviar as the centrepiece of your feast – surrounded by vodka, champagne, Borzhomi water, white slices of gelatinous sturgeon, fatty sausage slices on giant platters, skinny slivers of Dutch cheese, elaborate salads of vegetables chopped into tiny cubes and doused in sour cream, slice after slice of dripping red watermelon, and an oompah band cheerfully playing sad songs far too fast and loud – it just wasn't a feast.

So astonishing quantities somehow found their way on to tables, and it was all that a tired old Soviet state could do to keep the winks and the nods, the whispers and bribes, and the excited, furtive deal-making in check.

And then the Soviet state collapsed and died. The azart that had lain dormant in Russia for so long exploded back into life.

Everyone wanted caviar even more than before, and now there was nothing left to stop them getting it.

CHAPTER FOUR

No More Caviar
for the Masses

Pssst.

Pssssssssssst.

The man quietly trying to get my attention was carrying a cardboard sign with my name on. He was about fifty, with a barrel chest, Soviet specs, a neat grey padded anorak and a naughty, quizzical, befanged smile.

I put down the bag slung over my shoulder and formally shook his hand. This must be Victor, whose family I was going to live with for a month while I brushed up my very rusty Russian and tried to get a job here.

It was March 1991, and the airport in Leningrad was the same dusty old Soviet mess it had been ten years earlier. But everything else was supposed to have changed. I'd become a sleek professional in cashmere and polished leather. Outside, in the winter night, I was expecting to see a Russia transformed by the magic word perestroika.

'Pleased to meet you,' I said. I fumbled over the simple Russian words. Victor and I both reached for my bag at the same time, both recoiled, and both tried again, a bit harder this time, to grab the handle and control of the situation.

'It's not heavy,' I said in Russian, getting the ending of my adjective all wrong and silently cursing my own ineptitude.

'I will take your bag,' he said determinedly, at the same time, in English.

He won, He slung the strap of the bag over his shoulder, on top of his own shoulder bag. 'Please,' he said, in excruciatingly polite and incorrect English, gesturing towards the baggage reclaim. He set off briskly, trundling the trolley he had been smart enough to get in advance. There was nothing to do but trot obediently after him.

We had another battle of wills at the door.

By now Victor's trolley was loaded down with my luggage. In the five years I'd been working abroad as a reporter, I'd learned to travel light: a toothbrush, a computer, a change of clothes. So I was already embarrassed to have broken my usual travelling rule by nervously packing every warm item of clothing I possessed, along with about three dozen Pot Noodles just in case it was true what you read in the papers and people in Russia were starving. It looked incompetent and girlish to have too much luggage, I felt. But it was worse still if you had to have someone else – and especially a man – lugging it around for you.

So I held the door open for him. He looked at me in surprise. 'Please,' I said, correctly, in Russian, gesturing for him to go through first with the trolley. But Victor only stopped, smiled even more broadly, and took hold of the door himself. He clearly had no time for post-feminist angst about sharing burdens equally. Or perhaps he just found it funny. 'Ladies first,' he said, in English. 'Please.'

I hunched in the hot, fuggy car, feeling prickly and outwitted, trying to recapture my sense that everything was possible and that I could conquer the world.

I had only become a journalist so I could go to Russia. By some quirk of my bosses' institutional logic, I had somehow ended up learning Portuguese instead and covering the distant wars of Portuguese-speaking Africa for the last eighteen months. So I knew how to hitch rides on aid helicopters from Soviet and South African pilots. I knew how to be self-contained, wrap up small in the back of cars, send telexes whenever there was electricity, eat and sleep only when there was time, and always find a way to call the office even from the middle of a desert or a war zone. I was far too busy for romantic attachments or domestic dullness. I stood up my friends for last-minute jobs; I ran my love life across continents. I looked in the mirror in the morning and preened myself for being the queen of detachment, a trained observer watching history in the making. And I still only wanted to be in Russia.

It was ambition. In 1991, Russia was The Story. Whenever you turned on the TV anywhere in the world, you would see another reform, another strike, another tumultuous session of parliament somewhere in the Soviet Union. I'd learned the language for all those years; now I wanted the rewards. I had been working in France and in Cambodia while Eastern Europe fizzed and fermented; I had just been leaving for Africa when the Berlin Wall came down. I'd missed everything so far, but I wanted to be in Moscow when it became a democracy so much that it hurt.

Now, at last, I was getting a trial run at working in Russia. My bosses thought it was for a month. But I knew better. I was stubbornly, fanatically determined to stay on.

[55]

Part of my plan was to live with a family – not in a special hotel for foreigners – so my Russian would come back faster. An organisation that sponsored exchanges had found Victor's family for me, and would arrange for one of his children to go to England later. Part of the excitement of Russia now was that you could do things like that.

But my first impression of Victor was giving me second thoughts. The last thing I wanted was to find myself cooped up with some bossy middle-aged Soviet man with bureaucratic glasses and no soul, undermining my confidence, patronising me, telling me everything was forbidden and lecturing me all month in his good bad English.

I sighed, and looked at the crumbling palaces moving by behind the glass.

Victor's family lived in the ruins of Dostoyevsky land, off Peace Square, which until Soviet times had been Haymarket Square market. A packed, grungy, unofficial market still operated over and around several different building sites. A church had once stood in the middle, until it was knocked down to make way for something new that had later been forgotten. There was an old metro stop and a new one, complete with towers and cranes and rotting fences, which had also gone unbuilt for some years. The empty space was filled with currency sharks, drunks, hawkers and pickpockets. Somewhere out of sight, someone was playing a sad song on a squeezebox.

'Don't forget, this isn't London,' Victor said. 'Peace Square is a dangerous place. With your bag open like that, your passport will be stolen in a second. As that old darling Brezhnev said, be vigilant!' And he wagged a finger playfully in the air, as if I were a naughty child. I nodded with all the chilly dignity I could muster. But I also closed the zip on my bag. The darkness did look menacing.

It was better as soon as we got inside, and into a tiny kitchen full of warm yellow lamplight.

The kitchen is where you find the soul of any Russian flat. Kitchens are full of gurgling pipes and tea. There's never enough room for everyone to sit at the tiny table, on the tiny stools, but there's always a heart-to-heart talk going on, a radio or TV whispering, and something warm on the stove.

They put me on a stool in the window corner, by the orange plastic curtains, and they all came in to stare at me from the edge of the pool of light: a woman of forty, with a pretty, tired face, loose tendrils of hair coming down from a bun, and a flowery housecoat; a tall, blonde, snub-nosed girl of eighteen; and a pigtailed kid with skinny legs and her father's fangy grin. Oh, and Tobik the gerbil, too, wrenched out of his warm nest of torn-up scraps of *Pravda*, sitting in the palm of the little girl's hand, looking as though he'd rather be asleep. 'Named "Toby" in honour of England,' Victor explained deftly. 'Mama, is there any tea in the house?'

And suddenly an hour had gone by, and we were drinking tea and eating cake and showing each other photos, and Victor was improvising funny jazzy wedding music on the piano in the other room. His bossy Soviet personality had been taken off at the door with his coat. There was a soft, shining, expectant look in every pair of eyes, a little like being in love.

Indoors was always like this here: a little warm nest of books and blankets and bedding, eiderdowns packed under pull-out beds in the morning and brought comfortingly out at night, feet pampered in sloppy old slippers and socks, and a hallway of furry boots and woolly hats and scarves to lose yourself in before venturing out into the harshness of the winter weather. We lived as entwined together as a litter of sleepy kittens. In the morning, when my warm bed vanished under the divan next to the piano, the room became Nadya's homework desk and Victor's office. The rest of the family got dressed in the main bedroom, where everyone's clothes were kept and which was shut up by day. Lena, the mother, and the two girls slept in the double bed, and Victor, dressed for the night in blue tracksuit trousers with two white stripes down the leg, made himself a nest in front of the TV in the sitting room. 'May I enter your virginal vestibule?' he would say, little fangs gleaming gently, and slip to the desk to take out papers or books to look at on his sofa. There wasn't room for a bubble of personal space. Everyone was always darting in and out of everyone else's territory. If that annoyed someone to the point of snapping, whoever had provoked the outburst would raise his hands gently, rein himself in and retreat. We were a team. We couldn't quarrel. It was us, in the warm circle of kitchen lamplight, against the whole dark cold Soviet world outside.

One by one we tiptoed out in the mornings, wrapped up against the winter, full of tea and food. I crunched the snow and drew air into my nostrils with a cold thrill.

There wasn't much to stay out for after my morning language classes. Reports that perestroika had improved the quality of life seemed somewhat exaggerated. Bureaucracy was still frustrating. The girls swam once a week at a pool in what had once been a Lutheran church on Nevsky Prospekt, but I couldn't join them without a medical *spravka*. And that meant finding a doctor to give me a gynaecological examination. I passed on the swimming. I passed on shopping too. The shops seemed even emptier than before.

So I got home before five like everyone in the family. Our nights went on till midnight or later: tea, supper, television, chats, teasing, wandering from room to room, piano playing, record playing, word playing, and late tea before bed.

'Enema . . . enema . . . you're a filthy enema,' Mouse would hiss at tall Nadya, grinning wickedly, while the parents were safely in the other room. Mouse had an inventive line in swearwords. 'Enema yourself,' Nadya would answer, good-humoured and mature, and Mouse's eyes would instantly brim with unshed tears. 'Oh, don't cry! Please don't cry!' we had to chorus, and Mouse would peep consideringly up at us, like her gerbil, before smiling again.

Norkova! Mouse called me, turning my name inside out to make me sound like a furry mink. She brushed my hair; just like her Barbie doll's, she would say with satisfaction. But it wasn't enough to call me Minkievee or Barbie. To her, I was a walking bestiary, to be named, renamed and marvelled over. 'You tired crocodile! You old oak tree! You dancing giraffe! You twit!' she would giggle. 'Mouse . . .' Nadya would begin, warningly. 'Ah, who cares?' Mouse answered petulantly, her shrug turning into a whole-body wriggle. 'She doesn't understand what I'm saying, does she? She's a thick foreigner.' And then she would bound into my arms, hug me repentantly, and wheedle, 'Norkova! You don't understand, do you? And you know I don't mean it, don't you? I looove you!'

'I love you too,' I'd say, and mean it even when Mouse then

stuck her tongue out at me and hissed, 'You old oak tree!' again. But when Mouse was in bed, her mother would whisper apologetically, 'Nadya is our golden girl. She works hard, she speaks English, she plays the piano; how we love her. But Mouse is a problem child.'

We had no evening life outside the flat. We only went out very occasionally, and chaperoned, to worthy concerts or operas or ballets. The family was terrified that rascally Russians outside would rip me off. Foreigners were natural victims, in their view, and I was their personal foreigner, not to be hunted and preyed on by street criminals. Restaurants – rackety places full of black marketeers – were out of the question. Instead we sat at home and ate more than I had ever thought possible. Even if there was no food in the shops, there was an enormous amount to be got through inside. Every day, we had variations on this overwhelmingly calorific menu:

Cheeselets (fried soft cheese patties with raisins, sprinkled in sugar, drowned in sour cream).

Darling doves (fried cabbage leaves stuffed with fried mincemeat, drowned in sour cream).

Pelmeni (Siberian ravioli: doughy parcels of mincemeat, boiled then drowned in sour cream).

Vegetables (fried and refried potatoes, with garnishes of pickled cabbage, pickled cucumbers or pickled mushrooms).

A shelf ran around the top of the kitchen. Every inch of it was covered with greasy jars, full of dark liquid and dark, bobbing, salted, vegetable shapes. It was Lena's store against starvation. It made me feel anxious to look at it.

The food I liked least was black, rubbery, pickled mushrooms.

Lena: 'Have some pickled mushrooms! Tuck in! You like our pickled mushrooms, don't you?'

Me (doubtfully): 'Mmm . . . yes . . . delicious . . . mmm . . .'

Lena: 'Have some more!'

Victor: 'We bought a lot of vegetables cheap for pickling a few years ago. Very cheap. People were making so much fuss about Chernobyl, no one would buy stuff from the market. But I'd done my research. I knew something they didn't . . .' (fumbling through papers, triumphantly flourishing a dog-eared typed article). 'Look. My tables show that low-level radiation is good for you – that means that a Chernobyl cabbage could actually lengthen your life. We pickled a lot of cabbages in 1986. They were giving them away. Mushrooms too.'

Me (still more doubtfully, wondering whether it was possible that I was eating five-year-old pickled Chernobyl mushrooms): 'Really I think not . . . delicious, but I am so full . . . maybe later . . . No, it's a waste . . .'

Lena: 'So have some cheeselets! Tuck in! You like our cheese-lets, don't you? Have you got enough jam? Jam! Give her more jam, Victor! She likes our jam! It's made of cranberries I picked myself and I boiled it up myself. Wait, you haven't got any sour cream left, wait wait, I'll get you some. Sour cream! Mouse, look in the fridge!'

A basket of sliced bread accompanied every meal, half white bread, half black bread. I waved it away at first. I even said, 'I don't like bread.' That was a mistake. 'That is a Western luxury,' Victor said crossly. 'If you'd grown up here, during the blockade, you wouldn't refuse bread.' From then on, I made sure to take a slice of bread and tore bits out of it so it looked half-eaten. 'Bread is our riches,' Victor would say, half-mocking the Soviet propaganda phrase but half tut-tutting at me, clearing away the crumbs.

Victor had a free metro pass because he'd been born in Leningrad in 1941, when Nazi armies were beginning a three-year encirclement of the city and trying to starve and bomb the inhabitants into surrender. He didn't remember the siege, but like every adult in Leningrad was tremendously proud that they had not given in. Teenagers, however, took a dim view of the older generation's sacrifice. 'Just imagine, if they had surrendered, we'd be Germans! We'd have the highest GDP in Europe! I'd have a Swatch and Levis!' Nadya said sardonically. But she said it in a whisper, and never when her parents were in the room. She was a sensitive girl.

Calories meant love, and that made perestroika-era Leningrad a bleak place. Victor and Lena were issued with monthly ration coupons for bread, milk, flour, butter, sugar, meat, eggs and vodka. There wasn't enough food to go around. Lena queued on the way to work, queued on the way home, and came home from empty shops with queuing war stories and bulging carrier bags.

'How do you get your hands on so much food, Lena?' I finally dared to ask, after a couple of weeks.

'I've bribed and borrowed from everyone I know so we can feed you properly this month,' she answered with grim satisfaction. 'If only you knew the trouble we'd gone to!'

One night she made apple cake for midnight tea. It tasted fresh, of fruit and not fat. I often got up in the night and sat peacefully at the kitchen table, drinking tea, learning my lists of words, and watching the fierce black snowstorms outside through the window. That night I had a second slice of cake. I thought everyone was asleep. But Mouse and her mother were listening to me through the paper-thin walls. 'You were so sweet, padding down the corridor like a little hedgehog, looking for apple cake. Whiffle whiffle,' Mouse said, and wrinkled up her nose and paws. The cooking got even more frenzied: now Lena baked apple cake every day.

Lena never ate, but she was anguished by our inability to devour everything she heaped on our plates. 'Mouse! Mouselet!' she pleaded. 'You're my golden one! My darling! My little darling dove! Eat something! Just a little something! Please try!'

Mouse refused. She lived on a diet of bananas and flavoured foreign yoghurts ('So expensive! But what can you do?' her mother whispered), and she brimmed with tears if anyone tried to force her to finish her food.

Nadya was in quieter revolt against mealtimes. 'I don't want to be fat,' she said. She put up a list of things she couldn't eat on the kitchen wall: cheeselets, darling doves, pelmeni, fried potatoes, sour cream, and bread. She pointed to her list whenever her mother served her forbidden food. 'I can't eat that,' she said, and Lena's brow furrowed anxiously. She looked tearful and defeated. Nadya stood firm.

I surrendered completely. I gave Nadya my tightest jeans, and stopped doing up the top button on the rest. Secretly I loved being fussed over. I told myself I was taking the path of least resistance.

They still spent their days sitting in the kitchen, safe, static and hidden, but everyone in my Russian family was beginning to dream of going out and conquering the darkness outside.

Victor watched television. It showed parliaments of every kind, around the clock, Soviet, republican, regional, city, town, district, with people shouting, arguing, waving fists from the podium, and calling each other Comrades! or Dear Colleagues! or Respected Deputies! 'I was so excited for a year or so, when all this democracy began,' he said. 'But just look at them. What will those idiots ever do for us?'

Victor wanted to get rich and travel. He was a scientist, and he'd been named as a candidate member of the Academy of Sciences, but he'd never managed to join the Party or the Peace Committee or any organisation that could reliably get you abroad. Now he was trying a new route: he'd wangled a three-year grant from a British university to write a research paper that happened to have exactly the same subject as his old PhD thesis. He was translating his out-of-date work into English, presenting it as new research, quietly congratulating himself, and dreaming of air tickets.

Victor had a friend with business plans. He brought me his friend's leaflets, five or six faxed, stapled pages that he called 'advertisements'. They were lengthy promises of every kind of commercial help, in bizarre Soviet English. 'We can on Your behalf purchase diamonds; we can assist Your purchases of Golden materials, ingots, bars, rings & cetera; we can undertake Your travel insurance using coordination facilities of our JV (Joint Venture) enterprise; we have experienced to arrange Your concert tour of Israel, wholesale and retail commerce of shoes, boots, stockings and tights, contractual arrangements for Import-Export for books, documents, all types of publishing matter and face cream.' The sheer scope and hopefulness of the promises made your head spin. Victor only asked: 'Can you check the grammar?'

Lena dreamed on behalf of her daughters, and most often of Nadya. If only she could get Nadya safely out of the country. If only Nadya could study in America. The girls were learning tennis. Nadya had been on one school trip to France and was going again in the summer. She might also be going to England as the return part of the exchange scheme with me. Money was already put aside for tickets.

But the exchange trip vanished. One day the Soviet government devalued the rouble, from six to the dollar to twenty-seven to the dollar. Suddenly there were only a fifth as many dollars in the kitty to pay for the trip. 'The idiots, it was bound to go wrong,' Mouse said when she heard. 'Anyway, they always spend all their money on Nadya. Why should I be upset? What about me?' And she stuck her tongue out at her sister.

'I feel terrible about this – I'm taking your hospitality under false pretences if the exchange can't happen any more,' I said. Lena and I were on our way back from the ballet, rising through the air on a rushing metro escalator. 'Nonsense!' she replied stoutly. 'What you have to remember is that They are always out to ruin our plans. It's up to us not to let Them get away with it. If we just don't think about the exchange any more, and only remember the pleasure that we're having with each other, then that's one thing They won't have managed to destroy.'

While they waited for their own dreams to come true, they threw themselves into helping me achieve my ambition of getting a job in Russia. 'What will impress your bosses most?' Victor asked. And he started to think of feature stories I could write, and find me interviewees. Our list grew until it included: The Apparatchik Building The River Barrier Poisoning Leningrad's Water Supply; The TV Crime Show Star With Party Connections

And Links To The Underworld; The Teenage Ballerinas Starving In The Rat-Infested Dance Academy; The Priest Seeking Out Communism's Lost Souls; The Easter Midnight Mass Where Police Outnumber Worshippers; and The Woman Who Might Front A Hardline Communist Comeback.

I met the woman who might have fronted a hardline Communist comeback in the school chemistry lab where she taught, among shrouded Bunsen burners and chipped sinks. Chalky dust lay on the work surfaces. Nina Andreyeva was wearing a white coat. She was my first Stalinist, stout and sinister with tight terrier hair and a tight disapproving mouth. There was white powder on her cheeks.

Nina Andreyeva had shocked the entire Soviet Union three years before when a letter from her, headed 'I Cannot Betray My Principles', was published in a hardliners' newspaper. The letter appealed to good Communists to resist the reforms of Mikhail Gorbachev (who happened to be out of the country when it was published), since otherwise he would bring capitalism back to the Soviet Union. When the hardline Kremlin ideology chief Yegor Ligachev chimed in, saying editors-in-chief should be guided by ideas expressed in the article, Russians suspected Andreyeva was the front for a creeping coup against Mikhail Gorbachev. But nothing came of it. Gorbachev returned, Andreyeva was denounced, and Ligachev was shunted away from power. The chemistry teacher was left alone with her principles.

I asked her about her principles, but her answer was all about food. She came from a humble family of workers, she said. The Soviet system had given her all the chances: an education, music lessons, sports training and medical care. In the old days before Gorbachev's reforms (she said the phrase with a look that might as well have been a curse, or a gob of spit), it had all been freely available to everyone. In the old days, before reform emptied the shops and bankrupted the state, you could get any luxury you wanted to eat. A bit of goose. A bit of beef. A bit of sturgeon. A bit of caviar. (Not huge amounts, mind. Not all the time. Just enough to make you happy.) Yet now there was nothing. Millions of workers' families of the future might never again get the chance to enjoy their bit of goose, or beef, or sturgeon, or caviar. If Gorbachev went any further towards capitalism, only the rich would get the goose and beef and sturgeon and caviar. The poor would lose everything they had won. He had to be stopped, for the sake of the masses.

It was a poignant argument in a city where calories mean love. I surprised a soft, nostalgic look on Nina Andreyeva's big face, and were those tears in her eyes? She paused and licked her lips reminiscently. I was almost beginning to warm to her.

Then she dived into her handbag. She pulled out a handful of pamphlets and newspapers. 'These are the work of my political group,' she said – it had one of those fringy-sounding names, with the words Communist, Bolshevik, Stalinist, Soviet, Supremacist, and more, all thrown in. 'I brought them for you.'

'Oh, thank you,' I said, picking them up and eyeing the tiny typeface and long headlines with a sinking heart. The words and phrases that leapt out – from 'Jewish bankers' to 'international conspiracy' – did nothing to convince me that I would want to sit up poring over these documents late at night. I folded them politely into my bag.

'They'll cost you.' Her voice cracked like a whip as she displayed an unexpected talent for retailing combined with a teacher's knack for discipline. 'Seven roubles each. That's twenty-eight for the four copies, and two more for the leaflets. Thirty altogether.'

Her hand came out as fast as a cash register drawer. There was nothing to do but pay up and quietly dispose of her papers in a bin on my way out of the school. A strange fantasy picture followed me all the way home: a fat-cheeked child Nina Andreyeva, happy and full of hope, dandled on the knee of a big Soviet hero daddy in blue overalls, sitting at a rough-hewn table and tucking into tasty morsels of goose, and beef, and sturgeon, and caviar.

Three months after I left Russia, to begin the long wait to hear whether I would get a job there, there was a coup attempt against Mikhail Gorbachev by hardline politicians who thought like Nina Andreyeva. I phoned the flat. 'We're OK,' Nadya said, though she sounded shaky and high-pitched. 'But Papa's gone to Palace Square to join the demonstration against the coup, and Mama's not letting us out of the house. And can you imagine? I flew back from France yesterday – via Finland, it was cheaper – and got on the train home from Helsinki this morning, not knowing what I was going back to, and naturally the train was completely empty, no one else was such an idiot as to come back during a coup, and there was no one to meet me at the station, and when I phoned home to say were they coming, I got Mama's voice, whispering and sounding completely terrified, saying, "Nadya, are you *mad*? Why ever didn't you stay away?" '

I'd never phoned them since leaving Leningrad. I'd had to leave behind half the presents they'd given me – my bags had got too heavy to get on the plane. But I missed them. I thought of the gentleness of their tiny kitchen every day, the still air and cosy claustrophobia, as I rushed through my oversized, airy and very empty house to work, and as hurry and hassle sliced away my Russian weight until my clothes hung lean and dangerously off my hips again. For the first time, I'd realised my traveller's life was lonely. I'd been holding off from phoning until I had good news about a job. Without that, I'd been scared that we might have nothing to say. Now I was suddenly scared of something new: that the Soviet bureaucratic barriers would go up and I might never see my Russian family again.

But I did see them. They (and perhaps Nina Andreyeva, and perhaps the coup plotters, who had put the Russia story even higher up the news agenda than before) helped me beat the odds. The very next week, I was told I'd got a job in Russia. I drank champagne and organised parties and packed. By the time I started work in Moscow three months later, the failure of the coup was history. The Soviet Union was disintegrating, taking Communism with it. Nina Andreyeva's dream of caviar for the masses was dead.

CHAPTER FIVE

The Caviar Thieves

Pssst!

Pssssssssssst!

Girl! Pssst! Madame, *kommen Sie hier!* Psst! Psst! Wanna buy this? Psst!

It was winter again, but the next winter, when Christmas was officially celebrated on 7 January for the first time in many years, a few days after the Soviet Union vanished.

It wasn't a happy Christmas for most people. At first there was more, but still not much, in the shops in Moscow – only a lot of Western cameramen filming empty shelves, and rather fewer disappointed customers. Later, the shops filled up with food, but at sky-high prices that most people couldn't afford. In the phrase of the day, the old fixed state prices had been 'freed'. People were scared they might starve – though that didn't stop Lena from phoning me on weekend evenings and telling me to meet the Leningrad train at midnight: she'd given passenger x, in carriage y, seat z, an apple cake to make sure I didn't go hungry. The cakes, wrapped in paper inside shoeboxes inside Sellotape, were so huge they fed my entire office.

But fears of starvation didn't bother the very few people

with the money to shop in the private markets. We were free. There were no restraints on us.

I was in my market, shopping. It was a haggler's heaven. The air was heavy with scents and hissy, sing-song, exciting invitations to buy.

It wasn't a particularly safe or hygienic market. You reached it down icy back stairs, behind the circus. There was a sour smell of wild animal, and you could almost hear tigers roaring sadly in the distance. Once I saw a rat, slithering under the fence away from the bins. It seemed at least a foot long, and its fat, naked, rope-like black tail was twice as long again as its greasy body. It gave me a long, arrogant, considering look. Two women behind me gasped. We all paused and waited fearfully for it to skitter off over the black ice. It looked mean enough to go for us if provoked.

The market wasn't a quiet place either. A kopeck for the love of God, murmured the beggars at the door, crossing themselves and bowing almost to the floor if you put a coin in their rough hands. Come and buy! sang the stallholders, baring their teeth and kicking slimy rubbish under their tables. Policemen came in every day to shake down the stallholders. It was a noisy ritual war dance, in which the men in uniform demanded licences and proof of non-involvement in various sinister criminal activities, and it began with accusations (fingers raised, truncheons raised) but ended in mollification (truncheons lowered, fingers counting notes in pockets) and big smiles all around. Even the shoppers shouted and argued and haggled, prodding goods, tasting things, demanding a slice of this or a silver of that. 'But is that herring fresh?' they screeched. 'I don't know; it smells a bit funny to me. What did you prepare it in? When was it made? Where has it been?' Look at that rubbery texture, I think it's been around a while.' They wanted something good for all the money they were paying. They were all almost sure all the time that they were being ripped off. The noises they made were all interesting. Only the pickpockets and dodgy moneychangers worked furtively, in silence.

Inside, the market had one hall for meat, sausage, preserved meat, and suckling pigs in dead pink litters, and another separate hall for hard cheeses, curd cheeses in cloth wraps, sour creams and yoghurty milks. Here, full-bodied Russian milkmaids and men cut, churned and measured, expertly whisking wires and giant choppers. Grannies ran a honey zone where you could buy golden jars that smelled of summer, or slabs of waxy honeycomb wrapped in paper, or a strange dark powdery stuff that I found out from friends was a bee product, drunk in vodka, that warded off winter colds. I called it the bee's knees.

But the market was also the place to come if you wanted the things that the dark-skinned, gold-toothed, big-smiling, energetic traders from the southern republics came north to sell: dewy bouquets of dark roses, bottles of silver-topped Crimean champagne, rich red and orange spices in buckets and baskets, pyramids of watermelons and apricots and pomegranates, almonds and walnuts, fresh greens and salads and herbs, piles of freshly picked berries, pickles and potions, exotic southern sweets made of strings of threaded walnuts dipped in honey and grape resin, and caviar in quantities I'd never dreamed possible.

This caviar was clearly not legit. It was sold in dark corners, in old jars. It came without guarantees. Everything about it screamed 'poached'. But no one minded that then. There was no

Soviet state any more, so no one knew who they should believe was in charge. No one knew whether Communism should be forgotten and whether capitalism was just another word for theft (though the general opinion in the market was probably yes to both). Since no one was sure what counted as stealing, it was impossible to say whether, if the caviar was stolen, it was stolen from the defunct Soviet state or from the new replacement republican governments or from the caviar fisheries or from local people. And no one cared much about any of them. So everyone who dared was joyfully helping himself.

You saw the southern traders at airports, like busy, frantic ants under their mountains of produce. The story people told, even in Soviet times, was of Georgian merchants who bought two seats on the plane up from Tbilisi: one for themselves, one for a pyramid of their watermelons to sell on the street in Moscow. Now there was money about, and the southerners were going big time. I knew someone with a dacha on the edge of town next to a Georgian trading family. 'My dacha stinks of pickled garlic,' he said, though not unhappily. 'They've got a *whole barrel* of it buried in front of their house. And the wines! And the herbs! They've got salad there in mid-winter!'

Georgia was one of three little Soviet republics just south of Russia that had become independent that New Year. It was Christian and rich. Stalin came from there. It had hills and vineyards going down to the Black Sea. Armenia was Christian too, but poor: red and mountainous and fierce and landlocked. Azerbaijan was the only Muslim country, an expanse of desert bordered by the Caspian and flowing with oil. The hissy, alluring caviar traders, with their long eyelashes and gentle eyes and sing-song accents, came from Azerbaijan. They were the ones who murmured 'Psssst!' as you passed, and who winked and glittered and grinned at you from behind their jars.

Just how much stolen caviar was on sale in that new Moscow, alive with azart, could be guessed at from the statistics showing how fast the official catch was declining:

1990—15,056 tonnes of sturgeon officially registered caught in the Soviet Union.

1991—11,499 tonnes.

1992—10,779 tonnes in the newly independent Caspian seaside states.

1993—6,744 tonnes.

1994—5,422 tonnes.

In just five years, two-thirds of the sturgeon catch vanished into the poachers' nets. By 1995, local fisheries experts on the Volga and the Caspian believed that poachers were grabbing ninety per cent of the sturgeon catch.*

There was no one to stop them. What had once been one long Soviet coastline around most of the Caspian, policed by Soviet police, had suddenly become four separate, chaotic, new states: Russia, Azerbaijan, Kazakhstan and Turkmenistan. Even part of the Russian coastline wasn't quite Russia: it belonged to an autonomous statelet called Dagestan, where most of the people were Muslims and where so many different languages were spoken that it was called the Mountain of Language. Each of

---

* The situation has not improved since 1995, despite international attempts to limit imports to consumer countries and even stop exports altogether from the Caspian seaside states. Illegal fishing is now thought to account for 10,000 tonnes of sturgeon annually, compared with the official combined catch in 2001 of just 650 tonnes by Russia, Azerbaijan, Kazakhstan and Turkmenistan.

these places was now supposed to fight its own crime separately. But none of them had the faintest idea how to begin. So each state resorted to blaming the others for everything that went wrong with the sea. If that failed, they all got together and blamed the genuinely foreign state along the Caspian's southern shore, Iran.

Official caviar production wasn't only declining because people living along the Volga and the Caspian had taken courage as the Soviet state declined and got their boats and nets out to steal the state's fish. There were older abuses too.

During the winter that the Soviet Union collapsed, I went to a party in a Russian flat. One of the guests was an Englishwoman called Sian, who had been living in Russia for a while. She wouldn't eat the caviar. She had been making a documentary about caviar production. Long before the poachers had got their nerve up, she said, Soviet pollution had already been destroying the industry.

From the early 1950s, the Soviet government had been damming the Volga and other tributaries of the Caspian Sea. They wanted reservoirs and hydroelectric plants. When they began regulating the river's flow, in 1958, the spawning stock of sturgeons was vast: 20,000 belugas, 400,000 sevrugas, and 700,000 osyotrs. But the dams meant that the river's natural spawning grounds were reduced. Eighty-five per cent of the spawning grounds in the lower Volga were lost, among them almost all the beluga's spawning grounds. Spawning stopped altogether in the Kura, Safid-Rud and Terek rivers. The dams stopped the sturgeon swimming upstream, and so much water was removed from the rivers for industry and agriculture that some deltas were left dry except during floods. Just as adult sturgeon could not get upstream, young fish migrating downstream could not reach the sea. The 'sturgeon passages' designed by Soviet engineers to solve these problems didn't work. By 1987, only just over two thousand spawning sturgeon were counted heading upstream.

Industrialists liked to blame the fact that the Caspian Sea, a saltwater lake which mysteriously rises for several years at a time, before falling for several years more, was on the rise during the eighties. Yet the years of rising sea levels had once meant bigger, healthier, more plentiful sturgeon; now the weight of belugas continued to fall, from an average 110 kg in 1970 to 57 kg in 1991.

Environmentalists blamed pollution from the oil that bubbles up along the Caspian shore, and from industrial sewage. There was more oil production now: Western companies began to sniff excitedly at the Caspian from the eighties onwards, suspecting that the oil boom of the twenty-first century would come from here. Between 1980 and 1992, the copper content in the Volga increased 11.5 times, zinc 9.8 times, lead and cadmium 4.9 times. By 1989, concentrations of petroleum products in the northern Caspian Sea exceeded the maximum amount permissible by the Soviet government by nine times. Large-scale muscle degeneration and mass starvation were observed among Caspian sturgeon in the late 1980s, caused by these toxic pollutants. All eggs collected from mature sturgeon in the Volga in 1990 were deformed.

In some of the caviar Sian had seen, the membranes between each egg had failed to form. The result was a black, stinking goo. She couldn't eat it, she said.

Now the industries that had caused much of the havoc were shutting down. They had no work. But it was too late to undo the damage. And the poachers who were now preying on the sturgeon were doing even more damage.

Not long after that party, Sian began a sponsored bike ride around Russia. She was killed by a drunken lorry driver coming round a bend on the wrong side of the road.

Everything was dangerous in exciting, cruel new Russia. Buying caviar was an exercise in fast talking, glib or nervous. You always made the same jokes ('caviar emptor', or, if you remembered the title of a famous Soviet book, 'the fateful eggs') as you took a deep breath or two, ready to start.

The traders were short men, always with a gleam of gold in the mouth, always with enormous smiles, and always wearing old suit trousers a couple of sizes too big, leaving a floppy concertina of synthetic greyish fabric around the ankle.

There'd be a couple of them, eyeing you from a corner. They'd have a little table with a lot of pickle jars on it. Big pickle jars, washed and resealed with greaseproof paper and a rubber band. Half-litre jars, and each one packed with dark eggs.

These caviar eggs had no history. There were no labels. You didn't know which jar contained osyotr, or sevruga, or beluga. Nor could you tell from the colour or size of the eggs. Sometimes they were as black as dye; sometimes they were a pearly grey, or brownish, or greenish (a slightly scary palette of colours). Sometimes they were big. Sometimes they were small. 'What kinds of caviar are these?' you'd ask in mid-negotiation, pointing at two or three very different-looking jars. 'All sevruga!' or 'All osyotr!' the answer always went. 'Every fish is different!' Perhaps the experts who wrote the neat descriptions on Western menus, talking about nutty flavour here and big pale eggs there, making each type of caviar sound completely different from the next, had just never seen so much caviar together. Or perhaps you were being sold dud stuff.

A shocked voice in your head kept saying, 'Just imagine what it would cost to get all that caviar in the West!' and 'It's stolen, you know it's stolen.' But it tasted good. And another voice would say, 'Good for them!' as you looked at the merry traders, and remembered the taste, and were drawn towards their mischievous thieves' smiles.

So you'd stride past, looking busy and purposeful and as if you had better things to do, but slyly checking them out too from the corner of your eye. Then you'd turn back, slooowly, reluctantly, trying to make your body language say, 'Oh yes! I almost forgot! Not that getting caviar really matters today . . .' It was better if there were two of you; more scope for exchanging melodramatically despairing glances, for wrinkling your nose at the price, for beating the salesmen down.

OK-lads-we-do-want-to-try-your-caviar (is-it-good-is-it-fresh?) but-the-price-has-to-be-right. No-ripoffs-ok?

Ksss. Fresh as mountain dew. Expertly prepared. Delicious. We have it for breakfast. Mmm. You wanna try? Try some! Or try this one! Here!

They had cleanish plastic teaspoons or wooden lollipop sticks. They took the paper off all the jars you were interested in, and scooped an egg or two off the top layer of each for you to taste, with a fresh spoon for each jar. You threw them on the ground when you were done. I think they picked them up later and rinsed them for re-use.

The trick, everyone said, was to take a spoon for yourself and delve deep into the jar. You needed to check whether there was a layer of sand, or earth, or pebbles hidden in the middle. So canny buyers pre-empted the salesmen, snatching a spoon and plunging it in to make sure they were getting only caviar. Sometimes there was an undignified scuffle as vendor and purchaser each tried to conduct the sale according to their own rules. But there were no rules. The quickest on the draw always won.

Hmm . . . Hmmm . . . Hmm. That one's not bad (but I'm not sure). What do you want for it?

Kss. Whatever you're not embarrassed to offer . . . However much Allah tells you to pay . . . A fine big jar like this (imploring, beseeching looks, interspersed with more big grins).

You had to haggle and cavil. But it was worth it. In the end you'd pay somewhere between twenty and a hundred dollars for enough caviar to feel sick on for days. As you left the market, you'd hear them pulling the next punter in with a soft 'Psst.'

CHAPTER SIX

In the Dollar Bubble

At first, life in the new Russia was just formless, frightening chaos. For most people, there seemed no escape from poverty: the value of your money shrank every hyperinflationary minute. Men died at fifty-seven of drink or fear (they amounted to the same thing). Everyone else dreamed of wealth, but didn't know where to find it. Girls dreamed of getting rich by becoming hard-currency prostitutes. Women poured out of their flats, selling anything they could on the pavements of central Moscow. At night, the tons of waste they left behind were swept into the streets and burned. You could see the Kremlin silhouetted in fire. There were knife fights and gunfights and bottle fights and protection rackets. The cinemas closed down, or only showed dud Western porn. Crooked vodka manufacturers mixed the stuff they sold in street kiosks with industrial alcohol, and killed their customers.

Was it true, or just an urban myth, that ambulance drivers knocked passers-by on the head and whisked them off to sell their body parts for cash? And how about the story that personable young men knocked at old ladies' doors, got them to sign away their rights to the flats they could now own, and inherited when the old ladies were later found crumpled in the snow below their balcony, or dead at the foot of the communal staircase? You wanted to laugh off stories like that; but you couldn't.

In the countryside, crops failed. In the provinces, whole towns went hungry and unpaid because the old Soviet industries were dying. In one grim Arctic town, where the sun hardly rose all winter long, miners who had long ago been forced north as prisoners of the Soviet state – and who stayed now because they couldn't afford to go anywhere better – went on strike when both their wages and food supplies disappeared. They seized the mine bosses' offices. Triumphantly, guiltily, fearful men with anxious smiles took me on a tour, but I couldn't see any sign in those poky little rooms that the bosses were better off than the men they bossed. One of the miners grabbed the door of the managers' fridge and yanked it open. 'Just look at the luxury stuff they get to eat!' he yelled. Inside, curled up on a saucer, were two tiny half-gnawed sprats in tomato sauce, out of a can, getting a bit smelly. I started to laugh at this anticlimax, but hastily stopped myself. He wasn't laughing. He was grabbing the fishy tails and shoving them into his mouth.

I made friends with Volodya, a shy musician with a stammer and a big bush of Marc Bolan curls. Once he had made his living playing in a dance band on Volga cruise ships all summer long. Now no one had money to pay him, and he seemed to exist without money, living with a big black long-haired cat in a single room in a communal apartment in the middle of town, not far from my home. His ex-wife, his daughter and his mother-in-law (and a lot more cats) also had rooms in the flat, which made him embarrassed to take his Australian girlfriend home. In his pain-fully honest way, Volodya worried and worried about how to make a living under capitalism. He was good with his hands, and had lots of ideas for gadgets that musicians would like; but there was no point in trying to manufacture anything for sale, he said. The Mafia would steal the profits. Once Volodya sold me a clever plastic cutting-and-slicing thing for the kitchen; but even telling me how it worked embarrassed him so badly that his stammer stopped him speaking for minutes at a time. Trading wasn't his thing either. That was for wide boys and the Mafia. Then someone told him he could privatise the flat and sell it to one of the Western businesses moving into Moscow for half a million dollars. It was a huge place: five big rooms, slap bang in the middle of town. But it seemed an impossible price to me. Still, he dreamed about it for months. His share would be enough to get a nice little flat further out, all to himself. Late one frosty night, we shared a cigarette on the balcony of his girlfriend's flat. 'I really need to get some money together soon,' he said, flicking ash down eleven floors over the tiny figures walking on the gleaming snow. There was a glint of something I hadn't seen before on his gentle face. 'People are making millions wherever you look. If only I could think of a really good way of ripping people off.' It should have been a joke, but I didn't even think of laughing. He meant it.

Victor came to Moscow from Leningrad – now officially called St Petersburg again – to see my new flat. I gave him tea. I had no sugar. I never have sugar. 'Don't you have sugar in the house?' Victor asked, and there was a tinge of genuine worry in his voice. He bought a pack of sugar lumps before catching the night train home.

Victor's family was muddling along somehow. 'Lena's job . . . well, she hardly ever gets paid,' he said. 'I don't know whether there's even any point her going there in the mornings.' He didn't bother with his job at all at the moment; it had pretty much folded. He was doing bits of translation to make ends meet (he had an instant translation programme on his computer, which produced gobbledigook versions of a Russian text in English within seconds). He was trying to get a new academic research grant from a new Western body. He had applied to George Soros, the European Bank for Reconstruction and Development, and any embassy cultural office that had forms for grants. Mouse needed expensive braces on her teeth.

For the moment, Nadya was keeping them. Luckily, she had wangled a part-time job working in the business centre of the smartest hotel in St Petersburg, the Yevropeiskaya, recently revamped by Scandinavians and now swankily called the Grand Hotel l'Europe. She got fat tips from fat businessmen. They liked her pert nose and her smiling blonde resourcefulness in three languages. The fact that Russians were automatically supposed to be servants to foreigners irritated her; but the money she was earning between university lectures was enough to stave off disaster.

I stayed a weekend in St Petersburg soon after Nadya got the job. A middle-aged American hotel guest called her late in the evening; he wanted her to walk for twenty minutes through the snow at midnight and deliver him a fax to his room. She put the phone down, looking crestfallen. 'It's so late, and it's cold,' she said sadly. But she didn't seem to have words for the cheerfully coarse speculation I might have indulged in about whether the man was going to try and jump her (which he obviously was) and she was clearly about to obey and trudge off to fiddle with fax machines and dodge the client for half of the rest of the night. She just looked depressed about it. I felt she was being exploited. 'You don't have to go,' I said, playing the big sister. 'Just say it's inconvenient. That's not being rude. You could promise to take him the fax first thing, while he's at breakfast; he'd still have it before work.'

'You know I'm not a prostitute,' she said.

It was as if our conversation had suddenly shifted into a parallel universe. It took my breath away even to think that anything I'd said might make her think that I might think that she might be a prostitute. Nothing of the sort had ever crossed my mind. But her saying it reminded me of the desperation all around. 'Of course not, of course not, heavens, I just think you shouldn't be pressured into running errands so late,' I babbled awkwardly. 'I just meant he shouldn't have asked you, it's about respect . . .'

I was blushing. But there was no need. She had heard a new idea. She was taking in its possibilities.

'What was that word you said? Inconvenient?' Nadya was saying now, and dialling the number. 'It's a bit inconvenient to come so late, but I can come in early and bring the fax to you first thing in the morning if that suits you,' she said into the receiver, very fast. A minute later, she put the phone down. She was smiling, with pink patches on her cheeks. 'It worked!' she said. 'He didn't mind!'

'I want Nadya to be educated abroad,' Victor began later. 'I want her out of this mess.'

'. . . ?'

'Someone is offering to pay for her education and give her a home with him, in Switzerland,' he went on. 'She could live there for nothing. He would ensure that he studied for her degree. She could start a new life.'

'. . . ?'

'He's a businessman. He's middle-aged. He's Swiss. He's very respectable.'

'. . . . . . ?'

Victor paused. 'But do you think there would be anything, well, improper about it?'

'Yes.' I nodded my head forcefully.

'Definitely?'

'Yes.'

He nodded sadly. 'Yes, I thought so too. But it's a pity. It seems such a good opportunity.' He couldn't quite get the wistfulness out of his voice.

Victor was knocked down by a car. His hip was badly smashed. He was in hospital for weeks and on crutches for months. 'I came round when I was lying in the road. A man in a car saw me and stopped. I couldn't speak, but I was so happy that he was going to call an ambulance and get me rescued. But all he did was stick his hand in my breast pocket – and go off with my wallet.'

There were many other weekends in St Petersburg. Victor and I used to go outside after supper, to the dungeon-like communal stairwell, where there was rising damp and windows darkened by decades of dust, and talk about life over a peaceful cigarette. He had made an ashtray out of an old can of sprats. One night we came out to find a ragged man hunched in the doorway. Victor hissed at him to go away. With a flash of needle, the man scuttled down towards the street. 'It's those lads upstairs,' Victor sighed. 'The market traders. Now they're pushing drugs from their flat too. There's big money in it. You get some strange types coming in here.' He picked up the hypodermic, covering his hand with his jacket sleeve. 'I don't like it. I don't want the girls to be exposed to people like that.'

Victor didn't like violence or self-destruction, but he admired anyone who could put one over on the system. His hero was Ostap Bender, who features in a post-revolutionary novel, a cheeky chancer who wandered round Russia fast-talking his way into money. Victor was always quoting Ostap Bender. He wanted to be like him. In a way, he succeeded: he got another three-year grant to re-do his old research. 'It will pay for Mouse's braces; it will pay for Nadya's schooling,' he said, chuckling.

And Victor enjoyed some of the criminal talk that the new life was bringing back into the language. I did too. 'I hung macaroni on his ear,' he would say, fangs gleaming with laughter. It meant, 'I told him a tall story.' It was one of the lively bits of language that had been 'freed' from the Soviet prison zone now that some of its inmates, imprisoned for crimes such as profiteering, which no longer counted as crimes under capitalism, were trickling back into ordinary life. There had been no contact between the rough and smooth ends of the Russian language in Soviet times. The underworld had been another world, and respectable Soviet Russian had been unbearably prim. (I knew Russian swearwords, but I would never use them. It would sound too shocking. The equivalent exclamation to the English 'Shit!' is '*Blyad!*' which means 'cunt'. It was acceptable to say '*Blin!*' instead, which means 'pancake' and made you sound as schoolgirlish as someone saying 'Sugar!' in English.) Victor was delighted, early one morning, when he heard Nadya trip up in the corridor on her way to the bathroom. 'And do you know what she said?' he asked fondly. 'She hissed, "Oh shit!" In English, too. So now I know that she's free of the slave mentality. And somehow or other she'll get away.'

Yet Victor's fangy smile had a twist in it these days. He talked mockingly about people playing on your sympathy with their fake tears, and shoving their begging bowls into your face. He also talked mockingly about the deals that were making a few Russians rich – the iffy oil licences, and dubious exports of strategic metals, and strange loans from ministers to their families to be banked right away in Switzerland. This tiny tribe was known, and hated, as the New Russians. 'Have you noticed how the people getting rich now are the ones with the contacts?' Victor said. 'Party contacts, that is, or criminal contacts. The same people are still running this country.'

Gradually Russian society was separating into two layers: the haves and have-nots, the dollar-earners and the rouble-earners, the caviar eaters and the rest.

The haves, the dollar-earners and the caviar eaters lived in the dollar bubble that was beginning to cover Moscow. There were foreign stores – the Irish shop, the Finnish shop, the German shop – where you could get every possible luxury food, at a price. Foreign-run restaurants opened, where you paid one hundred dollars or more for a plate of sushi, or one hundred dollars or more for an overblown High Russian experience, complete with stuffed bear and balalaika players. There was a nightclub in a military ice-hockey rink, called Red Zone after the Soviet prison zone, hung with scary Soviet-kitsch propaganda, where nearly naked girls writhed in cages suspended from the ceiling. There was the casino at the Leningradskaya Hotel, run by Wacko Jacko, a Scot who had left wartime Serbia because it wasn't exciting enough any more; the casino was packed with tough-looking men in suits and tough-looking girls in glamour rags. It had a metal detector at the door. I won a thousand dollars there at roulette from a single fifty dollar chip that Wacko Jacko gave me on my first visit. 'For the young lady,' he'd said patronisingly; how I enjoyed cashing in my winnings later. There was another metal detector at the door of Night Flight, or Night Fright, the club near me where bouncers with broken noses felt your wallet and felt for your gun before letting you in to see more nearly naked girls offering businessmen champagne and haggling over prices around a tiny dance floor. Businessmen staggering home in the early hours were beaten up by the lowlifers hanging around outside. They even robbed Wacko Jacko.

Inside the dollar bubble, life was a non-stop, glittering, frenzied thrill. It was chic to pretend not to live in it – to boast about going out with Russian friends, to casually mention bohemian night spots and artists' dives, to drop Russian words into your conversation, and to discuss how your ready wit had saved you from paying a dodgy traffic cop a bribe for an imaginary traffic offence. I did all that. But I also paid dollars for my flat, for my food, and even for taxis when I couldn't be bothered to haggle over a few roubles. Dollars meant I could jump queues and bypass boredom.

Dollars were so alluring, and so corrupting. A few greenbacks in your hand gave you an instant buzz of azart. You felt you could go anywhere, and do anything.

I loved Victor's family; but most ordinary Russians' endless complaints about the way life was turning out seemed wearisome to anyone in the dollar bubble. No money? So get a job! Set up a business! Democracy means taking charge of your life! On your bike! we chorused cheerfully, like an army of Margaret Thatchers. But what about the Mafia? they answered. We sighed at their defeatism and passivity and lack of enterprise, and changed the subject. You couldn't go out in the evening with Russians, except to concerts that were over by nine o'clock. They had no money, and it was embarrassing to buy them dinner in places where a meal cost a month's worth of their wages. It was often embarrassing to go to their houses, too: they'd feed you a feast, then complain that it had cost them a month's wages. Or they'd try and sell you things. Or they'd just ask, over and over again, how much things cost in England: how many dollars for a car? How many dollars for a house? How many dollars for a life?

Impatiently, we lucky ones with money talked about our have-not, dare-not Russian friends as a separate sub-category of our busy, important, wealthy lives; impatiently, we made our most exciting plans without them. It was boring to think about the pain of the poor.

As well as foreign stores and foreign restaurants, the dollar bubble inside Moscow was attracting foreign Russians. The country's hidden past was coming back to merge with its present. You could walk down any street now and find every possible kind of Russian jostling every other possible kind of Russian. All the fragmented, mutually exclusive societies that had existed since the Revolution – the White émigrés in their quarrelling groups, the Soviet émigrés in their quarrelling groups, the Jewish émigrés in their quarrelling groups, the career criminals in their underworld of prison camps and tattoos and fierce slang, the prisoners of conscience, dissident writers and musicians – were here. Everyone was having a flutter with fate.

The man who would have been Tsar, if Russia had wanted him, came to have a look at his homeland. Vladimir Kirillovich was old and tall and imposing, with baggy eyes. His father, a cousin of the last Tsar, had been the first Romanov to betray Nicholas II by swearing allegiance to the new rulers in 1917. He brought his jolly Georgian wife with him, and a planeload of Paris Russians, for a few days in St Petersburg. They wore beautiful furs. They had nothing in common with the nervous, badly dressed people they met in St Petersburg. Vladimir Kirillovich said eagerly that he was ready to help Russia in whatever way it wanted. But if he was hoping to be asked to come back as Tsar, he must have been disappointed. No one knew what to make of him. No one asked. He died soon afterwards. His daughter's son, Georgy, became the 'heir'. The young man – Spanish-educated, pizza-loving, plump – has taken the royal Romanov name, but his own father was a Prussian prince called Hohenzollern. He has his Georgian granny's dark looks. For a while, the family kept hopefully in touch with the Russian government, and dreamed of being brought back in the same way as Spain's royal family. But most Russians snicker and call Georgy by his Georgian nickname and Prussian surname: Gogo Gogenzollern.

A tall blond British teenager came to work for the accountants in my office. He was a sweet-faced boy called Peter who had grown up in West London. He spoke a bit of Russian, and he was working in Moscow while he thought about whether to go to university. When the time came for him to get business cards printed, he wanted them to carry his full name and title: Prince Peter Obolensky. We teased him about it. We called him 'Prince'. The title never made it on to the cards.

I met another prince at an embassy dinner. He was about my age. He had an American accent. He had a German princess for a wife. He had a royal Russian name and a neat imperial beard. He spoke old-fashioned White Russian: he'd been brought up to say 'quill' instead of 'biro', which Soviet Russians thought hilarious. He had a jolly laugh. He had plenty to laugh about: like all the bankers here now, he was probably making millions. And he had two small daughters. 'They ask me: "Papa, are you a New Russian?" ' he chortled. 'And I tell them: "I'm an Old New Russian." '

Homesick Soviet émigrés who had been abroad for years came too. Unlike the aristocrats, they knew approximately what they'd find. But they were still often astonished at the inflation, the mess, the many things now on sale, and the desperate looks on other people's faces. They also found it hard to fit in.

Andrei Konchalovsky, a film director, came back to Moscow after decades in Hollywood. He was slim and fit and tanned and amusing and wore designer sunglasses. Once a year he went to a health farm and fasted for a week. He went to live in the countryside near Moscow, next to his brother, another film director, Nikita Mikhalkov. It would have been hard to find two men less alike. Mikhalkov was beefy and broad-shouldered, a vodka-and-sausage man. He had a wide face, and suffering, watery eyes with a shaggy Cossack moustache. He was a Russian nationalist. Andrei made a film mocking Russian greed and drunkenness; Nikita made a film weeping for Russian suffering under Stalin. They were both nominated for the same prize at the Cannes film festival. Mikhalkov's *Burned by the Sun* won.

Poetical, bearded Alex Bachan came back from New York, where he had lived since he was fifteen when his parents had managed to emigrate from Odessa. He had a strange time in Moscow. He was one of the first of the flood of perestroika-era American correspondents; but to Russians he still sounded like a Russian, so much so that women in banks and post offices and dollar shops sometimes refused to serve him. 'Russians can't use this facility,' they snapped. 'But I am an American citizen!' he would wail. It was Alex's tragedy that he had emigrated just too late to speak English without a Russian accent: he sounded Russian to Westerners too. 'If I'd been eleven when we reached New York, or ten, just a couple of years younger, everything would have been so different. I would have grown up really American,' he would muse. His accent had trapped him in New York's Russian ghetto, working for Russian services of foreign radio stations, never quite able to escape a past that he had never belonged in. 'No one ever called me Russian when I was child – I was Jewish then,' he said sadly. 'So when I was at school I made up stories about how I spent every holiday in Leningrad. It seemed such a romantic, sophisticated, Western place to me. It was the closest I could imagine to abroad. I knew every street, every restaurant, every theatre in the city. But the truth was that I'd never been there. And even now, now that I'm an American citizen, I've still never been to St Petersburg. I wouldn't want to spoil my dream.'

All those years dreaming of Mother Russia, but once they got here they all wanted to be special, and different from other Russians.

The returning Russians hid behind their dollars. Their foreignness meant status; even a few dollars meant millionaire status.

Some of the boldest chancers in the Moscow dollar bubble weren't Russian at all. Foreigners were flooding in, all saying fine things about helping to turn Russia into a democracy, but all also hoping to profit in some way from the Russian chaos. There were financiers and investors hoping to get their hands on Russian assets; advisers from everywhere, hoping to become the power behind the throne in the new country; retailers setting up shops, or dreaming of beating the bureaucracy so they could set up shops and rake in dollars; journalists with jobs, like me, hoping to make a reputation; journalists without jobs, hoping they could get lucky and land themselves a posting.

An American journalist I didn't know asked me to put him up for a few days. He was a freelance, a big man with an easy salesman's laugh, trying the patience of his long-suffering wife and daughter back in New Jersey with his lengthy travels, on a smash-and-grab feature trip here to relay his impressions of Moscow to the folks back home. He liked it. He didn't speak Russian, or know about Russia, but he made friends wherever he went, and brought them home to be fed. Whenever the phone rang, Scott would pick it up with a mock grimace. 'It's the Beast!' he'd say, and roar. 'Gotta feed the beast!' And he'd start dictating his copy.

He stayed and stayed, and gradually expanded out of the spare bedroom till his belongings lay everywhere. After a week or so, he brought a packet of a cereal he liked as a contribution to the household. Scott had got to know my boyfriend in Nicaragua, a few years before, in the same way. He'd ended up staying six months with him, and even went on living in the house after my boyfriend left Nicaragua for good. 'Scott's very charming, isn't he?' my boyfriend said casually. 'I wonder what you'll make of him.'

One night, Scott found me curled up on the only unoccupied sofa, reading a book about the last Tsar's daughter, Anastasia, and Anna Anderson, the most convincing of the many people who claimed, after the Revolution, to be Anastasia and to have survived murder by the Bolsheviks. 'My grandfather's in that book,' he said knowledgeably. 'He nearly married Anastasia.'

So he was. So he had.

Scott's grandfather was a conman. His name was Irvin Baird. He came across Anna Anderson in 1930, a decade after she had first claimed to be Anastasia, and shortly after she had been taken in by Annie Jennings, a wealthy society lady in New York.

Things had already started going badly wrong between the Jenningses and their eccentric, difficult guest. Anastasia hated her room. She hated the servants. She hated the food. She shopped extravagantly on Miss Jennings' money. She thought the Jenningses were out to steal from her. Miss Jennings' brothers wanted to have her committed to an asylum.

Into this battleground walked Jill Lillie Cossley-Batt, an English adventuress. She claimed to be the Dowager Countess of Huntingdon. She claimed to be writing a book, *The Adolescent Life of Christ*. She claimed to be writing a piece on Anastasia for the London *Times*. She claimed to have known Anastasia in Russia. And she claimed Irvin Baird was her manager and boyfriend.

Anastasia didn't believe all of their wild stories. She certainly didn't believe that Irvin Baird was the son of the King of

England's physician, who was a Scottish duke. But she was desperate to leave the Jennings' house. So she played along for the next two months, in an incredible-sounding game of cat and mouse that Peter Kurth recounts in detail in his biography, *Anastasia: The Life of Anna Anderson*:

> Jill Cossley-Batt and Irvin Baird told Anastasia the Jenningses were out for her royal inheritance. They promised to write her memoirs for her, making enough money to get her a Canadian passport and bring her to England to be recognised as royalty.
>
> 'They were talking always about bringing me to England,' said Anastasia, but how did they mean to do it?
>
> Well, said Jill, they could cross the border into Canada secretly, without a visa, and then get a letter to the Prince of Wales. He would take care of everything.
>
> Anastasia had reached the end of her rope. Whom was she going to trust? Miss Jennings kept calling and cabling and begging her to come up to (her country house), but Jill and Baird were warning her that 'for God's sake (she) should not go ... for they would do something to (her) there ... the Jenningses had told them that they intended to lock (her) up.' All the while Jill and Baird were getting bolder. 'They drank without my permission,' Anastasia observed sternly. They read her letters. One day, she found them rummaging through her closet. And then Baird had a plan: Anastasia should marry him, thereby solving all of her legal problems. And if the notion of marriage didn't appeal to her, maybe they could arrange something else. Did she get the idea?

It was only after the London *Times* cabled that Jill Cossley-Batt was 'entirely unauthorised to represent us', and it emerged that she was known elsewhere as 'Lady Lilian Mountbatten', that Anastasia parted company with these strange friends. Even then, the decision was not hers. Unexpectedly, they announced that they were leaving for good. Baird's final words to Anastasia were, 'Go to hell!'

On this ungracious note, Irvin Baird disappeared from history. As I finished the pages and looked up, Scott beamed at me, full of family pride. Did Irvin Baird look like him? I wondered.

'What became of your grandfather afterwards?' I asked curiously.

'Oh, you know,' Scott answered cheerfully. 'He had a wife and children back home all along. But he had this English woman friend in Europe too. And he'd just take off on long trips, for a couple of years at a time, for most of the rest of his life. Nobody in the family ever really knew what he was doing while he was away.'

Meeting Irvin Baird and his girlfriend was bad for Anastasia. Her relationship with Miss Jennings broke down completely when, 'in a fit of anger over Miss (Cossley-Batt) and Mr Baird', she strangled her hostess's parrot. A court ruled her insane, a danger to herself and others. One night, men broke down the door to her room, found her cowering in the bathroom, dragged her to her feet and took her off to an asylum.

Scott stayed three weeks with me before I asked what his plans were next. Charming though he was, I was beginning to want my privacy back. He was expecting the question. Without any fuss, he found a new place a couple of days later and moved on. But he had an affinity with the dollar bubble: the next time he came to Moscow he was on an official assignment, and his new bosses paid for a five-star hotel room.

The return of Russia's past was like something out of a book. A specific book: the comic fantasy about the future that a Soviet émigré novelist called Vladimir Voinovich had written a decade before 1991 – long before it had seemed possible that any of this might happen.

Moscow 2042 tells the story of a laid-back émigré narrator from West Germany, not unlike Voinovich himself, who takes a time-travel holiday to the 'communite' state of tomorrow. It is run by the Genialissimo. It is even more decrepit and cynical than the Communist state of 1982. Another, grander émigré – a terrifying, bossy, self-regarding old man called Sim Simych Karnavalov, who is living in Canada and is intended to be not unlike the real-life Alexander Solzhenitsyn – has made the narrator take a floppy disk of Karnavalov's over-long and pompous works to the future. Karnavalov wants his work spread secretly among the unfree communites, so they will rise up against their rulers. The narrator finds that this can't be done. There's only one state-owned computer in the future state – and it doesn't really exist. So he goes on his merry way, shagging a pretty communite honeytrap and poking predictable fun at communite corruption, laziness and jargon for the next four hundred pages or so.

Just when you're getting bored, the book ends with a bang. Without warning, thousands of supporters of Karnavalov, the Simites, appear in Moscow. They overthrow the communites. The old toadies and time-servers go to ground. Within minutes they have disguised their pasts with flowing hair and cardboard crosses. Sim Simych's body, which has been waiting in the deep freeze for this moment for the last sixty years, is defrosted; he somehow manifests himself, flanked by Cossack guards, as the new Tsar and Autocrat of all the Russias, Serafim I.

By the next day, Moscow is transformed. There are hangings and crucifixions and beheadings; compulsory baptisms in the Russian Orthodox faith; orders that machines must be replaced by horses, men grow beards, women wear ankle-length clothes, and Western dances be banned. Communite officials reinvent themselves in Cossack trousers and horse-drawn carriages. All portraits of the Genialissimo are somehow instantly replaced by portraits of the new Tsar Serafim killing dragons on horseback. A magazine called *The Imperial News* is displayed in government offices. Double-headed eagles, the insignia of the old Tsars, replace the red stars of the communites.

Even the street names change. 'First we drove down Marx Avenue; its age-old name, Hunter's Row, had already been restored,' the narrator notices with fascination as he is swept off to the Kremlin for a final interrogation by the Solzhenitsyn-esque Tsar.

By the time I got back to Moscow, life was furiously imitating art: the cityscape was changing almost as fast as it had in Voinovich's book.

The central street formerly known as Marx Avenue had really reverted to the old name of Hunter's Row. On the night the Soviet state died, portraits of the Soviet leader vanished. On tired Soviet sewing machines, mothers all over the country ran up neo-Cossack uniforms with red piping and epaulettes for their strapping sons. Strutting Cossacks with droopy moustaches began to appear at parliament meetings, in the street, and in church, shoving their way to the front. A growing number of men grew straggly beards to show their faith. Churches got fuller and fuller of devout women hissing at female newcomers to cover their heads with a shawl. Double-headed eagles, the insignia of the old Tsars, were restored, along with the Tsars' tricolour flag, as Russian emblems (though the red Soviet stars glowing on top of the Kremlin towers and on army tanks stayed where they were). The mayor of Moscow put up medieval-looking posters of St George slaying the dragon, the city's new emblem.

Moscow's restoration took on a cartoonish life of its own. Mock-medieval churches and imitation ancient gates shot up. So did luxury shopping malls, a replica nineteenth-century cathedral, a 300-foot-high golden statue of Peter the Great planted in the river, floodlighting that turned fountains the red of the blood of innocents, and flashing banks of neon lights that banished wistfulness forever from Pushkin Square. The real Solzhenitsyn stayed in America, in self-imposed exile, for another three years. Who cared about him? Everyone else with a few bucks for a ticket home was already here, watching history in the making, and making it up as they went along.

Even the Devil came to Moscow, and his appearance meant hope.

The devil in question was Voland, the charming, witty, Faustian Prince of Darkness of a cult novel that had been banned for decades, but that everyone had read.

Mikhail Bulgakov's hilarious, sad *The Master and Margarita* deals with the visit Voland pays to mid-century Soviet Moscow. He comes with assorted minor imps and sprites: a beautiful naked red-headed witch called Hella, a hard-boiled talking, flying, gun-toting cat called Begemot (Hippo), and a pair of cheerful befanged heavies called Azazello and Fagot (one short and fat, one tall and thin with a tendency to levitate). They take over a flat off the Garden Ring road in Moscow (where Bulgakov himself once lived). They hold a magic show at the Variety Theatre in which they shower a greedy, feverish audience with money and glamorous party clothes (which later disappear into thin air). They dispense rough, light-hearted justice: the many liars, cheats, hypocrites and timeservers they meet are duly beheaded, or kicked downstairs, or arrested, or suddenly find themselves in faraway seaside towns. But the good are rewarded. Voland rescues the Master, who once wrote a novel about the life of Jesus that destroyed his life, lost him his beloved Margarita, and left him shut in a Soviet psychiatric ward. Voland reunites the Master and Margarita, and restores the Master's novel, burned in a long-ago moment of despair; 'manuscripts do not burn,' he says. After throwing a magical Satanic ball in the flat on the Garden Ring, he lets the lovers escape their lives in Moscow to live forever in a quiet, lilac-shaded basement. Then, having briefly restored both darkness and light to this grey, cowardly city, the devils vanish, leaving only a vague memory that troubles one poet when the moon is full.

By 1991, anyone who crept into the rundown courtyard of a certain six-floor building on the Garden Ring could rediscover the Devil and his minions. The house where Satan's Ball had been held was a shrine to the people who dared to hope that the troubles of today might bring good tomorrow. They had covered the courtyard walls with chalky graffiti: pictures of Begemot the black cat and his demonic mates, and the novel's most famous, most defiant quote repeated over and over again in every imaginable language. The pictures carried on in through one of the staircase doors and up a dark, scary flight of stairs. The door to Bulgakov's old flat was locked. (People said it was a squat. I once knocked, but there was no answer.) Yet the silent top landing was a secretive riot of colour, mischief and imagination.

Hope was the most wonderful and surprising thing about Russia in those confusing days. Even if life now was terrifying, there was also a real sense that it was the beginning of freedom from fear. The powerful were less powerful; the KGB was being disbanded. It was a time of daring gestures and extraordinary revelations. Every day, more guilty secrets from the past were published in the newspapers. One day it might be photos of Lenin – in a wheelchair, clearly at death's door, with sick, mad, empty eyes – when he still officially ran the Soviet Union. Another day you might suddenly read an eye-witness account of exactly how the erudite, private, dignified poet, Osip Mandelstam, had ended his days mad and lost in the gulags. The subtext of every exposé was the same: the truth will out. Manuscripts do not burn.

Victor's gesture of faith in the future was to flog the Marx and Lenin volumes clogging up his bookcase. He and Nadya replaced the entire smug leathery set with just one book. Of course it was *The Master and Margarita*.

I made a gesture of faith in dollars. I went to Satan's Ball.

It was held on the first capitalist Easter weekend, in 1992, in a quiet little enclosed park not far from the Bulgakov flat. You had to pay a substantial amount in dollars for your invitation card, printed in curly, old-fashioned Russian writing. You had to pay still more if you wanted to dine in the inner sanctum, which would be made to look like the book's luxury restaurant for state-approved writers, the House of Griboyedov. The idea was to raise enough money to turn the flat on the Garden Ring into a museum. I'd never heard of anything like it in Russia. I went with two friends.

It is never very dark in Moscow in summer, and in May the first leaves are out and the air is fresh. We wandered under the trees of the Hermitage Garden and watched gypsies dance and eat fire. Girls in wisps of chiffon were screaming in the basket of a hot-air balloon. The snake-charmer offered us a hold of her eight-foot snake, and, in the little theatre at the edge of the park, a souped-up cabaret version of the Satan's Ball scene from the novel was being performed, with Lenin and Stalin lookalikes meeting the Devil in Hell. You could smell shashlyk on the air, and the moon was full. We bought champagne and passed the bottle round, because there were no glasses. The magic of the evening was that no one knew quite what to do, and everyone was too happy to care.

We'd only paid for the outer darkness, where the Master and Margarita lived, but when the breeze got too chilly my friend from London, who'd come to see whether he could make instant millions exporting something from Moscow, got bored of lending me his tuxedo and flashed enough dollars to get us into the inner sanctum. It was expensively gloomy inside, with chandeliers and ruched satin drapes. There were enormous platters of sturgeon and caviar on the overloaded table. There were glasses for the champagne here, too, but somehow no one seemed to be having quite such a good time as they were in the park.

It took a few minutes for our eyes to adjust to the thicker, smugger interior darkness. We watched the other diners: more dinner jackets than leather jackets in here, but an awkwardness in the air too.

'Look,' my friend whispered suddenly, and nudged me. At a corner of the buffet table, half hidden by a satin curtain, someone had drawn up a chair. It was an old woman in rags: an obvious gatecrasher. She was the only person in the room who didn't feel ill-at-ease. Ignoring everyone else, she was working her way through a three-foot-wide tray of caviar canapés, one by relentless one. Even when her mouth was full, her hands were picking out more black morsels and dropping them into a napkin in her open poacher's bag. She had a smear of forgotten fish eggs on her chin and a self-absorbed smile on her mouth.

We stared. We counted the improbable numbers of canapés disappearing down her throat. We grinned at each other in astonishment, amazed at her cheek as much as her gluttony. Other people were staring too. You could see everyone wondering whether she really was just a bag lady who had somehow got in past the bouncers, as it appeared; or whether she was a Bulgakov scholar down on her luck, like so many intellectuals nowadays; or whether she was actually part of the entertainment – some sort of parable from the book being re-enacted here to see if we'd respond like its less attractive Soviet characters. There was no way of knowing.

She didn't care. She knew no one was going to tackle her, even the waiters who should probably have thrown her out. You could see them thinking, 'Good for her,' as they tactfully steered a circular course around her, or put more enormous trays of caviar within easy reach. She'd got so lucky. It wouldn't have been in the spirit of the evening to give her a hard time.

We tiptoed back out to the light-hearted gypsies. It was dawn before we walked home. It was my best night in the dollar bubble. Perhaps it was the bag lady's best night too.

* * *

Inside the dollar bubble, everyone got mysteriously richer and richer.

My boyfriend visited me in Moscow and wrote a story for his paper about a young New Russian millionaire who had just bought his seventh luxury car, a Rolls-Royce. Now he had a new set of wheels for every day of the week. The young man took my boyfriend out for a lobster dinner with champagne. When he was asked how he had made so much money so fast, the young man answered laconically, 'Import-export.'

How had the trendy democratic mayor of St Petersburg got enough money to knock his flat through to the flats all around, creating a luxury penthouse with a glassed-in orangery on top? And who had bought him a country mansion? Why did the Moscow Patriarchate of the Orthodox Church have a licence to import fags and booze duty-free? Who was getting the licences to export Russia's fabulous oil wealth? And how were the lucky winners selected? The newspapers asked, but there were no answers.

The bubble was growing so big that it could accommodate more and more of the wily people who were finding ways to escape the terrors of life on the outside.

My musician friend Volodya sold his flat for half a million dollars.

How can we catch criminals in their fast cars when we drive clapped-out Soviet rust-buckets? the police complained. Soon they began to drive more glamorous crime-busting vehicles, with screaming sirens and flashing lights and orange go-faster stripes. They looked prouder, though they didn't catch any more criminals.

A Moscow husband and wife set up a Young Ladies' Academy. For a hefty consideration, young ladies could learn modelling, deportment, etiquette, fashion design and lap dancing. Graduates might be lucky enough to be sent to Western Europe on a nightclub tour. It smacked of white slave trade to me, but the provincial girls lining up to be relieved of their life savings didn't seem worried. The directors, a former circus ringmaster and lion tamer, were doing nicely.

Tanya came to our office sometimes. She was a life-long friend of Olya, who worked with me. Tanya wore sharp suits. She had a tiny mobile phone. But she always looked lost, and sat for too long in the office kitchen, where the drivers sat and smoked, whispering over cups of tea with Olya. 'Meet Tanya! Tanya's a real New Russian!' Olya would screech happily to anyone who came in, and Tanya would look embarrassed and wriggle and say shhhhhhhh. 'Poor Tanya,' Olya would say later. 'She's rich, but she has no life any more; she can only see her old friends on the sly. She's desperate for normal friendships.' Tanya's husband had managed to become the sidekick to a New Russian millionaire called Roma. She had been catapulted into a stiff, unyielding world of receptions and chandeliers. There was no give and take in it; you always had to be on your smiling best behaviour. Whenever Tanya thought she might be able to spend a relaxed weekend with her real friends from before, there'd be a last-minute invitation from Roma. It wouldn't pay to refuse. So Tanya would call Olya on her mobile. 'I'm so sorry,' she'd falter. 'Roma has called for us . . .'

'And what does Tanya's husband think about being a slave to Roma's whims?' I asked.

Olya's eyes glittered. 'Oh, he doesn't mind. He's a man making his fortune. It's azart.'

It was rare to meet anyone with the gift of serenity. But I did know one or two people who seemed happy without dollars.

Larissa Deville came back briefly from the Greek island where she lived now to organise a Moscow exhibition of her German lover's paintings. She was small, dark and still beautiful, dressed in dark, restrained, French clothes. She had left Moscow long before for love, marrying and going to France as she finished her medical studies. Now she had an eighteen-year-old student son in France, and an artist lover called Wolfgang to live with. All her life, artists had wanted her to be their model, or their muse. I met her through an English friend in Moscow, who had met her while honeymooning on her island. At home, she liked to help with the harvest, he said.

The three of us went out together on a magical summer evening, in a golden twilight that lasted for hours, into a Russia without dollars.

Larissa had a friend at the Taganka Theatre. She took us backstage to admire the famous people's signatures on the dressing-room walls. She introduced us to the peppery director, Yuri Lyubimov, who shouted at us. Then she took us to the races, explained the fiendishly complicated betting system, and showed us how to queue to place our bets. The horses trotted in, their little carriages flying behind them. We tore up our losing tickets and threw them to the exhilarating wind. It was a scruffy-men-in-overcoats sort of place, with fag ends on the floor and vodka swigged behind fences. But it was at one end of a ludicrously opulent yellow stucco palace, built for Stalin's horse-mad son; a New Russian had made a restaurant and casino at the other end.

So we crossed back over from the rouble zone to the dollar zone, and took her to dinner at the casino. There, we played roulette among the joyless wives of New Russian millionaires, and lost. We ate grand food, served by grand waiters. A violinist came to the table and bowed over his instrument to play soupy café music. The sun set through sparkling picture windows.

'We shouldn't have come here,' Larissa said. We were finishing our coffee. The violinist was pocketing our dollars. 'It's sleazy. We should have stayed at the races. We were having a much better time back there, proletarian style.'

There were other distractions from the dollar bubble.

Moscow was full of crazy artists who didn't care about dollars. Sasha Petlyura's squat was a big empty building on the Boulevard Ring. He had somehow fastened cars upside-down to the walls around the courtyard. The rooms down the long corridors were full of his treasures: dozens of curly-haired bright green caps, like mad wigs; dozens of Lenin busts; a huge aquarium filled with plastic lobsters. Sometimes he just had parties there. Sometimes they were parties with bonfires, or parties with Alternative Fashion Shows. Once, Pani Bronya, the ancient, wrinkled, sweet-natured ex-ballerina who lived with Petlyura and his German countess girlfriend, starred in an Alternative Fashion Show. She waddled down the catwalk, waving and smiling. She wore a stripy shift dress, one of the hairy green caps, a snorkel, a rubber face mask and a pair of flippers.

Sometimes Larissa took me away to the country. We looked at churches being restored, or walked in the quiet birch woods in the sun, or picked wild flowers. She taught me the affectionate peasant words for dandelion – a direct translation would be something like 'blowaway' – and ladybird – 'holy cow' – and buttercups – 'chicken blindness'. We stopped at roadside stalls, and came back to town in the evening with bags full of cucumbers and coriander.

I liked those brief reminders that quiet happiness was possible outside, but I was still always secretly happy to get back to the action inside the dollar bubble.

More and more raffish foreigners came to Moscow. We partied and feasted. We explored the past, the present and the provinces. I travelled around Russia alone for weeks on end, looking for stories. I didn't have a care in the world.

But it was too good to last for long. Another kind of foreigner started coming.

One night I went to a party where there were three people I'd been at university with in England. Everyone was talking tame, dull, expat talk, the kind you could hear anywhere, about international schools, dollar apartment prices, little Johnny's piano lessons and how to join the American embassy gym.

'There goes the neighbourhood,' my fellow adventurers and I said snootily, and took ourselves off in a cowboy cab to the new Indian restaurant on Tverskaya Street. It was half full. At a table near the door I saw four people I'd been at university with.

When summer was just beginning, a few days after Satan's Ball, I went to the market to buy a feast. I bought a giant jar of caviar, a suckling pig, salad leaves, a watermelon and sweet Soviet champagne (it tasted terrible, but it was fashionable to drink it, and fun when you had to saw the plastic cork off with a bread knife).

There was to be a celebration. My future husband was coming to live in Moscow.

I'd met him once or twice before I came to Russia. We worked together for a couple of days. Then he started to write to me. He signed himself 'your admirer'. He looked boyish and shy, but his letters were full of adventures. He went to New York and practised fencing with his Latin American friends. He had Nicaraguan friends whose idea of fishing was to throw a stick of dynamite in the river, and catch the fish as they rained down from the sky. He had Nicaraguan friends whose idea of a party was a pile of cocaine as big as a bag of flour. He even had one Nicaraguan friend who had assassinated a right-wing leader from her sports car, with her hair swinging loose, wearing a pink jacket. He had a red sports car. He drank champagne.

Before starting my life in Moscow, I had three weeks of holiday in London. He took me out to dinner. 'I'm going on holiday to the Isle of Skye tomorrow,' he said. 'Come with me.' We set off in the red sports car, but we only got as far as Edinburgh before he said, 'Marry me,' and, 'I know. I know you're the one.'

I said yes. We bought a ring. We drank champagne. And then I flew away to Moscow. I didn't know whether anything would come of it. But it was romantic and exciting. It was what you did when you were young and free and brave. Wasn't it?

'Marry me now,' he said on the phone every night.

'Not while you live in London and I live in Moscow,' I said. So he got a job in Moscow.

'Marry me now,' he said.

Now it was May. The wedding was to be in August. Mouse was going to be a bridesmaid; my casino win was going to pay for her family to come to London. It was all arranged. It had sneaked up on me before I'd thought about it properly. I could understand why blushing fiancées said, 'But this is so sudden.'

My friend from London, who could cook, came to the market with me to choose the sweetest of the suckling pigs for our feast. He called the dead piglet Eric. He laid him gently in the fridge, on a big plate, curled up as if he were sleeping. There were wedding invitations on the kitchen table where we unpacked our treasure.

The date on the invitations was in brilliant sunshine. It suddenly seemed far too soon. I knew nothing about my future husband. I didn't even know whether he'd want me to stop racketing unrespectably around and settle down to quiet nights of expat chat.

'Do you think I could just change the year on the invitations, and make the wedding next August?' I asked, only half joking.

That afternoon, I went back to the market. I bought more caviar for the feast that night. It was an excuse to sniff the summer wind, look at the light glinting on the caviar salesmen's teeth, and dream of making my escape to the wild south soon.

CHAPTER SEVEN

South Down the River of Azart

In Russia, to go south is risking danger and braving the unknown. But it also carries with it the possibility of rewards beyond the adventurer's wildest dreams.

When Ivan the Terrible sniffed the summer breeze and headed south down the Volga River, he not only conquered the last Tatar khanates of Kazan and Astrakhan, wiping out centuries of humiliation, but also transformed his small, backward northern principality into a fully-fledged Russian state with access to the outside world over the Caspian Sea.

Although the south has remained here-be-dragons territory on the edge of the map of the known world, the wilder kind of adventurer from Russia has been hunting for thrills down there ever since.

Adventures take the same route as young sturgeon, down the Volga to the sea. If they are lucky they come back north at the end of their adventures, following the mature sturgeon heading upriver to spawn and die, with heads full of travellers' tales and a fortune in Caspian commodities: silk, oil and caviar.

The great, shallow, sluggish Volga is the route down which the gleeful, questing, selfish spirit that the Russian state can't cope with is channelled: the river of azart.

Daredevil English sea-dogs were among the first foreigners to find their way to Russia, and then, once the authoritarian Russian state had given them prickles of claustrophobia, south down the Volga to freedom and sea wind.

The first visit to Russia, by Richard Chancellor in 1553, was an accident. His ship, part of a three-boat fleet trying to get to China, got blown into port at Kholmogory on the White Sea, and the captain set off for the barbarous, secretive town of Moscow to meet 'Ivan Vasilevich Emperour of Russia and great Duke of Moscovia' in person.

Dozens of Englishmen followed him to Moscow, lured by the generous commercial privileges offered by Ivan the Terrible in a trade treaty with England in 1555. The paranoid Russian Emperor hoped Elizabeth I would in return offer him refuge if the hatred of his own countrymen one day forced him from power; but the first travellers' appalled reports of outlandish Russian cruelty, savagery, hard drinking and general sinfulness ensured that no such offer would ever be made.

Chancellor was repelled by the contrast between the show-off gold plates and goblets at the Tsar's feasts and the Russian court's shabbiness when not on public display. Jerome Horsey was revolted to watch a treacherous Russian nobleman executed by being impaled on a stake and left for fifteen hours; the victim's mother was raped by a hundred soldiers and her remains eaten by the Tsar's hounds. Giles Fletcher was disgusted by a Russian tendency to cheat and break promises, as well as by the 'straungenesse of the murders, and other cruelties committed among them, that would scarcely bee believed to bee done among men, specially such as professe themselves Christians'. A generation later, George Turberville, the most amusing of the horrified travellers, expressed his distaste for Russian ways in rhyme:

> *I feel a thousand fits of deepe and deadly woe,*
> *To thinke that I from land to sea, from blisse to bale did go.*
> *I left my native soile, full like a retchless man,*
> *And unacquainted of the coast, among the Russes ran:*
> *A people passing rude, to vices vile inclined,*
> *Folke fit to be of Bacchus traine, so quaffing is their kinde.*

Just four years after Chancellor first saw the Kremlin keep's walls, Anthony Jenkinson, another Englishman in Moscow, became the first to leave for the south. Jenkinson's southern get-rich-quick scheme was to open up a trade route via Russia and the newly opened Caspian Sea to Persia. He planned to come back loaded down with Oriental silks and spices. It was a dream that tormented English adventurers for two centuries. They tried and tried to make it come true. But none of them succeeded. Danger was everywhere. English ships ran aground on the Volga's shallows in summer, or were crushed by ice in the winter, or sank in Caspian storms. English crews were attacked by Russian pirates or Tatar robber gangs. They naively challenged members of the region's tough trading nation, the Armenians, and usually came off worst. They walked into elaborate rivalries, or wars, between the Russians, Persians and Turks who all wanted control of the sea. They fell sick. They were beaten up. They committed suicide.

All Jenkinson achieved, after four years of stumbling into

the wars raging around the sea between Turks and Persians, was to raise the red cross of St George, the royal banner of England, on the Caspian.

Pursuing the same dream, another expedition led by Christopher Burrough set sail in 1579. The travellers lost most of their cargo when one ship was stranded, lost another ship which was cut to pieces by ice, and were ambushed by Tatars, but did finally make it back to Astrakhan. Perhaps unsurprisingly, they gave up.

More than a century later, John Elton, a merchant operating from St Petersburg under Peter the Great, tried one more time to make a fortune from the Caspian silk route. He came a cropper too. Feeling unstoppable, he got too greedy and overstretched himself. Elton's mistake was to go over to the side of the Shah of Persia, who made him an admiral and instructed him to patrol the Caspian, forcing Russian ships to acknowledge Persian paramountcy. The Russians were furious. Anxious English merchants in St Petersburg sent a young envoy, Jonas Hanway, to lure the lavishly turbaned Elton back home. He failed. Elton stayed on. In 1746, Russia banned the English from any more trade with Persia over the Caspian, and the dream died.

Back home, by their quiet firesides, the former adventurers recalled their travels at leisure. They argued over the Caspian's greatest mystery: the waters that drained away for years at a stretch, as if disappearing down a plughole. They wondered whether a secret tunnel connected the Caspian Sea to the Black Sea next door, and whether a whirlpool swept away the waters pouring into the sea from the Volga and other tributary rivers, and whether there was any truth in the fishermen's tales of boats swallowed up as the waters glugged away into the unknown.

They also remembered caviar, the taste of adventure, the taste of their lost glory days.

Russians ate caviar on fast days, especially during Lent, when meat was banned. But there was no noticeable sense of restraint about their fishy dinners. The *Domostroi* – the rule book for Russian households under Ivan the Terrible – permitted the following Lenten dishes:

> The little loaves used during a fast, pike caviar, pressed caviar, fresh sturgeon caviar, caviar gleaned from sturgeon during the autumn, fresh caviar from sturgeon and sterlet, liver of pike spiced with saffron, white salmon casserole, pink salmon liver, black pike liver, pike-perch casserole, sterlet casserole, fresh sturgeon casserole, fresh white salmon casserole, fresh sturgeon liver, pickled beluga liver, dried sturgeon, beluga liver, smelt, dried smelt, layers of carp and ide, boiled caviar, mixed caviar, dried sturgeon bellies, pickled fish bellies, fish spines stewed in vinegar, boxed sterlet, boiled tongue, smoked sturgeon bellies, smoked beluga bellies, beluga tongue, grilled sturgeon, noodles from dried peas, groats with poppyseed oil, split pea soup, mashed peas, two kinds of cabbage soup, pancakes, onion tarts, fritters, pies stuffed with poppy seeds, sweet jellies and unleavened bread.

The travellers remembered the extravagance of those groaning tables in Moscow or St Petersburg, but also the quiet pleasure of eating eggs straight from the belly of the fish at the sharp southern end of their journeys. John Cook, a Scottish doctor who spent the 1740s travelling around the Caspian, wrote nostalgically: 'I imagine no part of any fish, at least which I have tasted, is comparable to the fresh caviar.'

It was another century and a half before the Caspian drew another flood of adventurers to its shores. This time, it was the oil bubbling spontaneously up from underground around the port town of Baku, capital of the Turkish-speaking area, Azerbaijan, which suddenly promised untold wealth.

An oil boom began in Baku in 1870. The oil was shipped up the Volga to industrialised Europe. By the end of the century, Baku was producing more oil than the whole of the United States, and the industry was employing twenty-seven thousand men.

The big winner this time was Robert Nobel, a gunmaker whose brother, Alfred, manufactured explosives. Robert came down from St Petersburg to source wood for rifle butts, realised the potential of the region's oil, and stayed on in the south to set up a refinery. The Nobel company became one of the biggest oil firms in the world. Nobel was hastily followed by anyone with an eye for a quick fortune: British, French, German, Belgian and Dutch firms piled in to compete for leases, and even the canny local Armenians got in on the act, controlling nearly a third of Baku's industries by the turn of the century.

The fabulous fortunes being made from the Caspian's oil vanished as unexpectedly as they had come. Oil made Baku the prize to fight for at the start of the twentieth century, in the decade of the First World War, the Russian Revolution and the Civil War. Dozens of local political rivals, spies and foreign armies converged on the city and the seashore around it.

In 1918, nationalists in Baku declared Azerbaijan and its oil independent. Over the next two years, Baku was ruled in swift succession by a twenty-six-man Bolshevik Commune (arrested as they tried to escape the town, and later murdered), Armenians and Russians, a British military force, a Turkish-German army, the British again, and Muslim nationalists.

Finally, in the spring of 1920, power (and control of the oil) passed to the invading Red Army's choice of communists. The foreign oil millionaires lost the source of their wealth. The Soviet part of the Caspian closed itself off from the world.

The consequences of the Bolshevik victory were disastrous for one dashing young British spy, Captain Reginald Teague-Jones. He had been gadding about in the region all through these troubles, having a whale of a time, darting in and out of Baku whenever it was in enemy hands, stealing maps of the harbour, egging on the various ill-assorted factions fighting for Baku to act in line with British policy, and falling in love with a pretty Russian girl.

In 1920, once the fate of Baku was settled, the Bolsheviks accused Teague-Jones, personally, of having murdered the twenty-six Commissars. They weren't interested in Teague-Jones's story that the Commissars had in fact been executed by a rival political faction. Not wanting to wait for the vengeance of the terrifying Leon Trotsky, who, in those days, still held the power of life and death over millions and was thought to have a network of agents and assassins stretching all over the world, Teague-Jones went to ground.

It was only after he died, at the age of ninety-nine, that the world found out (through an obituary in *The Times*) what had happened to Teague-Jones. He had been forced to adopt an alias, becoming 'Ronald Sinclair' for the rest of his life. Nurses at the home in Plymouth where 'Ronald Sinclair' had ended his days were not entirely surprised. It solved the mystery that had puzzled them for years: why Sinclair's gentle Russian ex-wife had always addressed him not as 'Ronnie' but as 'Reggie'.

Teague-Jones was the last crazy adventurer of his kind. Soviet leaders had no time for selfish individualists brimming with azart. It was seventy years before the curious, the explorers, the romantics, the conmen and the get-rich-quick merchants looked at the dark oil smudges on the map, or sniffed the summer air in a Moscow street market, and came pouring back to the Caspian to try their luck again.

CHAPTER EIGHT

The Caspian,
Where Sturgeon Come From

It is after midnight, and hours after the start of the curfew (in theory, at least, this is a country at war). But if you stand on your hotel balcony and look out over the vast Soviet panorama of concrete and dust for long you will still see the occasional car racing along the seafront. The sudden noise is startling. You swing your head to follow its headlights until it disappears into the Black Town, and all that is left is the ghostly sound of panic, rattling and revving.

And then there's just you and the night, and the occasional burst of meaningless gunfire somewhere far away (or perhaps the bangs are backfiring cars). The square in front of you is enormous. The hot air is scented with exhaust fumes, but sometimes you think there might also be hints of jasmine and roses in it. The fountains don't work, but the sky is cloudless and swooning with stars, the main street behind you is called Nightingale Avenue, and the sea on your right, beyond the luscious garden promenade, is murmuring love songs in a language you don't understand.

I had made it to the south at last. It was 1993, the spring after I'd got married. I was waiting for the coup that seemed certain to happen here one day soon.

Most people in Azerbaijan didn't feel they had much to celebrate. Their country had become independent in 1991, and it had so much oil waiting to be extracted from its seabed that it would one day be very rich. But first the Azerbaijanis had to win the war they were losing, and that seemed impossible. Azerbaijan's enemy was a vague army of ethnic Armenian irregulars in the province of Nagorno-Karabakh, who were citizens of Azerbaijan but now wanted their region to be independent. They had kicked out the local Azerbaijani population before advancing out of their hill zone. They now held something like a fifth of Azerbaijan.

Azerbaijan's existing oil income was all going on losing the war. The new president was a nationalist, and his reputation depended on beating the Armenians, so his plan was to let Western companies in to extract the new oil from his sea and foot the bill for winning the war. The oilmen were waiting for the contract. The army was waiting for the funds. But the president was a new-style democrat too, which meant he was an anxious, skinny, touchy ex-dissident who had spent half his life in prison and didn't know how to run a country or take decisions; and the Russians who had once run things here didn't want Westerners to get their hands on the oil. So the oilmen sat in their offices and bars and waited, and the army chiefs sat in their offices and camps and waited, and nothing happened. (The president gave me an interview in a giant hall filled with brand-new gilt furniture, some still in its wrapping; we perched on it timidly, like interlopers, and for form's sake he insisted on having my Russian questions, which he understood perfectly well, translated into Azeri; when it came to answering, he had nothing to say.) For now, while I went through the motions of gathering material about the future of the oil business, and the future of Azerbaijan, there was nothing much to do but wait for him to make up his mind, and listen to the whispering of the waters. But one day soon something would have to give: the deal would get signed, or the president kicked out. That was why a coup seemed so likely.

Meanwhile I was talking to ministers and oil magnates every day, and I was in love. I stood on the balcony by myself every night, and listened to the Caspian Sea.

The Caspian lies beyond the Caucasus mountain range, which the ancients knew as the end of all the earth, and it does not obey the same laws as more familiar seas.

It does not empty out into a bigger ocean. It is not very salty. It has no white-capped breakers, and no tides. And its surface looks as iridescent as a soap bubble or a puddle of petrol. The Caspian glitters magically with oil.

Oil oozes spontaneously out of the ground along the seashore. If you leave town for a seaside picnic, you'll find murky, dirty, reedy sand, drenched in sweaty darkness. At night, when the bubbles of marsh gas catch alight, you are haunted by will-o'-the-wisps. There are places where the night is lit up by tall columns of burning gas.

Before they were Muslims, the Azerbaijanis who live along this stretch of the Caspian coast were fire-worshippers. So were the Persians to the south of the sea in what is now Iran. There's a Zoroastrian temple outside Baku, the capital of Azerbaijan. It's made-up history: a corny Soviet take on an eighteenth-century experiment by visiting Indian Parsees in reviving Azerbaijan's antique Zoroastrian past. But it does remind you how many people in this part of the world worshipped fire, for many centuries, and why.

Romantics call the Caspian Sea's oil, as well as its fish eggs, black gold. The first oil boom in the nineteenth century turned a Persian walled citadel, a poem in pale sandstone, into a boastful boomtown of curlicues and overblown opera houses and caviar banquets. Local people became urban. Now, in plastic shoes and too-big trousers hitched up by plastic belts, they live in their thousands on the flatlands and suburbs along the seashore.

In the sea itself is a human settlement called Oily Rocks, a strange second city composed of two hundred kilometres of oil drills, walkways and bridges suspended over the water. This huge manmade cobweb was proof that the Baku bosses could be relied on to triumph over the natural world. Before the international oil firms moved in with their floating rigs and modern equipment, thousands of oilmen were ferried out from land to work here for one-week shifts. They had wooden bungalows, buses, piers, a dispensary for the sick, a cinema and a café. There was even a bar, though it served no alcohol.

Onshore, there is a rust belt of acres of industrially developed oilfields on the fringes of the desert. Towers reach into the sky. They look like the skeletal steeples of temples to dark gods: fire, power, money. If you look too long, you get sand and grit in your eyes. (There's a wind; Baku means wind in Persian, and sometimes the city is swept by gale-force winds called *khazri*.)

Working people live beyond the Black Town, in little houses and big apartment blocks scattered along tracks that barely amount to more than a few tyre marks in the sand. The smaller machines that were used to extract oil a century or more ago, called nodding donkeys, have survived in some of those places. Their cranks still move up and down, braying rustily. On some, you can still read British manufacturers' names.

The workers' houses were built in booms, and left behind as one forgotten tide of fortune or another receded. There have been more booms than anyone remembers (no one said oil was stable). There's so much oil that people's houses sometimes flood with it. They hide upstairs in their bedrooms. But they shrug and come back down when the darkness recedes.

You can swim and sail in the sea off Baku, though it's healthier to avoid the polluted waters touching the Baku promenade. There's a picnic spot not far from town, where Soviet planners in the seventies built tables and chairs and parasols out of brightly painted metal, and bolted them together, and sank them into a concrete bed on the beach. But it's not much used any more. The tables and chairs and parasols are half submerged. The sea has risen several feet since those days.

'No one knows why the sea is rising,' said Suleyman, the taxi driver who had been with me since my first day in town, who lived in a little house beyond the Black Town, whose parlour had been flooded with oil. 'People say it rises for thirty years, then falls like a tide. But I don't know. I reckon they've done something bad to it, and that's why it's slowly flooding us. I used to swim in it as a kid, but I'd never let my kids in there now. I don't trust it. I don't trust Them.'

Perhaps it is the sea's mysterious behaviour that makes everything else here a little unreliable too. Legend has it that the squat twelfth-century Maiden's Tower in the old fortress was built for a princess whose father fell incestuously in love with her. 'I will be yours if you build me a tower to our love,' she promised. But she was lying; she had secretly resolved to die rather than be so dishonoured. As soon as the tower, called *Kyz-kalasy* in Azeri, was finished, the legend says, she ran up to the roof to admire the view – and threw herself down into the sea below. Today the sea is two or three hundred yards away. All that surrounds the tower nowadays is wind and pale walls, the sandy courtyards, domed bathhouses, wrought-iron balconies, spiral staircases and vines of the fortress, named Icheri-Shekher; and the foreign oilmen in check shirts, pacing through town. The truth has shifted shape.

In this topsy-turvy realm of legend, forbidden love, gales, black gold, shape-shifting, jasmine, kebab, pomegranates and general impossibility, only Suleyman was prosaic.

Most of the time he was just a brooding, resentful presence in front: iron teeth, grimy fingernails on the wheel, a death-rattle cough. He slammed doors. He grunted.

But sometimes he talked. He disapproved of, or was baffled by, a lot of things that were happening nowadays ('How Can They?' he would say, flatly, in almost any conversation about anything). As a principle he thought the Old Days Were Better. He didn't like the government, or the new president who was wasting the country's money on war. Most of all, he didn't like the war.

The war in Karabakh had begun before the Soviet Union collapsed two years earlier, but only just. People still regretted the local Armenians who had grown up in this holiday resort in Azerbaijan, but ran away a couple of years before. The war belonged to the savage new times, not the old days of smug, comfortable Soviet speeches about the friendship of nations.

'So have you been to Karabakh?' I asked on my first ride in Suleyman's car, with the impertinence of a foreigner. Another part of the joy of being here was that I was so glamorously alien that I could always ask rude questions, and be too naïve and too forthright for comfort, without being afraid of forfeiting people's interest or respect.

'Nah,' Suleyman answered phlegmatically. 'Well, I mean to say. Holidays and that, yeah, with my friends. Beautiful air there is up there, fresh mountain air, like Switzerland. But that was before. The good old days of the Soviet Union, as they say. Now some of my mates have gone to the war; and some of them are dead from fighting. You wouldn't catch me going off there, not now, no way. This war is stupid, and I'm not stupid. I'm a family man. I've got a life to live here.' His mouth shut tight with a steely snap. It was a moral position.

Among the special features of Suleyman's ancient car were pictures of two small children taped to the dashboard, as well as a plastic Hand of Fatima swinging from the rear-view mirror, a pine-shaped green silhouette swinging next to it which gave off a powerful scent of artificial woodland, and a back rest made of big wooden beads strapped to the driver's seat.

'Would you work for me for the rest of this week?' I asked, liking him on an impulse. 'I'll pay you in dollars.'

People would kill for a dollar job as a driver. Urban myth had it that every second driver in Russia was an astrophysicist, a philosopher or a film star, fallen on hard times. Suleyman was no astrophysicist, and the sum I named was many times what he could possibly ever have earned in a week, or a month. But he only looked cagey.

'Erm. What would I have to do?' he said. 'My car's old. I couldn't drive it far out of town.'

'I don't think I'll need to go out of town.'

'Not to the countryside?'

'Not to the countryside.'

'And not to the war?'

'Not to the war.'

'Are you sure? I'm a family man, see; I've got no business going near wars.'

'Definitely not to the war. I promise.'

Suleyman was his own man. He clearly didn't want to be bought. But he began to look cheerful.

'Well . . . if you're sure about that . . . let's see how it goes,' was all he said, and held his hand out for his fare. But he was still there an hour later when I came out, and his car stereo was playing dance music.

Suleyman was short and squat, a little man in mourning for the peace of the past. He had dirty fingernails and a grimy, lined face, which seemed older than his thirty-eight years. When he grinned, which he often did now we had a definite relationship, his teeth were a cheerful blend of gold and iron fillings and nicotine. He smoked one filthy Russian cigarette after another (the cheapest Belomorka papirosy, with an inch of instant-death tobacco at the far end and a long cardboard tube to be pinched and dented one way and another to stop the smoke rotting the lungs too fast). To be polite, he always hung both cigarette and cigarette hand out of the window.

And he grumbled.

'Your hot water was off overnight? Mine too. The cold was only on for half an hour this morning too. And it comes out rust-coloured. Or muddy. You half expect tadpoles.

'You shouldn't drink from the tap even when it comes back on, you know. They used to tell us that our water was the purest in the world. Drink freely! they said. Huh. Now I've heard that ecologists say the water's polluted. Full of heavy metals. Poisoning us a bit more every time we drink. And I reckon those ecologists are right. They deceived us good and proper all our lives, our rulers. Drink freely, indeed.'

He had plenty of opportunity to talk. We were mooching around the city, and I was interviewing people, but no one's heart was in it. Azerbaijan was stuck. So were we.

'They want to change the alphabet now, have you heard? Give us the same Roman alphabet that the Turks use. What's the point of that? I'm not a Turk. I can only read the Cyrillic alphabet. If everything is written in Turkish, how will I be able to understand road signs?'

We sat in the car between my meaningless meetings, listened to news of the latest defeats read out in mournful voices on the tannoys in the town squares ('It's hysteria, going on and on about losing, trying to get people's tempers up'), and smoked. The days were very long. Once we went to the war cemetery – the Martyr's Graveyard – a huge place of plastic flowers and solemn young dead faces on daguerrotypes, cemented on to gravestones. We put flowers on the graves. Mostly, Suleyman sat on his wooden beaded seat cover and worried over the way the war had changed life in the city. It was a hopeless lament; nothing could change things back.

'War, who wants it? No one, except the two mafia gangs who are making money out of the mess, of course. Look how young these boys are. Anyone old enough to have sense, or rich enough to pay a bribe, gets out of the war. Only the poor kids get sent to die. I ask you, How Can They?'

The war Suleyman despised so much was as far away as it could possibly be from this busy, whispering, frivolous city, with the sun glimmering darkly on its waters, with its streets packed with dark young men with fags in their mouths and fake military service deferral certificates in their pockets. Baku was hundreds of miles from the hills held by the Armenians. A hot, flat desert lay between the war and the city, which trembled on the easternmost edge of a peninsula sticking out eastward into the Caspian, looking on the map as if it were shoving and straining just like the cheerful deserters who thronged its streets to keep away from the war. Here, you only felt the echoes of the fighting.

'Ah, what a city Baku was before. Back when there were Azerbaijanis and Jews and Armenians, all living together in peace and friendship, before the Jews all went to Israel, and the Armenians all went to Armenia. The Jews were the intellectuals in those days, and the Armenians were the craftsmen. The cobblers. The watchmakers. We were all city people together; it never bothered us what race we were, we just got on with our lives. And people came from all over the Soviet Union for their holidays.

'But then these Events all started, and the Armenians, our own Armenians from Baku, got scared and ran away.

'The city still feels empty without them. Empty.'

One of the reasons the war seemed unreal was that there were hardly any casualties, the diplomats said. People evacuated their villages and fled to the city if they heard even a rumour that the Armenians might show up sometime. They didn't have to hear guns. They didn't have to see sieges. There was no fight in the Azerbaijani villagers.

'They're lovers, not fighters,' said one shy American I talked to. 'They talk a kind of tough Turkish, but ethnically they're gentle Persians. Just look at their eyelashes.'

'You must tell the world about how we suffer,' said the refugees I met, full of terrifying trust that I was important enough to have a hotline to presidents and palaces everywhere. 'Tell Washington. Tell the International Community.'

'I can't; I can only write my story, and hope a politician somewhere reads it over breakfast,' I said, making helpless gestures with my hands.

But part of me felt important anyway when they clustered urgently around me, and told their frantic stories. I felt entitled to be told. I'd been to their war, bumping around in jeeps, looking through gunsights, hitching rides on army helicopters; I'd taken the risks so many of them had run away from. I wasn't braver than they were. It was just that, unlike them, I felt almost immortal. I was only observing their world, so I never thought their war might hurt me. It didn't have anything to do with me. I was always sure I'd get safely to a phone by deadline time.

And this life at the end of the world, where no one dared to go, was so alluringly full of people who needed me. I didn't have to do anything special to win the trust of the refugees, or the bored oilmen hanging around aimlessly in the hotel: just appear, listen, watch, and take notes. They were desperate to talk. I scooped up their stories, one by one, and feasted on them. I loved the easy way we slipped into instant intimacy, and the loving note we parted on a few hours later. I felt as blessed and magical as if I had a cloak of invisibility and seven-league boots, as if I could weave spells with words to invoke powerful forces that would save the defenceless from suffering. There was no one I couldn't talk to, and nothing I couldn't do. The next day I forgot their names, turned a page in my notebook, and went on to a new adventure.

Every morning, we drove off to interviews. Every night, back at the hotel, I'd look at the plastic phone in my room, so useless it could hardly connect guests with people down the road in Baku, and think briefly of going to the post office to phone home to Moscow and chat. But everything took so long . . . and the lines would be so bad . . . and I could tell my stories when I got back . . . and it would be so hard to explain by phone how infatuated I was with this mad, muddly land of love at the end of the world. You feel shy and self-sufficient at the shining-eyed beginning of falling in love; you want to stay immersed in the poetry of your feelings, and not have to venture out and explain yourself in prose to people who might not understand. Even your husband. So I loitered on the balcony instead, and looked at the stars, and mulled over what I had observed, and felt proud and independent, and wrote my stories for the next morning, and went to bed.

Suleyman hated the Azerbaijani refugees, his own people, with their plastic bags wadded up with towels and rugs and blankets, with their rage. 'Coarse, angry, thick peasants. Stirring up trouble. Stirring up hatred. Making things worse for everyone.'

The tired surgeons in the hospitals bore out what Suleyman said. They always treated Armenian patients the same as Azerbaijanis. 'But you have to take precautions. Say you've got a young lad in one bed who's had his foot blown off by a mine. Naturally his family will be angry. Naturally they'll be out for revenge. If you've got someone in the next bed with an Armenian name, they're at risk. So we give the Armenians false names, for their own protection.'

I imagined being an Armenian, lying in one of those metal cots, scared and in pain, and listening to someone else's mother and aunts and sisters cursing my people's blood in earthy farmer-speak. I imagined wriggling down and pulling the sheet up high, to avoid them all turning on me with hate-filled eyes, and trying to remember to answer to the name Magomed when I was really called Ashot. It made me shiver.

Even the supposedly civilised city people could turn nasty at times. One night a young Turkish journalist eating dinner at the hotel with me was grabbed from behind by a bunch of five or six drunk men. He yelped in Turkish. They yelled back at him in Azeri (almost the same thing), and hauled him to his feet. They looked furious. I got up too. 'Stop! What's going on?' I said in Russian. 'We've been watching this one, and we suspect him. We reckon he's Armenian,' the ringleader answered truculently. Their plan, it turned out, was to observe the decencies by dragging him out of the dining room, away from the ladies, and then debag him. If he wasn't circumcised, it would be proof he wasn't Muslim. Then they would beat him to within an inch of his life for being an Armenian Christian. We waved our passports. The thugs retreated, a little bit abashed at having nearly rearranged the features of an honoured foreign guest, but not very. One of them gave him a longing look as he let go. I wouldn't like to have been the next suspected Armenian the group came across.

'No, no. There've never been hard feelings here,' Suleyman insisted. 'We all grew up together. My best friend at school was

Armenian. I've even got a friend with an Armenian wife. That's how close we all are . . . And do you know, she was stuck home alone with their baby during those Events [the Azerbaijani weasel-word for pogroms]. She was terrified. There were gangs racing around in the street, setting fire to things, and taking the Armenians away, and everyone knew where to find her. But the neighbours took her and the baby in, and hid them both in a cupboard. She hid all day. It would have been bad for them if she'd been found, but us city folk stick together. She's still here now.'

'I'd like to meet her,' I said, enthusiastic for a new story. 'It would be so interesting.'

Suleyman eyed me cautiously, and answered, 'I could ask my friend Chingiz if he'd mind.'

'I'm bored. Let's go and look at carpets,' I said later, when my last oil interview was cancelled.

There were carpets everywhere. On floors, on walls, on balconies, on stairs; being admired, beaten, shampooed, or sold. They were only carelessly Muslim, dotted with little stick-pictures of birds, dogs, camels and combs. But I liked the idea that they had been knotted by people's grannies in the villages, with sly allusions to local people and events woven into their design. I liked the idea of women's art, made at home, unsupervised by stern husbands and fathers and full of quiet family jokes. These rugs were more than a rustic equivalent of the photo album, too. They were a record of Azerbaijan's history: bold and geometric as Turkish carpets, but with stylised foliage that also suggested a memory of a flowery Persian past. They had the reds and blues and browns of ordinary carpets, but they were also threaded with bright pinks and fiery orange, in the jagged flame shapes of the Caspian.

'We'll go to the Old Town, then,' Suleyman said. 'Everyone's selling them there.'

We parked and walked past the houses with their ripening vines and lacy iron and glass balconies. Women with rolled-up sleeves were whacking rugs on all sides. The sunshine was full of carpet dust.

'Oh ho! You keep your eyes off those carpets. They're not the ones for sale. They're just being cleaned,' Suleyman said, following my gaze. 'You don't want people to think you're one of those greedy crooks who are going about now, rich people tempting poor people to do wrong by their families for money. I had a beautiful carpet myself not so long ago, homemade by my granny, a lovely thing and a picture of our past, until some crook saw it hanging out on a day like this. He offered two brand new carpets in exchange, each one bigger than ours, if she'd let him have it. And can you believe it, my fool of a wife let it go?' He smiled, but his face was sad.

'Why are there so many carpets for sale?' I asked.

Suleyman grimaced. It was a stupid question. He ticked off the answers on his fingers. 'A, because there are a lot of foreign oilmen with dollars and nothing to do who want to buy luxuries like carpets and caviar. B, because there are a lot of refugees with carpets, who need money to survive and make a new home here. So our past is being sold off, and soon we'll have nothing left. You go along by yourself and have a look,' he added. For a moment, he didn't like me much, and he was too polite to say so. 'You'll do better without me.'

And he went off, looking proud and stiff-necked, to find some more cigarettes.

I sauntered up and down the squares and spiral stairs, past the domes of the bathhouse, over the cobbles, and into more courtyards. I gave the glowing oblongs spread all around me flirtatious sideways glances. I listened to the gentle calls of 'Pssst . . . ksss . . . *dyee-vushka?* Girl?' in the sing-song rising tones of Azerbaijanis speaking Russian, and passed by with a smile.

What could be more magical than a carpet? Carpets fly, they're the backdrop to *The Thousand and One Nights*, a thousand and one stories told by the feminist's wily first role model Sheherezade. Her listener was an angry, humiliated, woman-hating prince, who had earlier been disappointed in love; now he was lying back on the intricate carpets of the harem, blind to the mute women's love that had gone into embroidering, knotting and weaving them, tapping his fingers impatiently, and thinking how he would kill this girl as soon as she finished her story. But Sheherezade saved herself with her beautifully crafted stories, weaving them so artfully that, every night, her execution in the morning had to be postponed for another day, so the prince could find out what happened next and see how the pattern developed. Gradually, her tales turned the listening prince's hatred into love, a planned rape into a seduction, a planned murder into marriage, and transformed the violent language of knives and fists into the art of conversation.

In history, the most beautiful carpets are made after a surge of rampaging testosterone – which has brought armies, invasions, bloodshed and destruction – is finally transformed into civilisation. In the history of the desert, whose ghostly nomads move through a mournful landscape of endless grey-brown rock and sand, the carpets woven by women dreaming of peace represent gardens.

'The garden, with its avenues of cool and shady trees, beds of colourful flowers and brooks where water flows endlessly, is the desert dweller's Paradise. When Timur overran Central Asia in the fourteenth century, he had thousands of craftsmen brought from all over his empire to embellish the capital, Samarkand, on the other side of the Caspian Sea. But Timur never built a palace, remaining a nomad to the end. Instead, he built nine gardens in which his tent could be set up . . .'

I was talking to my second carpet salesman now, after escaping a first flirtation with a gruff chancer at the bottom of a sunken courtyard. He had insisted, in his jungle Russian, that the ugly rug he wanted to sell me for somewhere close to a thousand and one dollars was an 'antique thing, I swear to Allah'. When I flipped over a corner, I saw that the very modern-looking label sewn into it said 'factory production'. This second salesman was altogether classier, with a suit and a shop and a silver tongue. I was sipping sweet coffee sludge in a dark room behind his rugs, watching dust motes dance in a ray of sunlight, and he was spinning me stories.

'All Persian carpets are woven gardens, full of flowers and curves, the artistic fruit of the nomad's dream. But some are still more explicit, with designs that directly imitate the formal layout, in panels, of the Persian garden . . .'

'Perhaps the carpet that the sheikh sprawled over, fingering his dagger, thinking his murderous male thoughts about how best to dispose of Sheherezade, was as beautiful as the legendary garden carpet of the Persian Emperor Chosroes . . .'

'. . . Chosroes, one of the last Persian emperors before the Arab conquests of the seventh century, had a carpet in his palace at Ctesiphon that was ninety feet wide and five times as long, embellished with silk and thousands of pearls and jewels. Chosroes used it in winter to remind him of the spring. The Arabs tore it to shreds when they sacked Ctesiphon in 641. But the sacred garden remained enshrined in the Koran, where the faithful are promised a Paradise containing "four gardens, beneath which waters flow" . . .

'The carpets you see here are influenced by the Persians, and the Mongols, and the Turks,' Idayat said silkily. He was a big man, with sleek smoothed-down hair, big, soft, clean fingers, a signet ring, and a gold watch. Selling carpets to Western oilmen was clearly good business. 'Azerbaijan is the gateway where the great empires have always met. I can look at a carpet and tell, not only which region it comes from, but which family; I can decipher the colours and the dyes and know which phase of the moon the plants that made them were picked in; I know the secrets of every shape and symbol in every pattern dreamed of in these lands. It was banned knowledge in Soviet times, but I was taught by my father and my father's father; we have known our secrets since the dawn of time . . .

'I can make you a collection, with carpets from the mountains and carpets from the desert, from the seaside . . . I can find you the most beautiful treasures . . . living art that will light up the rest of your life, even back in the north, even in the snows.'

His voice grew still softer and more hypnotic. 'Come and see.'

*   *   *

Suleyman was standing by his car, on the cobbles, in the calm shade of a mulberry tree, when I rushed out of the shop a few minutes later.

'Are you all right?' he asked.

'Of course,' I said breathlessly, running fingers through ruffled hair, checking my shirt. A button was still undone.

Idayat had taken me to see his internal courtyard, where a model loom was set up against a wall with two dusty mannequins in traditional dress weaving at it. He had lifted my empty coffee cup and put it on the end of the loom. In the same movement, he was suddenly on me. He pushed me against the wall with one of those big pink palms with its soft clean fingers. He thrust his smooth face roughly on mine. His other hand was yanking at my clothes. He was much bigger than me.

We struggled. There was no time, just raw breath and angry muscle. Very slowly I thought, I won't get out. But I did, and stepped back, and picked up my bag, and heard myself saying, in bright, ladylike tones, almost as if nothing had happened only a bit more shocked: 'Well, perhaps I'll come back on my next visit and look at your carpets again, how fascinating, thank you very much for the coffee, goodbye.'

And then I was out in the sunshine, out of breath, and Idayat was in the shadows inside still looking through the glass at me. Trying to look composed, I turned my back on him and smiled at Suleyman.

'He attacked you!' Suleyman said indignantly, following the body language. 'That crooked, no-good, greedy bastard went and attacked you! He did, didn't he?'

'No, no . . . not really. He kind of made a pass. But it's nothing, honestly. Let's go.'

'That bastard! Those people are all the same! They want to screw everyone! I feel like going in there and sorting him out!' Suleyman was puffing up with rage, like a small, bedraggled, fighting cock. He was half Idayat's size.

'No, please don't. It was just silly. Let's go,' I said again, and opened the car door, feeling ashamed and embarrassed to be in this foolish position, not wanting Suleyman to get hurt, longing to get away. But I was touched all the same.

We drove back to the hotel in silence. My moment of panic had passed; I was getting back my confidence that I could trust my judgement of people, and if that went wrong trust my reflexes to be quick enough to get away from trouble. But Suleyman was planning what to say next. He pounced when I was ready to get out.

'You're married, aren't you?'

'Yes.'

'You should be at home with your husband. You should be having children, not wandering around here. What's your husband thinking, letting you go off unprotected, meeting grasping brutes like that one and hanging round wars?'

'Oh Suleyman,' I began, patiently. 'It's different for foreigners. We don't do things like you. My husband's got his job in Moscow, I've got my job and I'm here. We're supposed to put our jobs first. What would I do with children while I'm travelling?'

He let me go, but he shook his head resignedly and looked at the photo of his children taped to the dashboard. I could see him thinking, 'Foreigners. How Can They?'

*   *   *

Suleyman turned up the next morning with an unknown man, balding and as small and down-at-heel as himself, in the passenger seat.

'This is Chingiz,' he said. I raised an eyebrow privately at him, signalling a question: the Chingiz with The Armenian Wife Who'd Stayed Behind And Survived A Pogrom? 'Nonono, not that Chingiz,' Suleyman said hastily, looking shifty and failing to meet my eye. 'Just a neighbour. I get bored in the car by myself.'

So we talked inconsequentially, between interviews, about how common the name Chingiz – Genghis in English – was in Azerbaijan; about the ridge of cool hills you could drive along to avoid the desert if you had to get to the war zone; about the partridges fluttering along that country road, the pomegranates at the roadside stalls, and the old men playing chess under shady mulberry trees.

'Have you heard the rumour?' Suleyman suddenly asked. 'They say the military chiefs in Gyandzha, the headquarters near the war, are organising against the president. They say there'll be a coup. They say it'll be any day.

'There shouldn't be war at Gyandzha. Do you know, it was the birthplace of the most famous love poet in the Orient. Nizami: a Persian. There's even a great beauty of a statue to him at the entrance to the town. They shouldn't have besmirched Nizami's memory by filling the town with soldiers.'

I came out at midday from a government building. It was hot. Suleyman and Chingiz had let down both front seats and slumped back in them. They were snoring.

They woke up with a start when I opened the door, as stubbly and shy as a pair of hedgehogs. I could smell vodka on their breath.

'Why don't we stop early today?' I said gently.

'Yesh, good idea,' Suleyman slurred, revving wildly, stifling a yawn. 'And I'll take you for lunch tomorrow. You never seem to eat, and it'll be your last day. We'll have a feast.'

I'd been planning to spend the hours before the plane finding some really fresh caviar to take back to Moscow for my husband. But perhaps I could get some at the airport, and if I couldn't it wouldn't really matter, I thought. Moscow was full of caviar. I nodded.

The tannoy in the square in front of my hotel was giving out war news. Two generals at Gyandzha had been fired.

'Sho much for the coup,' Suleyman said, and he looked a bit dejected. 'We're stuck with that old goat of a president after all.'

'We got drunk yesterday,' Suleyman announced when the morning wind was still fresh on his greyish cheeks. 'Did you know?'

I laughed. 'Of course. Why d'you think we knocked off early? You were swerving all over the road.'

He giggled, and looked suddenly young. 'We both got a letter, see,' he said. 'It put the wind up us. A call-up letter. But I reckon there must be a mistake: we're both pushing forty. We've got families to look after. I'm not a Westerner, I'm not leaving my wife with no one to look after her. And just look at us: even if we wanted to, we're far too old to fight.'

'What will you do?'

He laughed. Everything seemed easy today. 'Oh, don't you worry about us. It's not a big deal. My brother's always getting letters, and he just goes and stays on people's floors for a few nights, till the call-up's over for the season. Or perhaps I'll go to the conscription office and show them my wrinkles, get them to say they made a mistake. I dunno about that, though. I don't fancy paying some git in a uniform a bribe.'

So we had a sentimental farewell lunch under a bower of vines, in an open-air kebab place on the edge of town. We settled up, furtively, under the table, so no one could see the dollars changing hands, while we sniffed the sizzling meat and downed slugs of vodka. We dawdled for hours over tiny plates of cucumber and coriander and caviar. In a week, we had nearly become friends.

'I like feast days like this,' Suleyman confided. 'Quietly does it. Good local food, a drink or two. Everything simple, everyone happy.'

I'd have picked up the bill, which was cheap for me but expensive for him, but he insisted. It was a question of honour.

'Please come back,' he said, as we drove to the airport later. He was swerving a bit again. 'Come back for the coup when it happens. Or come back to take a holiday and enjoy the beauties of our seaside! We'll work together again. I'd like that.' He wrote down his phone number in my book, painstakingly, with the tip of his tongue sticking out of his mouth. 'Now can you read it?' he said. 'You must definitely call.'

I looked at the photo of his big-eyed, smiling kids. I'd never even asked what they were called, and now it was nearly too late and I was already nostalgic for the missed opportunity. 'Do they look like you or your wife?' I asked, wondering why there was no picture of her.

'Oh . . .' he sighed. 'Like Annush. Anna, I mean: my wife's called Anna. She's a beauty. Thank God they don't look like me.'

He took my bag out of the boot.

'You know something?' he said, hesitantly. 'The Chingiz you met was that Chingiz I told you about, with the Armenian wife. Only we were a bit nervous about talking about it. It's dangerous. You can't be too careful.'

I didn't mind at all. But I didn't know why he was telling me this now, with that imploring look on his face, or what to say back. I patted his elbow. 'I understand,' I said lamely, not understanding. 'I should have realised.'

He was still waving, dropping ash on the floor, when the grumpy customs men took me off for the annoying pre-flight ritual of dismembering my computer and phone in case I was a spy. I wondered whether Suleyman might miss me in the next few days, riding round town in his gypsy cab, looking for fares, getting bored. I thought I might miss him.

My husband laughed when I got home, a bit browner and a lot dirtier than when I'd left, but with only the same small bag I'd started with. 'I thought you'd come back all loaded up with war trophies. Carpets. Kalashnikovs. Caviar,' he said.

I couldn't play Sheherezade without a carpet to lounge on, without caviar to spoon luxuriantly into our mouths while I told wonderful Oriental stories. But it didn't seem to matter now I was back. Reality was the ice still in the Moscow wind; I quickly forgot the smell of jasmine and the euphoric sound of the sea.

The coup in Azerbaijan finally began a few months later. Halfway through the first TV news bulletin, I phoned Suleyman to ask him to work for me again when I got back to Baku. I called him from Moscow, but no one answered. I tried him, from the hopeless hotel phone, when I reached Baku. I tried him from the post office. I tried variations of the numbers in case I'd been reading the digits wrong. I tried mornings, evenings, and midnight calls. No one ever came to the phone.

I never found out what happened to Suleyman: whether his house had flooded with oil again and he'd had to move, whether he'd got drunk and killed himself in a car crash, or been poisoned by the polluted drinking water, or hauled off against his will to fight in Karabakh. There were so many murderous fishers of men down there, waiting to trap the defenceless and the innocent in their nets. Anything was possible.

I could only hope that he hadn't come off worst in a fight with one of the violent anti-Armenian gangs who he didn't want to admit even existed in his beautiful city. They would naturally want to kill him, I realised, belatedly piecing together all the obvious clues he'd given but I'd failed to observe, because he loved his Armenian wife.

CHAPTER NINE

A Coup on the Caviar Coast

There's nothing like a good coup for getting a party going.

I came to the celebration straight from Baku airport. The moon had already risen over the restaurant. The air was sizzling with kebab. The fountain in the main courtyard was splashing over the cobbles, and some happily drunk Baku wedding guests were dancing and yelping manically around it. (It was Thursday, 17 June, and in four days' time there would be no more weddings. In all Shi'ite lands, the annual month of mourning, Makharrami, was about to begin. This lot were making the most of the good times while they lasted.)

In the other courtyard, our courtyard, the foreign journalists, diplomats, pundits, academics, busybodies, lovers, assistants, snoops and spies (in no particular order) who had rushed to town at the first sniff of a coup had assembled for shashlyk, lyulya-kebab, beer, red wine, vodka, iron-water, sweet basil, coriander, cucumber, caviar, and a frightening number of cigarettes, all at the expense of unseeing bosses far away.

There were at least thirty people in our courtyard. The look was pared-down and carefree – lean, mobile, muscular, efficient, with scuffed war boots and faded jeans and macho photographers' waistcoats with dozens of sandy pockets – but you knew everyone had their little vanities. The most obvious were funny embroidered caps or belts or knives or pens from previously visited trouble spots. Mine was a photocopied map of the Caspian and Caucasus area, kept in my pocket, with every road I'd gone down marked in orange pen. And the vanity I liked best was someone else's story about putting on his expenses the price of half a horse bought to get illegally into Afghanistan. (The horse threw him and the friend who'd bought the other two legs and disappeared over the border solo, but the accountants paid up anyway.)

Young and single, not so young and single, or not so young and about to be single: there were always pretty much the same guests partying at every troublesome border and front line and hot spot. You could tell them from the pockets bulging with useful not-too-new but not-too-old $20 and $100 bills from the office, the practical bits of kit in hidden pouches, and the ready packs of Marlboro, officially bought for bribing tricky officials with but always being smoked by their owners. They were full of tips about the lie of the land in Georgia, South Ossetia, North Ossetia, Armenia, Chechnya, Dagestan, Tajikistan, Uzbekistan, or wherever your finger fell on the map. They might have been strangely shy somewhere else, where people lived at peace; but here the mood was almost cosmically confident. It was a movable feast, this party, my home from home. All adrenaline junkies and freethinkers welcome, anytime, any place. Leave your troubles behind.

Here, after hours, among friends, white knuckles could relax their grip on pens and cameras and grab forks and glasses instead. Here you could flash manic smiles across the table, whisper with your travel buddies, flirt or plot or tease or be teased, swap gossip and conspiracy theories, discuss rumours, make predictions about the future of the oil deal or the economy or relations with Russia, pursue the diplomats to give you a new lead confirming something you'd heard elsewhere, compare notes on near-misses you'd had with tanks or bullets or crashing vehicles, and move your pepper-pot or knife-and-fork armies around on the stained table top. 'If the president's men move *here*; if the Russians left weapons *there*; if the rebels have got hold of *this* . . .'

There was still scope for endless theorising about this coup, because it was only starting. A week before, a mysterious army had appeared at the other end of the country, at Gyandzha, near the war zone, led by a beautiful thirty-year-old with a hawkish Michael Douglas profile. The rebels seized the city, and got their hands on the guns at the old Soviet base that Russian soldiers had just given up. They wrote an arrest warrant for the hopeless president, who just couldn't stop losing the war in Karabakh. Now they were marching towards Baku to force him to 'rule or resign'. Every day Suret's men came a few miles closer, laughing, swaggering and sticking posters of the president on trees and road signs, for target practice. No one resisted. The locals loved the rebels. The president's men kept resigning. The president kept panicking.

Sometimes it was hard not to feel ambiguous about being a foreign reporter in this unstable region, when (as often happened) you turned up in a revved-up, excited, manic pack at a scene of terrible suffering. That was too much like vultures homing in on a death: rushing around among the grieving and stricken, asking your banal questions in your foreign accent and rushing busily off, competing like children for the best montage of the pain you were watching together. 'It's our job to tell the world what you're going through,' we would explain, feeling sincere. 'We're doing our best for you.' But it was impossible to be comfortable with what our angrier or more cynical interviewees said back: 'No you're not. You're just making your careers out of our troubles.'

But this story was one we could enjoy with a clear conscience. No one was suffering. Every Azerbaijani we talked to seemed happy that the president looked doomed. We journalists got the usual bonuses: freedom from Moscow office routine, and lots of exciting adventure travel on the wild side. The story had enough big oil money sloshing around to get editors' attention back home (and ensure us some good headlines). For our Western readers, it was blissfully simple to understand: an elected president under threat, a new post-Soviet democracy under siege. And pundits and analysts liked the promising conspiracy theory it had engendered: that Russia was secretly sponsoring the coup, to stop the oil companies getting the deposits in the Caspian Sea. They were placing bets that the Soviet-era boss here would soon be back in power.

So there was a special happy buzz in the courtyard, as our glasses clinked and the wedding guests danced and the sea murmured outside our walls.

At the height of the evening, as a cloud passed over the moon and you could feel the first chill in the air, a knife rang against a glass, clear and insistent as a bell. Throats cleared, chairs scraped, whisperers were shushed: an impromptu, emotional, melancholy speech was coming.

'Who knows how all this is gonna end?' declaimed the American voice of one of our group. 'It may not be long now before external pressures force the elected president of this young democracy to get on a helicopter or a plane and flee the land he has been chosen to rule. He may be making his escape from this increasingly dangerous situation even as I speak. If he is, we may look back and remember tonight as the night when democracy died on the Caspian.'

There was a hush. It touched your heart, that forlorn picture of the president, with his anxious eyes and his thin beard, slipping away in the dark, his head bowed with the knowledge of his failure, his shoulders hunched with fear. The warm night seemed suddenly very dark behind the swimming stars. How true, how sad, I thought confusedly, how sad, how true. And my heart swelled with contradictory happiness at being there, as maudlin as my tipsy friends, watching history in the making.

No one had the heart to go on moving armies around the table. No one had the heart to go on flirting. Quietly, in twos and threes, we left. We glided over the cobbles, home to the hotel, talking French, American, English, or Georgian in hushed voices.

It seemed just a typically fanciful Caspian evening, full of feverish excitement and hot air. We woke up the next morning with hangovers. But we also woke up to news. The president really had fled Baku in the middle of the night, and had gone into hiding in the most distant province of Azerbaijan. The coup was hotting up.

Friday. Scorching heat. We foreigners run up and down the hill, from presidential palace to hotel to parliament building to foreign office to oil offices and back, longing to stop for cold drinks or food, but too busy, making do with cigarettes, asking frightened officials what's happening. This is what. The Soviet-era boss of Azerbaijan will stand in as caretaker president while the real president is on the run. He is seventy, but most men half his age don't have half that sun-kissed, energetic, glowing charisma. He tosses his great glamorous lion's head and smiles with his cunning eyes and winks his discreet Rolex from under his spotless tailored dark sleeve. How dismayed he is, he says sorrowfully, that the president 'could have left us at this difficult moment'.

As we run around, I count three wedding parties in cars with ribbons and flowers, speeding aimlessly round, honking and waving bottles. The thin happy sound of *mugam* music drifts out of the windows. Who's afraid of the rebel army?

Saturday. Scorching heat. We take a taxi and find some rebels on the road about seventy kilometres from Baku. What butch guys they are: spotted bandanas, reflector shades, fat bandoliers of bullets across their chests, T-shirts ripped to show off muscly arms: Sylvester Stallone clones. Their names are Rambo and Mr X, and the reason they're swaggering through the dust, swinging their hips, looking for trouble, is loyalty to their hawk-faced young boss. They paint him as a saint: Suret looks out for them, Suret protects their families, Suret ensures the poor never go hungry, Suret is a hero on the battlefield. And the president is an old goat. Goat means 'takes it up the bum' in Soviet gulag jargon. Mr X gets a real kick out of saying 'goat', and when he's said it a few times he cackles and sticks a fag end through the nearest mutilated poster of the president. The president's mouth already has three tree branches stuck through it.

We get back to town late in the afternoon. I come across only two wedding parties. In the evening, some of us stand in the square in front of the hotel, asking passers-by if they voted for the president last year when he won the election with a huge majority. No one admits they did. Everyone wants the rebels to reach Baku. We give up on straw-polling and go for a drink, and spend the evening smugly agreeing with each other that Azerbaijanis haven't got the first clue about democracy.

'Democracy is all very well,' my taxi driver of the day opines. 'But it's not for us. Democracy is like my pet parrot. My parrot was brought up in a cage. And people say now that it's better for parrots to fly around freely, but the way my parrot was brought up was like the Soviet-developed socialism we used to have. If I let my parrot out of its cage now, it would shit on the floor and tear holes in the curtains because it doesn't know any better. It wasn't brought up for freedom. If I got a new young parrot tomorrow, with no bad habits, naturally I'd give it democratic conditions and let it fly free. But I'm keeping my old parrot locked up in its cage, and the bosses should keep us locked up in our cage too. We weren't brought up to understand freedom either.'

Sunday. We're getting the hang of this joke coup now. At dawn, before the heat gets too overpowering, we take a taxi out of town to check on the rebels. Today they're camped just fourteen kilometres from the centre: three hundred men, three APCs, ten trucks. They are unbelievably dirty and unbelievably pleased with themselves, helping themselves to fags and beers from journalists, preening in front of the cameras. The defence ministry says it's persuaded them to stay there for now. We go again at dusk. They're still loafing around, grinning.

I see only one wedding party today. At the hotel, the maids and the cleaners are rejoicing about the coup. It was high time the no-good president went, they say happily; they can't wait for the rebels to get here. And they're not rebels anyway; they're heroes.

'Look around you,' urges the next taxi driver. 'Look at all the wonderful big buildings that used to be built here in Soviet times. Who built those? Not the president (that old goat), that's for sure. He's a nobody. He didn't know how to get on in the corridors of power. It's high time we had the old boss back. He's a big guy. He made this city the beautiful place it is. He has vision. He knows about wheeler-dealing. And he can handle the Kremlin. Not to mention the war – there was no war when he was in charge – and the crime – there was no crime then either. That's the kind of ruler we want, not some [dramatic pause, elaborate mime of spitting] DEMOCRAT.'

Monday. Another dawn check. Suret's men are still outside town, stubbly and hungover and running out of fags. The hotel is heaving with foreign journalists. The hotel management has started amusing itself by bursting into all the rooms where men are sharing with women and demanding to see their marriage certificates. We snicker like naughty schoolkids, try and bamfoozle them, nickname them the morality police.

But the fizz has gone out of the story. I don't know what to write any more. My editors want several pieces a day, and there is no news.

The stories I have to write are dictated by the day's announcements, about where the 'rebels' are and what is happening in the 'coup'. But the reality is so different it's impossible to take that information seriously. No one minds the 'coup'. No one is scared of the 'rebels'. Everyone local is sure now that the whole spectacle is just a way of legitimising the return to power of the old Soviet boss, and hardly anyone's against that. Then the oil deal with the West will be called off, and Russia, the old ruling power, will hold sway again. It's only a question of how, and when.

Plus the water at the hotel is switched off. I'm out of clean clothes and Moscow Marlboros. And it's always so hot. A hopeful, puppy-like Baku boy has attached himself to me as a translator, and keeps saying annoyingly that we should forget the coup and go off for a day's fishing at the seaside. We can't, of course, I snap, closing my mind to the sea breezes. We're far too busy. But we're not.

It's stopped seeming romantic to eat dinner in a courtyard by a fountain. I've started to hate lyulya-kebab.

There are no weddings today, either. It is the first day of Makharrami.

Most Westerners have heard of some Muslim religious dates – Ramadan, or Eid – but not Makharrami. It was even a problem for the Turks who hung around the hotel lobby, snickering in a superior big-brotherly way at the way that the backward Azerbaijanis mutilated the language they almost shared ('When they want to say "stop the car, I want to get out", it comes out like "Halt the carriage, I desire to jump down from the treetops"!' these sophisticates would cackle; or, 'Politicians are always talking about how it's a crime to misuse the oil money, but what they actually say is, "It's a murder"!'). Makharrami made the Turks feel uneasy. It underlined the real differences between them and the Azerbaijanis. For the Azerbaijanis, unlike most other Muslims, are not Sunni but Shi'ite, and Makharrami is a Shi'ite date.

The story of the split among Muslims goes back a millennium and a half to the Arabian peninsula, and the confusion that afflicted believers after the Prophet Mohammed's death in AD 632. Mohammed's disciples elected a new leader of their movement, the Caliph. But factional rivalries in Mecca soon exploded into civil war.

In AD 656, the third Caliph, Uthman, was murdered by supporters of Ali, Mohammed's cousin and son-in-law. They proclaimed Ali his successor. But Uthman had been head of one of the most powerful pre-Islamic clans of Mecca, the Umayya, and conflict between the Umayyads and Shi'at Ali (Ali's followers, who came to be known as Shi'a) raged on for the next twenty-five years.

Ali himself was murdered. The climax of the fighting came when his son Husain, the Prophet's grandson, was murdered with his Shi'ite followers on the tenth day of the month of Moharram in AD 680.

To this day, Shi'ites go into mourning at the start of the month of Moharram (Makharrami in Azerbaijan). Their displays of grief build up to a peak on the tenth day of the month.

The Umayyads won the feud. Like all winners, they wanted everyone to accept life as it was (with them on top). They were strict and conservative, and they became known as Sunni from the word Sunna, which means acceptance of convention. That carried over into their view of religion: the Sunnis stopped thinking of new interpretations of the words of the Prophet.

But the Shi'a sect carried on existing too. And it remained in opposition for centuries, questioning the validity of the powers of the Caliph, insisting on the right to go on arguing over Mohammed's spiritual and intellectual legacy (and incidentally being much more liberal than the Sunni majority about letting artists and craftsmen and carpet-makers use animal and birds and people in their decorative designs).

Today there is only one overtly Shi'ite state, Azerbaijan's neighbour Iran, a land which shares caviar, oil, the Caspian Sea, a fire-worshipping past, flower-strewn carpets and a big Azerbaijani minority on the border with the new post-Soviet country next door.

Azerbaijan isn't exactly a religious state, even if there are quiet, neatly-bearded Iranians living in the hotel and building mosques. It's almost a surprise that Azerbaijan's sleepy-eyed people, with their sing-song voices and happy-go-lucky attitude to life and politics and war, remember they are Shi'ites for long enough to bother with Makharrami.

But they do. Adil told me about it. Adil, one of the three modest Reuter TV cameramen who were only half-members of the excitable foreign press pack because they actually came from Azerbaijan; Adil, who got into his small car and went home to his wife and child somewhere in town when the day's work was done instead of carousing with us; soft-spoken Adil, with his compact frame, reassuringly square face, soft round eyes and philosophical level-headedness.

He was giving me a lift back to my hotel from the Reuter room at the other end of town. He'd rescued me from pecking fractiously at my computer, unable to think of a new lead to my story.

On the way back, he drew in for petrol. There was a long queue at the pump. He turned to me with a big gesture, part shrug, part smile, part sadness. 'Can you believe it? A petrol queue in an oil town. That's our reality for you, eh?'

At least it meant there was time to talk. I interrupted Adil sighing comically at the beauty of the English TV producer he was working with to ask him why there were no more weddings. 'It's a penance for sin,' he said. 'From today there are no weddings for a month. But that's only the beginning. After the tenth day of the month you won't be able to play music or eat by daylight either. This is a very serious time.'

Nightlife at the hotel was as frivolous as ever, though. The bar was packed. There were businessmen from Turkey. There were tanned aid workers in from missions in the provinces, looking for fun. There were oil workers, big anxious-looking men in plaid shirts from Texas or Inverness. The podgy Moroccan graduate student who had somehow forgotten to go home for a decade was there, cackling in Azeri with the barman. There were diplomats, tight-lipped about whether orders had gone out to send their wives and children out of the country. And there were journalists galore.

I loved the hotel. Everyone said it had been a marvel when it opened in the seventies, but it was scruffy enough now. I was getting to know every elderly blonde floor maid (for some reason they were all Russians) and every decrepit nook and cranny. It had rats on the fourth floor, a restaurant and a café on the ground floor, a hard-currency café on the third and two bars on the fourteenth.

Some hotel guests kept themselves to themselves. The Iranians obviously never came to the bar. Nor did the tough-looking Afghans, who were pretending to be Pakistanis, who were taken off every morning in a defence ministry minibus and were widely supposed to be helping the army fight the war in Karabakh (an open secret much discussed by the floor maids).

Some of the people who did come to the bar were very queer fish indeed. 'Spooks,' we muttered to each other as they walked through the door, and perhaps they really were. There was the American who claimed to be a tobacco grower from Virginia, looking into investment possibilities, who for some reason came to all the press conferences with his translator. And a young man who said he worked in the British press always turned up to drink with us, even though we never saw him in the daytime. One night he said he worked for *The Times*. Then *The Times* correspondent turned up, and didn't know him. The next night the young man said he worked for the *Telegraph* – until the *Telegraph* correspondent turned up. The next night, he told me he worked for the *Sunday Times*. 'That's interesting,' I said. 'My husband's their correspondent, and he's on his way here. You must meet.' He looked embarrassed. The next night, I heard him tell an aid worker he worked for the *Observer*.

'When do you think Suret's men will get bored of waiting and come into town?'

It was the next afternoon (and the second day of Makharrami), and the relaxed Texan oilman I was talking to had feet in cowboy boots up on his desk. 'Hey, one of them just came in here ten minutes ago!' he said. 'He knocked and asked if we had a spare beer. I gave him a six-pack out of the fridge. Gotta keep tomorrow's leaders happy.'

Everyone was talking about it that afternoon. It was like sightings of Elvis after his death. Suret's men had been seen here, there and everywhere: lunching at the Caravanserai restaurant, sauntering into oil offices, checking out the sea breezes. And then they went quietly back to their bivouacs on the edge of town.

'Everyone's cool about it, so I'm cool about it,' chortled the oilman. 'We've started calling it the bed-and-breakfast coup.'

Azart was in the air. While the big chancers gambled with the future of the state, little chancers everywhere were trying their luck on a smaller scale.

We were nearly robbed that evening. I went with another Western reporter for our pre-curfew check on the rebels outside town. The sleepy-eyed driver we found had a sleepy-eyed friend with him in the front of the car. We wanted to get back to the hotel as fast as possible after our perfunctory rebel inspection. But the two men in the front had different ideas. They weren't listening to us repeating, first calmly, then in a panic: 'This isn't the right way home!' and 'We're late for the curfew!' Instead they were driving us, faster and faster, down smaller and smaller empty streets in districts we'd never seen. Then a police siren sounded behind us; we speeded up, the police speeded up, our driver began to sweat and told us, 'You've got to say you were coming into my house' – he pointed at a little building on the side of the road – 'as guests.' Yes, yes, we chorused obediently, but 'no, no' is what we were thinking.

The driver pulled over to submit to police interrogation. The police were thrilled to see foreigners breaking the curfew. 'It'll cost you, mind,' the boss cop said, his face wreathed in smiles as he began to assess how much to sting us for. His face wrinkled when we launched into explanations that were far too frank and noisy for our driver's liking: 'We're very scared of this man! We're very pleased you stopped him! We wanted to go back to the hotel and he brought us here against our will! And we'd like to go back to the hotel with you!' The policeman didn't want to believe that we were in the right (and thus couldn't be fined of some of our dollars) and that the driver, an ordinary Azerbaijani like him, was in the wrong. But his sidekick did a perfunctory search of our car – a kick at the hub caps, a glance under the bonnet – and found a pistol taped to the underside of the bonnet. So things went our way after all, and the driver and his friend were arrested, and we got a free ride home in a police car.

Also on that day, as I decided reluctantly I might as well make a trip to Gyandzha and see where the rebel leader came from, Azeri customs men at the airport arrested a Turkish antiques collector. He was trying to smuggle a priceless Stradivarius violin out of the country without bothering with any of the usual permits, duty, bribes or hush money. The fiddle had a genuine 'made in 1730' tag on it, the news report said. He'd bought it on the black market for three hundred dollars, a pittance, and his idea was to quietly take it away to Istanbul and sell it for millions.

Sona Guseinov used the uncertainty of the times to get the ransom on her son's head halved. He was twenty, and a conscript soldier, and had been taken prisoner in the war. Now he was being held hostage in a private flat in Armenia. (One of the oddest things about this war was the flourishing trade in prisoners like young Ayaz, chained to radiators and penned in cellars, fetching high prices fixed by brokers with jokey names like Phantomas.) The Armenians whose booty Ayaz was had started by asking for $11,000 – right out of Sona's price range. But when the coup started they'd suddenly dropped the price to $6,500. She'd scraped together $1,300, and sold the rights to her flat to a loan shark for another $5,000 (which meant she'd be in debt for life, but it was worth it). Now she was trying to get the last $200 by wandering around the hotel lobby, looking for foreigners, and trying to sell anyone in imported clothes a huge, hideous, gold-encrusted soup tureen that she said was an antique. I felt sorry for her. She only had that day to raise the last $200 she needed; her husband had to get the bus that night to the swap venue, which was on neutral territory on the Georgian-Armenian border. So I gave her the money and told her to keep her family heirloom. Even though the marble lobby was chilly, she broke out in a sweat as she doubtfully took the notes. She clearly couldn't believe her luck.

How much to Gyandzha and back?

Fifty thousand.

On the third day of Makharrami, a soft-voiced Baku rip-off merchant took me across the country, chatting courteously in a way that the sometimes surly, often drunk, and possibly violent drivers of Moscow never did. It was only when we got back to the hotel in the evening that we discovered that the deal we'd made on a fare – 'fifty thousand' – meant to me the old roubles that everyone still used here, but to him the new nationalist currency, the manat. Manats were worth ten times as much as roubles. That made his price for the day trip half a million roubles, or $250: weeks of an ordinary person's wages, and more than I had. 'Why ever would I want to pay so much?' I asked repeatedly. 'I could have bought your car for that.'

'I swear to Allah, I have a family to feed,' the chancer answered repeatedly, in his sing-song Russian, fixing me with liquid eyes fringed with long dark lashes. 'I would never have taken a fare all that way for fifty thousand roubles. A tiny, miserly pittance like fifty thousand roubles. Tell me truly, how can a man live on fifty thousand roubles in these troubled times? How is such a thing possible?'

In the end, we both got bored with standing on our dignity. 'Give me what Allah tells you to,' he said. 'Give me whatever you're not ashamed to give.'

I tried an extra fifty thousand roubles, only twice what the fare should have been. He let it hang between thumb and fore-finger, full of dainty disgust (though not quite dropping it in the gutter). Hastily I added another few notes.

'I swear to Allah, girl, I wouldn't deceive you,' he said, visibly cheering up, and pocketing them before I could change my mind. 'A deal's a deal, and when you said fifty thousand I naturally thought you meant dollars. I mean, manats. But, so be it. God sees everything, and God knows everything. So let the fare be what it is.' Sighing and melodramatically shaking his head, with little looks at me to see if I might give in and pay more, he got slowly back into his car, and drove off. I was left uncomfortably aware that he'd handled the encounter with more charm (if less honesty) than I had.

It took four hours to get to Gyandzha. The air was so hot it looked wavy. The fields stretched brown and parched on either side. The driver and I lay back, fanning ourselves, panting like dogs.

When we reached the town – a strangely Middle Eastern-looking place, with pale square buildings and flat roofs and dogs in the sandy streets – we looked in Suret's barracks, and in the ex-Soviet barracks that now also belonged to the rebels. Suret wasn't there. It was a wasted journey.

We idled away another hour cruising around the countryside, looking at the thousands of refugees camped out in the fields in tents made of sheets draped over their carts and cars, half-heartedly trying to find a story by asking them where they hoped to go. But they were subdued. They didn't know the answer.

And I couldn't think of the right questions. In this open space, with dappled sun under the few wilting trees where we'd stopped, it was easier just to admire the beauty of the scene: the birdsong and buzz of insects, and the panorama of women and children in gaudy clothes, moving softly from carpet to carpet, boiling sparkling water over fires. All the individual lives and fears in front of me were reduced in my mind to a bright, remote picture in two dimensions. I felt guilty, but not very. It was too hot.

On the way back out of Gyandzha, when we first caught sight of the long pale road home to Baku, the driver suddenly swerved and pulled in under a giant concrete statue that stood just beyond the last building in town.

Adil was standing under it, grinning at us and waving. He ran over and jumped in. 'Knew I'd find you here,' he said with quiet satisfaction.

'But how did you manage to get here?' I asked, delighted but even more astonished. Adil had been wondering whether to come with us the day before, but had decided by the evening to stay in Baku in case something important happened. He was the last person I'd have expected to find at this end of the country now. But his apparently miraculous appearance had suddenly dispelled the airless monotony of the day.

'It was easy,' he said. 'I listened to the news in the morning, and when there was nothing on it I went to the airport and got a plane here. You were bound to go past the statue sooner or later.'

Adil already knew Suret wasn't around. He'd stopped off at the barracks, like we had. But he didn't seem too bothered. 'It happens,' he said absent-mindedly. The statue had caught his attention and he was looking up at it.

'Do you like it?' he asked, with that tinge of sadness in his smile again. 'It's Nizami, our poet. He wrote the greatest love song ever in the Middle Ages. It's a pity it isn't a more beautiful statue, but at least it's nice that our Soviet bosses remembered Nizami with respect.'

I hadn't really noticed the statue until then. It was a great Soviet lump. 'It's good that they didn't destroy it when they were fighting here a few days ago,' I said, trying to be tactful. 'Tell me about the poem.'

We set off, with Adil and the driver reciting bits of poetry at each other and translating them awkwardly into Russian.

Nizami wrote about love and the wind. Qays, his hero, fell so in love with Layla that he went mad. Now known as Majnun, the madman, he took refuge in the desert, where he composed poems that were so beautiful that they were sung everywhere and carried on the wind to his sweetheart.

'Though devoured by sorrow, Layla would not have told her grief for anything in the world. Sometimes, when no one was awake, the fountains of the moon made her step outside. There she stood, her eyes fixed on the path, waiting. But only the wind blowing from the mountains of Najd brought a breath of faith from a lonely man, or drove a cloud across, whose rain was, for Layla, a greeting from afar.

'Yet her lover's voice reached her. Was he not a poet? No tent curtain was woven so closely as to keep out his poems. Every child from the bazaar was singing his verses; every passer-by was humming one of his love songs, bringing Layla a message from her beloved, whether he knew it or not.

'Now Layla was not only a picture of gracefulness, but also full of wisdom and well versed in poetry. She herself, a pearl unpierced, pierced the pearls of words, threading them together in brilliant chains of poems. Secretly she collected Majnun's songs as they came to her ears, committed them to memory and then composed her answers.

'These she wrote down on little scraps of paper, heading them with the words: "Jasmine sends this message to the cypress tree." Then, when no one was looking, she entrusted them to the wind.

'It happened often that someone found one of these little papers, and guessed the hidden meaning, realising for whom they were intended. Sometimes he would go to Majnun hoping to hear, as a reward, some of the poems which had become so popular.

'And, true enough, there was no veil which could hide his beloved from Majnun. He answered at once, in verse, and whoever received the message saw to it that Layla should hear it at once.

'Thus many a melody passed to and fro between the two nightingales, drunk with their passion. Those who heard them listened in delight, and so similar were the two voices that they sounded like a single chant. Born of pain and longing, their song had the power to break the unhappiness of the world.'

The desert was flashing by, and the driver sighed happily. 'I can feel the wind again,' he said. 'The weather's changing.'

*   *   *

Adil wanted to be dropped off at the home of his relatives, on the edge of Baku. 'You like carpets, and they're refugees,' he said. 'I could ask them to show you some carpets they might want to sell.'

I didn't know any city people who had refugee relatives from the countryside. But it turned out that they were only in Baku because Adil had rescued them the year before, when the war came to their home.

'It was pure chance that I was going to see my great-granny anyway,' he said. His voice had got back the soft sing-song quality of someone reciting poetry. 'Luckily, I even had my Hi-8 camera in my bag. I turned up in the middle of winter, just as the Armenians moved into the hills in Kelbadzhar district, and found the road from the airport full of women walking towards me, through the snow, in their bare feet, weeping.'

I remembered the pictures now. He'd filmed the women, and Russian TV had shown them, and he'd got a pay rise for initiative reporting. But I didn't know he'd been looking for his great-granny at the same time.

'It was lucky all round,' he went on. 'Lucky that I found her. And very lucky that she's a tiny little thing, all skin and bone, because it was winter in the mountains, and anyone who was going to get out was going to have to get out by helicopter, and there were crowds of people in a panic around every helicopter, fighting for places. But she was so light that I lifted her over everyone's head and handed her to the pilot, and we sorted out a good place for her inside, with a seat and everything. We even got two of the carpets she wove for her dowry in too. She'd have been lost without them.' Adil shook his head reflectively, deep in his memories. I kept very quiet, not wanting him to stop. The sun was setting, and the wind was blowing dust against the car windows.

'How strange it is to think that the people doing these savage things may be the same Armenians we grew up with,' he said. His voice was low. 'And how strange that one day we stopped being able to talk to each other. I even remember it happening. We used to have chess tournaments every year. We loved them. But one year the Karabakh Armenian team arrived in a touchy, aggressive mood; they wouldn't speak to anyone except to accuse us of cheating. The next year, they didn't come at all. And now . . . well, who can think of chess tournaments now?'

We were driving through a strange area: a wilderness of furniture containers and dusty lanes on the edge of the city, clumps of cars, and clusters of improvised houses made from scrap.

Adil's relatives lived in a furniture container. They'd made windows in it. It had a sleeping area at one end, with lots of rolled-up bedding against the walls and overlapping carpets all over the floor. And it had a kitchen area at the other end, with a table and a lot of saucepans in a box. That was all. There were eight or nine people living in it, including the tiny great-granny in her loose black dress. There were a couple of dozen more wandering around in the dust outside.

'Everyone in this group of houses is from the same village in Kelbadzhar,' Adil said. 'It makes it feel more like home to them.' It was the same all over the edge of Baku, he said. Entire villages from Karabakh and the surrounding land were reconstituting themselves here, sticking with the people they'd known before their exile. A kind of imaginary Karabakh was being created, unnoticed, in the junkyards of scrap around the city.

Adil's relatives and their neighbours were very excited to have guests. The old lady didn't speak Russian, but she smiled a toothless, cheerful smile, and gestured me to a seat that two of the children were building from heaped-up mattresses. Glasses of steaming tea appeared from nowhere. Neighbours kept sticking their heads round the door, giving me bright-eyed, inquisitive stares. I gave the children some chewing gum I found in my pocket, wishing I had something better to offer. A jolly matron in a flowery shawl brought along a plate of sliced tomatoes. They showed me photographs of the house they'd lost, and their view of the mountains, and their former selves, all spruced-up and chipper in their best clothes, looking at the camera in solemn Soviet style.

The carpets came out too: big ones, small ones, ragged ones, crooked ones, all in bright pinks and oranges and reds. But the one I really liked was a modest, cheerful picture of two primitive lions roaring, with a name woven into the edge and the date 1961 next to it, that lay under the kitchen table. It was badly worn on one side.

'You like that one?' the granny asked, in foreign-sounding Russian, looking surprised.

'You like that one?' Adil and the two smudgy-eyed children echoed, looking equally surprised. ('The children have bad dreams,' he told me later, explaining their pale exhaustion. 'They still wake up screaming. It's the stress.')

I bought the lion carpet and another one. Adil said it had been part of his great-aunt's dowry. The price they wanted was cheap. I paid it without question. It would have been ugly to do anything else. The granny said something excited in Azeri, which Adil translated: she was going to use the money to buy a big, pompous, Soviet sideboard in bright brown wood veneer for the container. A *stenka*. Then they'd be able to start living like normal people again. She looked delighted at the thought. She was already planning which part of the *stenka* would have the linen, and where the plates would go.

'I'll look after your carpets well,' I said sentimentally. But I didn't think she minded seeing them go.

'Didn't you feel ripped off, paying so much?' Adil asked the next day, when he brought the carpets to my hotel room. I shook my head. I was delighted with them.

'No, no,' I protested. 'I love the idea of knowing the people who made the carpets, and seeing photos of the house where the carpets were made, and knowing the story of how they came here. And I wanted to buy carpets anyway . . . and it made me feel useful to be able to do something to help nice people who've had such a hard time. I don't think I paid too much at all.'

'You felt sorry for them because they were refugees, didn't you?' he said kindly. 'But still, you should always haggle a bit.'

My husband turned up later that day to join the press pack. He was laughing over his plane ride south. 'It was so hot that everyone had gone straight to sleep in their seats by the time I got in. All I could see was dozens of dark heads, all slumped back, and dozens of mouths wide open. It sounds cruel to say this, but they looked just like one of those torture-protest pictures of Kurds who've been gassed,' he said. His lip curled in easy, unkind laughter at the natives. I felt the distance between us grow.

The coup took a few more days to wind up. On the fourth day of Makharrami, parliament voted to strip the president of his powers.

On the fifth day of Makharrami, Azerbaijan suspended talks on the Western oil deal. On the sixth day of Makharrami, three ministers loyal to the president were arrested at the end of a press conference. On the seventh day of Makharrami, Suret flew to Baku to negotiate with the old Soviet boss. On the eighth day of Makharrami, the talks were still going on, and the rebels, who weren't bothering to spend the night on the edge of town any more, were wearing blue berets and guarding the parliament building. On the ninth day of Makharrami, the Azerbaijani oil boss resigned.

Finally, on the tenth day of Makharrami, parliament elected Suret prime minister and put the power ministries – police, spies and soldiers – under his control. After that it took a few months longer to organise presidential elections. The old Soviet boss won. (Not too many months after that, he got rid of PM Suret, too, but that's another story.)

By the tenth day of Makharrami, too, refugees were streaming away from Karabakh in their thousands. The enemy had sensed the chaos over the border. The Armenians were coming, faster and harder than ever.

On the tenth day of Makharrami, the month of mourning was in full swing in Baku. Men in black processed through the streets, beating their chests, chanting: 'Our weapons are in heaven, our imams are in battle.' But I'd gone to Moscow and wasn't there to see it. My party was over. The coup had been out of the headlines for days.

I didn't go back to the Caspian for a few years. By the time I did, Baku had changed dramatically for the better. It looked prosperous. There were restaurants everywhere, and Western-style bars with names like 'Ragin' Cajun' and 'Wild East'. There was a new hotel. There were flash cars waiting sedately at traffic lights, driven by oilmen in cashmere coats. By 1997, Baku was a boomtown again. All those foreigners' fears that the undemocratic old Soviet boss would today up to Moscow by tearing up the Western oil deal had proved unfounded. All he'd done was cut the Russians a small slice of the profits. He governed a country that was still a mess – it had refugees, corruption, and damage from the war – but he was using all his old Politburo wiles to keep Azerbaijan independent. The taxi drivers still sang his praises, delighted that they'd known better than the smart-aleck Westerners who would be the best ruler for them. You could buy his smiling official photo portrait in every street market.

By the middle of the 1990s, most of the fantastical coups and crazy semi-wars in most other parts of the madcap south had ground to a halt too. That was because, by then, a real war had broken out in the Russian mountains nearby, in Chechnya. A Russian army of a hundred thousand men was stomping all over the Chechens. Moscow's terrible revenge there gave people in the little statelets all around pause for thought. They grew frightened that any more rashness on their part might bring the Russian army their way, too, and they scurried nervously back to their schools and offices, hospitals and building sites, to get on with their ordinary lives.

The last time I saw Adil was in Chechnya. It was January 1995, at the start of the war. I was in a snowy wood on the edge of the capital, Grozny, and I was very frightened. Round a bend in the road, beyond the cover of the trees, the part of the city where I'd been early that morning was still being shelled. The apartment building I'd been standing under when it started had been hit. My driver and I had managed to escape from under the falling rubble, in a damaged car, chased by mortar bombs. But my photographer was still in there somewhere. I hoped he was hiding in a cellar till things quietened down. But thought he might be dead. We'd been waiting for him all day, first hot with adrenaline, then cold with fear. We'd been watching people stream out to safety, on foot through the woods, or in cars as battered as ours. We were stopping everyone and asking if they'd seen a big gentle bearded Lithuanian with a camera. No one had. A UN jeep had written down his name and given me a first aid pack, containing a bandage and a dressing, before roaring off away from the fighting. I looked at the useless things, bewildered, and put them down somewhere. Now it was getting dark, and Chechen guerrillas were unloading grenade launchers from a truck next to us, preparing for a night of fighting.

Suddenly, a group of Western photographers came out of the trees, striding jauntily away from the city, pink-cheeked and untouched. 'Have you seen the Reuters photographer?' I asked, imploringly, starting to describe him, feeling hope. They smiled vaguely. They hadn't. They had pictures to develop. They walked on.

I stopped the next car. It was a big black armoured thing, heavy and low on the road. Its bullet-proof window was cracked. I started asking about my photographer. The driver shook his head, then looked up from under his blue helmet at my face under my blue helmet. 'Surely that can't be Vanora?' he said wonderingly. It was Adil.

He was in a hurry to file too, but he was a kind man. He stopped the car. 'Here, sit down in the back for a bit, and have a rest. You must be frozen,' he said gently, and pulled out a bashed-up bar of chocolate from somewhere. 'We'll wait with you.'

I couldn't eat. But Adil sat in the front, leaning over the seat, telling me little bits of stories about an English reporter he'd been with yesterday who'd wanted to rescue a dog with bleeding paws from the ruins of Grozny; and about the failings of the armour-plated car, which he called the coffin, which was a reject from Bosnia, which was impossible to manoeuvre, whose window had shattered the first time a bit of shrapnel came near it. His smile didn't take away the sick black horror inside me, but it was a comfort of sorts. I didn't want him to go.

'We shouldn't stay here too long,' he said, and there was a hint of worry on his forehead. He gestured at the Chechen fighters setting up their position. 'It looks as though they're building up their defences here. This isn't a safe place.'

While he was talking, another tiny car full of big fighters had made its unsteady way to us. My missing photographer got out. He was alive. And he was all relieved smiles, talking nineteen to the dozen about the bombs that had dropped around the cellar he'd hidden in. The darkness cleared. I hugged him. I hugged the driver. The driver hugged him. We looked around, and Adil was grinning too, infected by our joy, and half his face was obscured by the Hi-8 camera he always carried. He was filming the reunion.

There wasn't time for more. It was dangerous to stay chatting. We didn't say goodbye. We all waved, and smiled, and ran to our different cars, and set off in opposite directions for our different temporary homes on the edge of Chechnya.

Later that year, while I went back to England for a few months and got divorced, I found a copy of *Layla and Majnun* and read it. How beautiful it was, and how sad. The point, it turned out, was that Layla and Majnun's love was impossible – too ideally perfect to exist in real life. They died apart. The place I'd thought of so happily as the land of love turned out to have a darker story in its heart.

I never managed to tell Adil I'd read it. He was killed a couple of months after I last saw him, in one of the final pointless outbursts of azart in Baku – some stand-off between the police and army, or police and security forces, or army and security forces, that caused a day's shooting on the streets of the city, but was forgotten immediately afterwards. Adil went out at six in the morning, with his Hi-8, to see what the noise was about. He didn't come home. They found him later in the morgue.

CHAPTER TEN

How Fish Die

It's hard to say exactly when in the nineties life in Russia lost its crazy get-rich-quick sparkle and desperation. But gradually people went back to living their real lives.

I date it to the moment when my fangy friend Victor, in St Petersburg, stopped scoring three-year grants from rich foreign organisations (and repaying them with a retyped version of his doctoral thesis from long before), and went out and got a job. It was a peculiar job: helping an American wannabe entrepreneur source cranberries in the swamps around St Petersburg, and export them home. Victor's role was to ward off on-the-make customs officials and run the office. At night, at home, he told mocking stories about the on-the-make Russian ladies the American didn't quite manage to ward off for himself, and recalled sardonically that the Russian word for cranberry – *klyukva* – means 'pie in the sky'. As a scientist, Victor felt that doing administrative work was a bit beneath him; still, he had an office to go to again, a work phone number, and, for a while at least, steady money.

Victor had managed to get his oldest daughter Nadya off to a university in America. She was doing business studies there.

Victor's earnings had been enough for a new computer, so they could email each other every night. 'How I hope Nadya never comes back to work in Russia,' he and Lena would say to each other, as devoutly as if they were praying, over the kitchen table, over their darling doves, cheeselets, and sour cream. (They'd got a new kitchen, and the mysterious jars of dark pickled things overhead had gone for good.) 'How I hope she makes a life for herself over there.'

Only Mouse, not a little girl in pigtails any more, was still wild, and getting wilder. She played truant. She failed her exams. She sulked for weeks when her parents refused to let her have a photo portfolio shot by a man who said she had the legs to become a top model – and make millions. 'I'm not having my daughter become a prostitute,' her mother said. So Mouse waited till her parents went to the dacha, then asked her wayward teenage friends over. The parents came back when the flat was crawling with young people with slurring voices and crazy eyes; there were two unknown teenagers in the bed. Mouse was gated but elated. 'We were all off our faces!' she whispered excitedly in the bedroom.

'Mouse is a problem child,' her mother whispered in the kitchen.

'She's just a teenager,' I said. 'It will pass'.

That was in the middle of the nineties, when Petlyura's boho squat on the Boulevard Ring was repossessed by the Moscow City Council. They bulldozed the building and built a nine-storey business and leisure centre (with casino) on the site.

At about the same time, my friend Volodya gave up his dream of finding a 'really good way to deceive people and make a million'; instead, he set up a one-man firm making stage sound systems, and moved into a suburban flat with his new wife. When I went to concerts now with my musical friends, Sasha and Natasha, I noticed that they'd stopped exclaiming at the high price of groceries and started praising the high quality of the CDs and trinkets on sale with the programmes. 'Really very cheap,' Natasha said happily, trying on earrings.

Most people were sick of excess. Everyone I knew had a respectable job to go to in the mornings, and – now that there was no hyperinflation – a taste for dull bourgeois luxuries. My friends compared brands of imported yoghurt, and talked about cars, foreign holidays, new sheepskin coats, and their relentless home improvements.

The caviar-eating classes were calming down too. The foreigners who came to make their fortunes in Russia now were neat bankers, management consultants, and lawyers, living in former inner-city slums that had sprouted smooth white walls and polished wood floors. Even the lawless new rich, still scrapping over their crooked deals to buy every last national asset on the cheap, were learning fancy manners. They sent their kids to public schools in England; they wanted tough laws to protect a status quo that favoured them. The old style of problem-solving, the *razborka* (a violent encounter featuring knives, guns, and blood) was being displaced by board meetings.

You didn't even have to go to the market to buy your stolen caviar any more. That was being institutionalised too. One of the British correspondents had a source, and sold caviar on for a modest mark-up to everyone he knew. If buying caviar from the safety of another correspondent's freezer seemed too tame, soft-tongued Caspian caviar salesmen would come a couple of times a month to the offices where rich foreigners worked, letting you taste and inspect their big, neat jars of gleaming, unbroken, fish eggs, sealed with fat rubber bands to keep in the tang of the sea.

On one hot summer afternoon, as I whiled away an hour waiting to see a government official, his slow-moving assistant sat down to tea with me and put the new mood into words. 'Ah,' he chuckled. 'If you were in Russia during the early 1990s, you'll have seen us all carrying on like lunatics. Rebellions, riots, shootings, ah! Those were the days. You must have been impressed by Russian azart! But you can't carry on like that forever, you know. Sooner or later they were bound to stop it happening. Now it's the *knut* and the lash if we misbehave. Quite right too. That's what we Russians need. It's the only way to get us to knuckle under and go back to work.'

The only people who still lived by the laws of azart were the tiny elite of Kremlin politicians and their millionaire cronies, the ambitious, driven, ruthless people closest to the president. They filled the headlines with eye-popping tales of corruption and skulduggery. They won the president's re-election in 1996, beating the Communists – but then it turned out they'd omitted to mention that he'd had a heart attack before the voting finished, and was now an invalid who needed major bypass surgery and couldn't rule. Hair-raising peacemaking in Chechnya brought an end to the war – as well as accusations that both the war and the peace were lining top people's pockets. The president's bodyguards were caught creaming off millions by importing duty-free fags and booze through what was technically a fund for sportsmen. Incriminating secret phone calls were tapped; secret pictures of steamy sauna orgies snapped.

It all got into the press. But no one paid any attention. There wasn't any point in journalists investigating all this wrong-doing because no one bothered to read the papers. Normal people, living normal lives, thought all these gangster politicians were a bunch of power-hungry animals, ripping out each other's throats, each as bad as the next, incapable of change. So they ignored their bosses, and got on with life.

The craziness was ebbing away out of Moscow to the fast-nesses of the Kremlin and the banks, or to remote places on the edges of the map, places you only saw on TV. Being a journalist in this smug, cynical business burg could feel as anachronistic as being a Communist Party member. When I let myself into my empty flat at night, I sometimes wondered what I was still here for.

We all know the ways of insomnia: lying in a warm bed in the dark, our bodies unwilling to get up, our minds racing, aware of the creaks and sighs of the building settling closer to the ground, listening to the whistles and snores of other people's peaceful sleep. Even time seems personal. Some of the people awake just before dawn in any block of flats anywhere will have jolted into consciousness, in a cold sweat, to worry at leisure about the problems of tomorrow. Others, who have stayed up late, eating or drinking or talking, might still feel they're in yesterday.

At 58 Lenin Street, Kaspiisk (another dingy dormitory town on the Caspian shore, a dispiriting place with buildings made of battered prefab concrete panels stacked nine floors high and sagging against the grey sea), a few residents were awake, for one reason or another, before sunrise on Saturday, 16 November 1996.

This is what the survivors remember.

There was a muffled bang from the basement. Two sections of the building seemed to jerk upward, hung for an instant in mid-air, and then, very slowly, came roaring down.

The rest of the story was on TV all through the day: men in military fatigues clambering over piles of rubble and furniture, grey with dust, digging. More than eight hundred rescuers dug through Saturday and Sunday. They were still digging on Monday.

Tuesday was a day of mourning across Russia. Flags were lowered to half-mast in memory of the dead. Television entertainment programmes were cancelled.

The rescuers found fifty-four corpses and dozens more smashed, broken, bleeding bodies of people who had somehow managed to stay alive. Eighteen of the dead were children. Their motionless little feet, sticking out from under tarpaulins, brought tears to the eyes of the TV audience.

The victims lay on slabs, like gutted fish, until vans from the morgue took them away.

The explosion wasn't caused by a gas leak. Someone had laid explosives in the basement and set them off in a deliberate attempt to murder all the sleeping families at 58 Lenin Street. The blast became a crime case.

The building turned out to have housed Russian military officers – the 41st Detachment of Federal Border Guards, as well as a helicopter squadron and the operational staff of the local military. Conspiracy theories quickly began flying.

Kaspiisk is in the very south of Russia, in a region called Dagestan, a poor, crime-ridden and mostly Muslim place next door to poor, crime-ridden, mostly Muslim Chechnya. After two years of war between Russian soldiers and Chechen separatists, it was almost a reflex action to suspect Chechen terrorism.

That theory didn't hold for more than a minute, once people remembered that the war was over and that the 41st Detachment had in any case never worked near the Dagestani border with Chechnya or had any chance to provoke Chechen resentment.

The vital clue came from looking at what the 41st Detachment did. It patrolled the Dagestani coast, policing smuggling routes for weapons, narcotics – and black caviar.

'People are saying that Valery Morozov, head of the border troops detachment, was "on the outs" with local organised crime bosses who were involved in the arms business and caviar smuggling,' ran a typical piece of speculation in one of the Moscow papers. 'Members of the border troops, looking warily over their shoulders for a sign of their superiors, whisper that the local caviar Mafia had repeatedly threatened Morozov both secretly and openly. There allegedly had even been threats to blow him up along with his family . . . The straw that broke the camel's back, people say, was a recent operation in which border troops at the airport detained half a ton of black caviar that was heading for the Arab Emirates . . .'

The Russian border guards had started doing well against smugglers that year. In the first three months of 1996, they had seized 1.6 tonnes of contraband black caviar. In May, guards operating at Dagestan's international airport (in Kaspiisk) had intercepted 560 kilos of caviar on its way to the United Arab Emirates. Fake waybills accompanying the cargo suggested that local customs officials were involved.

Lieutenant-Colonel Morozov was killed in the explosion, so he could not confirm the stories that his professional successes had led to threats against his life. But a year-long investigation by the Russian security police bore out the rumours. It ruled that the explosion was the caviar Mafia's revenge for losing a consignment of illegal caviar that would have been worth millions of dollars on the world market.

'Our sources say the caviar Mafia had been bargaining for a long time, in an attempt to get their cargo back,' the newspapers said. 'They applied invisible forms of pressure, but failed to bribe the border guards. So they decided to blow up the building where the officers and their families lived.'

The culprits weren't named, or caught. There was no chance of a trial.

The Kaspiisk caviar murders were pushed out of the Russian news within a few days. Other things were occupying minds across the nation, including the whereabouts of the president, who hadn't been seen in public since having major heart surgery a fortnight before. (He turned up again soon afterwards, like a bad penny.)

But when spring came, and the sturgeon set off upriver to spawn and be slaughtered in the fishermen's illegal nets, I went south to Dagestan.

Even the idea of Dagestan filled my hot-headed office fixer with glee.

He was quite often bored with his Moscow desk job: too much kow-towing, too much irksome phoning of bureaucrats. He'd once got in a rage and thrown a chair at an American correspondent. What he liked best in the office was flexing his huge biceps against the Heath Robinson-esque resistance machine in his drawer, or writing the screenplay he wanted to show Arnold Schwarzenegger, who he'd once done some interpreting for and who, in the photo pinned lovingly above the desk, looked just like our fixer (only bigger). The screenplay starred an Arnold Schwarzenegger type, named Arnold, heroically muscling Chechen terrorists to the ground.

Dagestan was just the kind of place he liked getting his teeth into – the badlands, where anything might happen. It was one of the poorest places in Russia. It had mudslides, Muslims, cholera epidemics, twenty per cent unemployment, knife fights, Mafias and kidnappings. He phoned and phoned, yelling the formulas of international bonhomie down the crackling lines, gasping and tutting pleasurably and stretching his eyes as he listened to what people there told him.

'The fisheries minister will meet you to talk about caviar,' he said solemnly at the end of the day, chomping one of the energy-giving chocolate slugs he kept in his desk. 'The head of the National Council of Muslims will talk to you about religion. There. I've got you meetings with the two biggest men in Dagestan. I did well, no?'

'Brilliantly,' I said obediently, keen to move on to the joke he was visibly only just managing to hold in.

'And guess what?' he said, as a crazy, delighted smile lit up his face and his eyebrows wiggled joyfully. 'They're brothers! The pair of them control everything, and they're family! It's just like the Corleones! You'll have a wild, wild time!' And he threw back his head for a good belly laugh, and clutched his sides.

When I looked in the files for more information about the Dagestani brothers, I found that our fixer had exaggerated (it was a weakness of his), but not by all that much. The brothers weren't quite in control of Dagestan, a place with so many competing nationalities that it had long ago evolved a Swiss-style form of local government. Quarrels were avoided there by letting each of the main ethnic groups rotate in and out of power, almost unnoticed by the man in the street. But the brothers were beginning to upset that delicate balance.

Dagestan was a long ribbon of land, with one side running along the Caspian shore, and the other running along the mountains next to Chechnya. The mountains were home to Dagestan's many religious shrines; the sea was home to the sturgeon. Now that the end of Communism had killed off old-fashioned Soviet industry and subsidies along with Lenin, Dagestanis had little choice but to place their faith in God and make their living from caviar. By taking charge now of God and caviar, Dagestan's only growth areas, the brothers were cannily positioning themselves for power tomorrow.

The religious brother, Nadyr-Shah, scored the most headlines. He was an MP in the Russian parliament, and he wrote forceful articles in the Russian papers denouncing (a) Dagestan's old-fashioned Muslim leaders, for being corrupt stooges of Communism, KGB agents, British spies and so on, and (b) hotheads from the younger generation who were rebelling against the cowardice of their Soviet parents by adopting a dangerous fundamentalist form of faith, a Saudi import called Wahhabism.

The Wahhabis, with their wild beards and trousers hitched above their ankles, might have seemed comical if one group of them hadn't somehow got their hands on a lot of guns and taken over a hill village called Karamakhi a few months before. Three people had been killed in a battle of a thousand men. The village had been sealed off ever since; outsiders who tried to get near were stopped, searched, and scared away.

Nadyr-Shah's answer was to set up something called the Muslim Council; he wanted Dagestanis to adopt a religious Third Way – and become his followers.

The fisheries brother, Magomed, got much less of a look-in in the Moscow papers. But I found one mention, in a piece about how the Kaspiisk killings were part of a caviar war, in the investigative monthly *Top Secret*. The point of that article was that the caviar Mafia and the law-enforcement officials who were supposed to fight it were one and the same. It said the timid Dagestani papers were always telling readers that the caviar smugglers were a mysterious 'brotherhood of the reeds', outlaws and ne'er-do-wells who operated on lonely beaches along the region's long Caspian coast. But what people in Dagestan really believed, it added, was that it was their own fabulously wealthy bosses, in their trawlers and helicopters, who were stealing from the sea.

All this should have sounded intimidating, especially when you added to the picture the growing risk of being kidnapped when you travelled anywhere on the fringes of Chechnya. Dozens of Russians had been kidnapped. A French relief worker called Vincent Cochetel had been snatched during the winter; he was still a captive. Even though masked men had seized Cochetel from a town on the other side of Chechnya, the whole of the ethnic south was considered high-risk; Dagestani officials were among those helping get him out.

Two Russian male photographers refused point blank to take all those risks just to find out about illegal fishing. The American woman photographer who often did stories with me was squeamish too.

Yet I found myself working hard to persuade her to come, with no way of knowing that we'd be safe but with a strangely light heart at the prospect of going back to a realm of risk and chance and wildness. 'Of course no one's going to kidnap us,' I said, sounding more sure than I felt. 'We'll go to the mountains, and see the secret shrines, and the Wahhabis, and make friends with the poachers, and eat caviar for breakfast. There'll be fantastic photos. And Moscow's got so quiet, and so boring. It's time for an adventure. Please come.'

She was a trouper. She came. But she was still in two minds. 'Of course no one's going to kidnap us,' she repeated as we got off the plane in the capital of what we'd started, a little nervously, calling Dagger-stan. 'Right?'

Briefly, I wished I'd paid more attention to those very reasonable worries about bandits and kidnappings when we tried to check into a fleapit hotel in the middle of Makhachkala, and found the surly cashier sitting inside a metal cage, flanked by a man with a gun, and bars on all the flaking windows. Bedbugs were the best thing guests could expect there. We took our bags away.

But we cheered up once we started wandering through the sunlit park and squares, among the weekend crowds in their headscarves and embroidered skullcaps, under swaying trees. There was a holiday atmosphere. People were eating ice cream. A middle-aged woman who had once taught atheism but now devoutly wore a white headscarf gave it to me because mine was the wrong colour. I bought a little green booklet of prayers from a street stall, whose title, in mock-Arabic writing, was: 'How to Ward Off the Evil Eye'. We sniffed the kebab clouds coming from tatty cafés done out in pastel-coloured paint for innocent Soviet tourism.

Things began to go well. We found a local newspaper office, and made friends with some young journalists who promised to show us around. 'You can't stay in that dump in town,' one said at once, and whisked us off to a former Party hotel on the beach, where we were accepted as VIPs and checked in. 'I *think* you'll be safe here,' our new guide, Marat, said doubtfully. 'Just don't for God's sake go out for midnight walks on the beach, and if anyone knocks on the door just keep quiet until they go away.' We were grateful: it was rundown, and hot, and the fans didn't work, but it felt a lot less frightening than the fleapit.

We were even happier when we found the first of our brothers on a stage in the central square, where the crowds were beginning to converge. It was equipped with microphones, giant speakers, and oversized green banners in Russian and Arabic letters. Nadyr-Shah Khachilayev, who was about to speak to the rally of the faithful that he'd organised, was watching his side-kicks fiddling with the sound system. He looked more rap star than cleric. He was athletic: unusually tall, long-legged, lean, muscled, tanned and toned. He walked with a big-cat lope. He had flashes of gold at wrist and throat. He couldn't have been much older than thirty, and he was casual in jeans, a T-shirt, and a flying jacket. Above a trim beard, his face was lean and impassive and his eyes were empty.

'I can't speak to you today,' he hollered down from the stage. 'I have my big festival to look after, and it will take all day and all night. The faithful are waiting.'

'Tomorrow?' I tried.

'I'm a very busy man,' he began, shaking his head importantly. But the international press was too alluring a prospect to resist for long. 'We-e-ell,' he went on, curling a lip, looking tough. 'I could fit you in at eight in the morning. One hour max. I'm a very busy man. Are you girls hard-working enough to be up in time for eight?'

We assured him we were, thanked him prettily, and left him to his festival. Nadyr-Shah didn't seem to be a particularly subtle man. He was so taken with his pleasantry that he yelled it again at our departing heads. 'That's early, mind; I don't suppose you often get up that early, do you, girls?'

Nadyr-Shah wasn't up at eight. We knocked at the gates of his fabulously vulgar nouveau-Russian palace, admiring the stone lions rampant inside the wrought-iron fence, but got no reply. At nine, we tried again. This time, we finally managed to raise a couple of cross-eyed heavies, who yawned and clutched their heads and mumbled that we should come back at ten. 'Hangovers,' was Marat's grinning diagnosis. 'And these New Muslims are supposed to be teetotallers. It must have been quite some religious festival.'

Silence at ten o'clock. Suppressing laughter, we tried one last time at eleven thirty, ready to knock off for lunch if we got nowhere again. This time, at last, there were shuffling footsteps and slammed doors from inside the house. The guards were still holding their heads and looking tired as they opened the gates to us.

I wouldn't have liked to have had Nadyr-Shah's headache. He was showered and in fresh clothes, but his face was grey, he could only move cautiously and he gave the impression of being in terrible pain. He couldn't meet our eyes, either, when he finally loped down the curving staircase to the great hall, full of carved wood and enormous sofas, where we'd been told to wait. Perhaps because he was ill at ease over having overslept, he chose attack instead of defence. 'Didn't think you would make it for eight o'clock,' he sneered. 'And I was right. Where were you?'

Slightly to my surprise, young Marat blushed, cleared his throat and piped up bravely, 'Here. We came, as agreed. But no one was up. The guards told us to come back later, and we've been trying all morning.'

Even more to my surprise, Nadyr-Shah humphed, said, 'We were praying,' almost as an excuse, then subsided into sick silence. There was no real fight in him.

What followed wasn't exactly what I'd have called an interview. I'd ask questions about religion in Dagestan, and he'd half listen, exclaim, 'WHAT?' at apparently random moments, then go quiet again. He was clearly more a man of action than a man of words. He didn't have anything much at all to say about God. Every now and then he would get his cue, and half say, half shout a criticism of one of his rivals, or boast about how some of the separatist leaders in Chechnya supported him and wanted to create a 'single spiritual space' with him (not an idea that Chechen-hating politicians in Russia were likely to appreciate). It sounded like hot air. He didn't seem to remember the trenchant arguments made in his articles.

A bit desperate, and a bit bored, I found myself looking at Nadyr-Shah's splendid furnishings. There was a life-size portrait of a tall, rangy, bearded young man in a judo costume: not Nadyr-Shah, but clearly a close relative, perhaps yet another brother. There was a collection of heavily decorated daggers on one wall. A tiger skin hung on another.

After a few cups of sweet coffee, Nadyr-Shah did cheer up enough to tell us about how he'd gone to Chicago and met Mike Tyson, the ear-chewing boxer, and the controversial black American radical activist and Muslim Louis Farrakhan. He wanted Farrakhan to visit him in Dagestan. 'You don't think I could get him, do you? But he'll come,' he said, defensively. 'He'll come.' Wide-eyed, we promised to cover the visit when it happened.

But it was Mia, the photographer, who fully restored his good temper. 'Can I take your picture?' she asked.

His face lightened. 'Just a minute,' he said, and flew upstairs. When he trotted back down, as eager as a schoolboy, his hair was glossily combed and he smelled of cologne. She gave directions. He was happy to obey. He'd become a pussycat purring against his tiger skin.

Brother number two, Magomed, the head of the fisheries business, who swam into our net right after Nadyr-Shah, was even longer and leaner and more muscled and toned than his brother.

Magomed lived in a ghetto-fabulous palace too, down the road from his brother in a millionaires' district that, despite Dagestan's official poverty, was sprouting mansions in all directions. (Marat mockingly called the whole area 'Santa Barbara'). We waited for an hour for Magomed in an outer lobby, drinking coffee with his excruciatingly polite aide, watching workmen put together the pale sandstone arches of what would soon be a full-on, Hollywood-style Moorish courtyard.

Inside was another shadowy great hall, and a study featuring more carved hardwood than most Gothic churches, where Magomed, another man of action, spoke to me only in the vaguest of generalities.

How much money did caviar poaching drain out of Dagestan's official economy? I asked, hoping for some facts. 'Oh, statistics, they're all published . . . I don't know about statistics,' he answered, waving a magnificent hand. 'Anyway, we have no official economy here, just chaos. People are swept along by the tide of life and stay alive as best they can. Smugglers clearly work for the people in power, and a lot is lost. But I can't say how much.'

Trying to ask the most general of questions, just to get him talking, I asked whether what newspapers called a 'caviar war', pitting poachers against police, was really going on in Dagestan, and whether the Kaspiisk killings had been part of it.

Magomed's face changed. Veins stood out on his temples. He went red, then pale, then red again with anger. I'd clearly touched a raw nerve. He stood up, all six-foot-something of rangy rage, and a sheaf of papers went hissing unnoticed to the floor.

'*Top Secret* wrote an utterly absurd and brazen article about me in connection with that,' he fumed. 'They as good as came out and called me the head mafioso, the King of Fish. They are trying to label me as a criminal! They want all the mud they're slinging to stick to me!'

'Do you have an idea who might really have done it?' I quavered.

He stabbed a finger at me. 'No one with a human soul could possibly blow up a houseful of people for caviar or money,' he cried. 'How could they? I ask you, how could such a thing be?'

Magomed gave no further clues about who he thought was behind the killings, but his fury over the *Top Secret* article was dissipating. He chose to be photographed with an arm draped lovingly around his Humvee armoured vehicle, the envy of half Dagestan. Afterwards, he took us into a huge kitchen, where there was a big mixing bowl full of caviar on a marble work surface, and left a housekeeper instructions to feed us.

She made us caviar sandwiches that were greedy even by Moscow standards: great ladles of glistening black on bread. 'Go on, eat up,' she said cheerfully. 'How much would that cost at home? Hundreds of dollars. Thousands. Eat it: it's power food.'

We felt as euphoric as hunters after a killing to have got both Khachilayevs in a single day, even if they hadn't told us much. Out on the street, eyes still popping at their sheer larger-than-life flamboyance, we interrogated Marat about their reputations.

The brothers were the newest kind of new rich, he explained, with the disdain of the middle-class intellectual. People still remembered when they were just kids with a lot of muscle from the wrong side of the tracks, mad about sport, always working out at the stadium. Then one of the brothers became a martial arts champion (which meant prize money, but in Russia also often meant getting into crime). He was killed in a murky shoot-out soon after the Soviet Union collapsed, something to do with some Chechen business partners. The other brothers had gone from strength to strength. No one knew how they'd acquired quite so much more money since (though everyone could hazard a guess). They had power, they wanted more, and they might easily get it; but the brothers were still a bit of a joke.

It wasn't just the brothers who seemed funny. We laughed all the time in the car as we went hunting for poachers. Our boy journalist guides entertained us with stories about the drive-by shootings, mysterious explosions, and suspicious suicide leaps that killed so many members of Dagestan's new rich these days. 'I was just over the road when one of the first bombs went off,' Marat grinned, 'and I rushed into the nice solid bathroom and lay on the floor. It took me ages to realise it wasn't an earthquake. Now I know better.' No one ever got caught, and, whenever they were covering these assassinations for their paper, the boys always counted more bodies than were officially supposed to have been killed. 'Usually it's the bodyguards who die, or just people who happen to be out on the street,' they said. But the killers did get lucky sometimes. Finance Minister Gamid Gamidov was killed by a car bomb in 1996; his rival, Deputy Prime Minister Said Amirov, had survived four attempts on his life and now went around in a wheelchair. The boys called him 'our Roosevelt'.

Life was so cheap here that it was wise to take precautions. Before we dared venture into the secretive coastal villages to try and meet poachers, the boy journalists had insisted we find ourselves a friend of a friend of a friend who knew people there.

Our insurance policy with the caviar thieves was hunched in the front seat, a small speccy youth with spots and a cheeky grin. He was enjoying the adventure. He had a cousin who had a friend who lived in a smugglers' village halfway down the coast, near Izberbash, by a picnic spot where a cliff at the roadside looked like Pushkin's profile. Holidaymakers pulled up their cars there and grilled kebabs.

We turned left towards the sea, over lumpy tussocks of oily grass and sand. When we made a wrong turning, and ended up on the rubbish-strewn beach, near a couple of upended wooden boats and a fence from which nets were hanging, Specs and the other boys got visibly worried. 'Turn round here, quick,' Specs said sharply, even though none of us could see a soul. 'The last thing we want is any unpleasantness.' We reversed away, revving wildly.

The village, a few streets of white-painted breezeblock topped with vines, seemed as deserted as the beach. Specs knocked on gates and consulted watchful women peeping out. We sat tight. 'One never knows, does one,' Marat said cautiously.

But when we did finally track down Umar, our smuggler, he wasn't anything like the desperado I'd been expecting from this tense build-up. He was a light-haired, well-spoken, jovial man of about forty, who walked with a limp. When he welcomed us into his courtyard, we saw he'd been looking at a chess problem laid out on a board under the vines. Like the boy journalists, his eyes were full of laughter.

Umar had every reason to laugh at his bargain with fate.

His job canning stolen caviar was simple. His equipment was easily hidden from prying eyes. And his work netted him thousands of dollars every spawning season.

He had a workshop off the courtyard, with a solid metal date stamp screwed to a table. An ungainly device with more levers than a small cappuccino-maker – used to seal lids onto Russian caviar jars – was plugged into the wall. There were fifteen of these machines circulating in the village, he said, covering it with a discreet dishcloth; someone would be along soon to borrow it for the afternoon. Boxes containing hundreds of the glass jars, identical to those used for official exports and openly on sale in Makhachkala, were piled against the walls. There were also boxes containing big silver half-kilo cans, marked IRANIAN CAVIAR. Behind the courtyard, in another tiny room, Umar had stashed his only expensive piece of kit: a ten-thousand-dollar sterilising machine the size of a tall fridge. He banged his cane happily on its white side. He was investing in himself. Things could only get better.

Once upon a time in the Soviet Union, he'd been a middle-class engineer, with a job at a big military radio factory, a small but adequate pay packet, and a law-abiding future in suburbia. Then the Soviet Union collapsed, his factory shut down, and there was no more state work and no more command economy. The present was all hyperinflation and hunger; the only way forward that Umar could see was crime. So he became a smuggler. 'Look, what choice did I have?' he said philosophically. 'I had responsibilities, and kids to feed. This was all I could do. It's not a bad life.'

From where we were sitting, it looked idyllic. There were chickens clucking peacefully somewhere behind the kitchen, the smell of hot bread rising from the basket in front of us, a couple of women flitting to and fro with cool drinks, a dish of caviar and a big tray of watermelon, and happy children playing underfoot.

[197]

Umar's regular clients were in Makhachkala, but he didn't know, or care, who they were. He didn't see them. Phone calls came, sporadically, right through the season, and he would get orders to can up to 50 kilos of caviar a time. A 50 kilo job would take three days, and earn him a thousand dollars. All he had to do was limp down to the beach in the mornings, buy from his neighbours the fishermen as they brought in their catch, and get to work. Once his cans were ready, he'd load them up in his little minivan, top them off artistically with some nice tomatoes, and deliver them to Makhachkala.

The worst thing he could imagine happening to him would be to be stopped by a policeman who confiscated his consignment. But even that thought made him laugh. 'You just have to keep your wits about you,' he said happily, and he rubbed his fingers and thumb together, making the rustling noise of roubles changing hands, looking reminiscent.

The last time he was stopped on the road, a nosy policeman eager to investigate his boxes of vegetables poked his head into the boot and asked, 'So what's at the bottom of your van, under all that salad?'

'Ah,' Umar replied smoothly, passing over a banknote with plenty of noughts. 'At the very, very bottom of my van, all you'll find is bare boards.' Chuckling, the policeman waved him on.

'The only police who might arrest you are the ones you haven't paid off,' Umar concluded triumphantly, polishing off his caviar sandwich. 'The truth is everyone's at it: everyone in my town, everyone in every village up and down the coast. Look at the statistics: ninety per cent of caviar in the world comes from the Caspian, and ninety per cent of Caspian caviar is poached.

QED: we're all criminals. Nowadays, what else is there to make money out of except the shadow economy?' We all laughed with him.

We went to the beach, and sat under a decaying beach hut with Umar's two fishermen friends, gazing out at the sea, watching the sun set. It was very quiet. A breeze lifted the nets, scraping them against the barnacled boat bottom. The fishermen reminisced.

In the old days, fishermen only ever got killed by the sudden Caspian storms that turned the flat water we were looking at into a boiling grey nightmare, and washed bodies up on the beach every year. Now there were dangers everywhere. Fishing on the sea was illegal, and half a dozen different police forces patrolled the waters, ready to arrest smugglers and clap them in jail for years, or shoot anyone who made off towards the horizon. Or you heard mysterious gun battles out at sea – ba-BOOM! Ba-BOOM! – but never found out who was firing.

The local water police didn't cause too much trouble, as long as you paid them over the odds for boat permits (but if you came across Russian border guards in a gunboat, you'd be wise to tip your catch over the side smartish before they got close).

They cackled.

In the old days, there used to be so many fish that you could stand right here, on the beach, and see them wriggling and squirming in the water. And if you threw out a line, you could catch a sturgeon without even getting up; that's how many fish there used to be in the good old days.

The fishermen didn't know why there were fewer fish

nowadays. But they didn't think it was because they were taking too many fish from the sea. It was probably the poachers from Azerbaijan, they said, who came in big ships and stole fish from Dagestani waters, who were doing the damage. Or else it was the oil-drilling off the Azerbaijani coast, which might spread so much pollution across the sea that it would kill the fish off.

Umar could see I wasn't quite convinced.

'There's always been smuggling here, even if there wasn't so much before. And look how many eggs a sturgeon lays. Even if only a few survive each generation, it's still enough,' he said. Nothing bothered Umar if he could explain it away scientifically. 'Anyway, we're only little people, making our living from the sea. It's not our fault.'

I lost count of the number of times I heard the phrase 'not my fault' that week. No one took responsibility for the annihilation of the sturgeon. Everyone had someone else to blame. Azerbaijanis were the favourite scapegoat, followed by the Central Asians on the other side of the sea. And what about all the villages that lived by poaching in Russia proper, on the thousands of little rivers in the Volga delta where the sturgeon went to spawn? The pair of young fishermen I took out to dinner in Makhachkala the next day – neat, respectable-looking ex-bank clerks, making ten times their old salaries – went so far as to blame the Iranians.

The rival police forces patrolling the waters blamed each other. The Russian border guards accused their Dagestani colleagues of negligence. The Dagestanis admitted that they'd come across smugglers among the Russian border guards.

In the great game of life with caviar, there were no rights and wrongs, just the exhilarating thrill of the chase. Everyone in the business was having too much whispery, furtive fun to worry.

Sales of caviar and red fish – the different types of sturgeon – were banned all along the Russian Caspian. It was another way of trying to crack down on the smuggling business. It was everyone's pleasure to ignore the law.

'Would you like to see how you can't buy caviar in Dagestan?' Marat asked.

A whole side of the bazaar was given over to stalls selling red fish. The fish corpses, smaller than in pictures (there were so few fish now that they even caught the young, immature ones), lay on their sides, waiting mutely to be axed into saleable chunks.

We dropped in first during the morning, when a nervous policeman was hovering, ignored by the market people. 'Don't worry, he's tame; he's been bought,' a gold-toothed saleswoman said reassuringly, loud enough for the policeman to hear. He blushed and shuffled away. She laughed. Still, there were no cans of caviar laid out for sale, only cautious whispers from the lazily grinning men floating by. 'Pssst?'

But, by the time we came back, late in the afternoon, there was a party atmosphere: vodka on the traders' breaths, reck-lessness in the air. Drunken men with gold teeth and dirty trousers, streaked with sticky fish blood, were standing on top of the stalls, bawling rock-bottom end-of-day prices. The policeman had faded away altogether. Now you only had to ask, and big cans of caviar would be pulled out from under the stalls. Fifty dollars was what half a kilo cost, give or take an energetic haggle.

Fifty buksi was only half the Moscow price. We left, grinning from ear to ear, with a big going-home present. We didn't bother hiding it. There didn't seem any point.

Only people who had nothing to do with caviar trafficking had time to worry. Even they worried more about God than Mammon.

We had dinner with a university professor who worried about the rise of the Wahhabi ('Where did they get those guns from? Who will they turn them on next?'). He was the father of the most thoughtful of the boy journalists, Timur; he would probably have worried even more if he'd know that his son was taking us to a secret Wahhabi meeting the next morning, to see the men in black at prayer.

'They're banned, how did you know how to find them, Timur?' I asked curiously.

'I think what they preach is interesting,' Timur answered. 'I'm not ready to follow them yet; I still like smoking and drinking and nights out with the guys, and my wife doesn't think much of the idea of covering up. But in a few years – once we've all got more used to religion being a part of our lives – I could easily see myself joining.'

The Mufti of Dagestan, an intellectual with a beautiful, mobile face and great charm, worried about the rise of the Wahhabi and about the fight Nadyr-Shah was picking with him. 'Me and Nadyr are the two real leaders here,' he said wistfully. 'We should be working together, but in the last year I've begun to feel that we're jinxed.'

Before we left, we went to the mountains to pay our respects to the Dagestanis' God.

The boy journalists took us praying all the way through the deep puddles and rockfalls of a terrifying five-mile tunnel whose rock walls were dripping with water. It collapsed sometimes, the boys said; but nothing could harm us. We drove triumphantly out the other end, into golden sunshine, into a land of mountains piled on mountains, locked-away valleys, soaring cliffs, waterfalls, and eagles circling overhead, a land so remote it had taken most of modern Russian history to conquer it.

My first idea had been to go to the mountain village where the Wahhabis, with their guns and fanaticism and too-short trousers, had taken over. But the boy journalists flatly refused. 'Too dangerous,' they said. 'No point. They won't talk to you. And they might shoot us.'

So instead we went on the more romantic trail of Imam Shamil, the great anti-Russian resistance leader and religious figurehead of the nineteenth century, from the tiny mountain village full of crones in black where he'd been born, past the bizarre outcrops of rock where his battles against Imperial forces had been fought, to the mighty natural fortresses that were his in his heyday. A couple of other journalists had been there before, and dropped in at the Shamil museum that an old man kept in his front room in Shamil's birthplace, and, a little drunk on mountain air, signed the visitors' book with puppyishly heroic phrases ('Shamil lives! And the great battle against Russian domination continues, and will always continue! Allahu Akbar!').

We laughed at that, but it was easy to be carried away. Everything seemed so simple in this innocent golden air. As evening drew on, gazing at whitewater dancing down a hill below us, Mia and I found ourselves planning to hold my next wedding there. We were going to billet aunts in the village, hire helicopters and bodyguards, and, of course, source the caviar locally. 'It would be so cool. Just get the man, and we'll be back!' Mia said.

We went to a real wedding, too, given by Shamil's clan, the Avars (one of our boy journalists was an Avar, and the bride was his cousin). We danced the angular *lezghinka*, ate hunks of garlicky lamb, drank hooch, and were interrogated about the LA film business by tough old villagers. We heard the whispers of the feud with the neighbouring village. We were told the villagers' proud family stories of robbery and rebellion. We were given a wild ride in an open car at the top of the world, through a flower-flecked meadow, by hawk-nosed men in shades.

And we stopped at every roadside shrine. Traditional Dagestani faith is a folksy kind of Sufi mysticism, which favours holy men and holy places. Some shrines are wishing wells. Others are trees tied with rags, each one left in memory of some pilgrim's prayer. We tied ribbons. We tossed coins. We made our secret wishes.

The hundreds of rags were proof that we weren't the only pilgrims. 'No one used to come here,' Timur said. 'These used to be really secret places. But now everyone wants to find God. In summer, they turn up in coachloads.'

Perhaps we will come back and see the tourists too, I thought. Anything was possible. And then we left: a day losing height, feet on brakes, squealing round every bend, feeling the air lose its poetry, until we could see the flat sea ahead, and the coastal road running back to Kaspiisk airport, and the plane to Moscow.

High in the sky, we gloated over our memories. Nadyr-Shah's tiger skin! Magomed's Humvee! The drive-by shootings! Wahhabi trousers! 'Our Roosevelt!' Umar's canning machines! Dancing at the wedding! The gold-toothed market traders!

'And to think I didn't want to come at first,' Mia sighed. 'And it was so great.'

Silence fell. The plane began its descent over Moscow. The sun was setting. For some reason, I found myself thinking of the fish corpses in the market, and how small and defenceless they'd looked. Perhaps Mia was remembering them too.

'You asked everyone about who might have done the Kaspiisk murders,' she said. 'And no one answered.'

'No one knew.'

'And no one cared.'

Uncomfortably, I remembered our big can of caviar. We hadn't cared much either; certainly not enough not to buy.

'No one's ever going to find out who blew up that house in Kaspiisk, are they?'

'No one will be able to stop the poaching, will they?'

We both shook our heads.

It was dark when I got home. My flat felt too neat and too empty. I could have started going through my notes and tapes, and begun working on my story. Or I could have phoned someone and asked them round to celebrate my return by eating my caviar.

What I actually did was scrape the caviar into the bin. It suddenly seemed dirty. I didn't want to be the kind of person who ate it. Then I phoned my St Petersburg family, invited myself to stay for the weekend in their cosy, overcrowded home, and headed for the Leningrad Station to get the midnight train.

The St Petersburg flat was as warm and sleepy and full of furry slippers and comfort food as ever, and there was new wallpaper in the hall to mark Victor's return to employment.

My wedding photos, with a little-girl Mouse smirking in her braces and bridesmaid's dress, had been quietly put away in a cupboard.

There were other, more worrying, changes. Mouse at fifteen was a foot taller than in the photos. She was long and slim and lovely, but she had a tough new swagger too. She wanted the world, and she wanted it now.

A St Petersburg journalist I knew had come across her twice recently, in the middle of the day when she should have been in school, in expensive bars on Nevsky Prospekt. 'Your friend is turning into one of those cheap girls who'll go with any tacky New Russian who'll buy them a drink,' the journalist said disapprovingly. 'You should talk to her.' But Mouse was hard to talk to. Her favourite reply to any question these days was 'FK' – 'Fuck knows' – and a knowing grin. When I'd plucked up courage, once before, to ask the impertinent adult-to-adolescent question of what contraceptive she used, she'd just grinned harder than ever. 'The Holy Spirit,' she answered pertly.

She'd run away after the last row with her parents, and only been brought home by her father's policeman friend. They sent her to a holiday camp for difficult teenagers, but it didn't seem to have helped. 'You should *see* her friends,' her mother whispered. 'Tarty girls with no brains and too much make-up. No wonder she keeps failing her exams. How I wish she was a good girl, like Nadya.'

At the moment, Mouse was only allowed out of the flat to go to school. She had retakes in two weeks. If she failed, her parents would have to pay for her to repeat the year.

This time, Mouse wasn't at the flat when I turned up from the train. She'd already gone to school. I had breakfast with her parents before they went to work, then lazed around the flat on my own, half watching daytime TV, enjoying having nothing much to do, feeling as drained after Dagestan as if it had been a week-long binge instead of just a reporting trip.

No one was supposed to come home until four. So I was surprised to hear the key in the door at the end of the morning. Mouse walked in. She didn't know I'd be there. She did a double-take, then yelled, 'Norkova!' and snuggled up affectionately against me, leaving lipstick traces. It was suspiciously early for her to be out of school, but she shrugged off any questions. 'My lessons were cancelled. Let's go out.'

We mooched off to the park.

'Oh Norkova, you've got to help me get away from my parents!' Mouse suddenly wailed, and her eyes filled with tears. 'I'm so bored! Nothing ever happens! And I hate school, and I'm not allowed out to see my friends any more! All I do is sit in that stupid little flat and lead a stupid little life and get told off. I'll be ripe for the nuthouse if I have to go on like this much longer.'

She was upset about the modelling her parents wouldn't let her do ('The guy said I could make a fortune! And I know I could! But they just don't want me to be successful!') and about all the quarrels since.

But what she was most upset about was being accused of trying to burgle the flat of an old friend of mine, an Englishman called Nick. It seemed Nick had come home one day to find someone had picked half the lock off his front door. Earlier the same day, his neighbours had noticed three teenage girls — including one with legs as long as Mouse's — hanging around, smoking, outside the door.

'It's crazy! I looo-o-ove Neek! You know how much I love Neek! I'd never dream of doing anything bad to him! Of course I wouldn't! Think how many teenage girls there are in St Petersburg! And think how many burglars! It could have been anyone! But everyone automatically says it was me! It's disgusting!'

Hunched up on our park bench, with her hands bunched at her nose like a gerbil, Mouse looked like a child again. It was bewildering. I thought privately that I'd try and find out more from Nick and her parents later.

Meanwhile, I tried hankies and hugs. I tried comfort clichés, including 'it's-hard-being-a-teenager' and 'only-two-years-till-you-finish-school' and 'if-you-still-want-to-do-modelling-at-twenty-you'll-be-even-more-beautiful'. With rather more success, I tried an offer of hamburger lunch. We went to a smart American-style restaurant on Nevsky Prospekt, where she promised to explain to Nick that she hadn't been his burglar. Thinking how easy it would be to be jealous of a grown-up sister studying in America, I asked if she'd like to go and stay at my mother's house in London. But she shook her head. 'I'd be quite happy where I am, right here, with my friends, if only everyone would get off my back.'

Halfway down a chip, she suddenly grinned.

'Oh Norkova,' she pleaded. 'I'd be so good if I lived with you. I'd study all day, eat all night, never go out . . . Oh, can't I come and stay with you in Moscow?'

We walked back through the jostle of market stalls and building sites in Haymarket Square, which somehow managed to look squalid and grey even in summer.

Mouse was all smiles again now, looking around brightly, busy and purposeful. Suddenly she caught sight of someone. It struck me she might have been watching out for him for a while. 'Seen a friend. Wait a minute – don't come with me,' she ordered, and darted off to talk to a scruffy man in his twenties.

I recognised him; he was the market trader from the flat upstairs, whom Victor didn't like because he dealt in drugs. I came up behind her. She pocketed something, waved at him as he vanished back into the crowd, and trotted home with me. 'What was that about?' I asked, with a vague sense of disquiet.

'Nothing,' she said. 'Just something I'm getting over.'

Because it was Friday night, Victor and Lena relented and let Mouse go out with her friends for the evening. Nick came to the flat to take me out to a concert, and we sat in the bedroom with her while she danced around, humming, telling surreal lewd jokes, basking in our attention, brushing her hair and choosing earrings.

Suddenly she leapt on to the bed, enveloped Nick in a spidery hug, and blurted, 'Oh Neek, it wasn't me who tried to break into your flat, you know I wouldn't ever do a thing like that, I love you, you do believe me, don't you?' There were tears in her eyes again.

Holding his young-fogey's unlit pipe in one hand, Nick gave her a one-armed hug and said, in his carefully enunciated very good Russian, 'I know you love me, and you know I love you, and I know you wouldn't do anything to harm me, so it's all right.'

He twinkled at her, and she giggled and said, 'That's OK then!' and went back to dancing around and humming, but I thought it was a cagey answer.

'But I know she did it,' he said later, when I asked. 'There's no doubt about it. She's been to my flat before. She's taken dollars from my drawer before, too. But the point about this time is that the neighbours know her and they saw her, stabbing away at the lock with her scissors. Poor little Mouse.'

St Petersburg was full of girls like Mouse, who couldn't stop dancing. They stayed up all night at the Planetarium nightclub. They went off in flash cars with their dates, acting cool, and wiped off their smeary make-up on the metro home to their little family flats.

St Petersburg had one of the highest proportions of drug abuse, and AIDS, in Russia.

'What drugs have you tried, Mouse?' I asked, when she finally got up late the next morning and crept into the kitchen. She looked happy, if shattered.

'Oh, everything,' she said. 'I'm an addict, ha-ha!' And she stuck her tongue out. 'Is there any tea?'

I didn't like the idea of telling her parents about my suspicions yet. They were only suspicions, after all; I might be wrong, or Mouse might just be dabbling in a harmless teenage way with whatever her reckless, knowing, post-Soviet friends did at parties. Drugs were everywhere, but *narkomania* was still a serious crime, still brutally punished. I wanted to be sure before I meddled.

I asked Mouse to stay in Moscow the next weekend (calming her parents down every time they phoned to say, 'But she might misbehave!'). Mostly I thought she'd enjoy being spoiled rotten for a few days; part of me also thought I could interrogate her properly about drugs if I got her on to my home turf. But she turned up with a boyfriend in his twenties, so I never got the chance. We went out to clubs and restaurants. The boyfriend, who looked scruffy and studenty and sweet, was surprisingly well-off. He wouldn't let me pay for them. They had enough dollars, he kept saying. On the night they left, he and Mouse went out to watch the sunset. They came back two hours later. They'd been to McDonald's, and Mouse pressed a greasy farewell package into my hand. 'Your supper,' she said, childlike and innocent, making her gesture towards housework. 'So you don't have to wash up.'

It went well, I reported hopefully back to Nick, even if Mouse and I never had the drugs pep talk, even if the boyfriend had a lot more money than I'd expected. (Nick and I were drifting into a kind of affair: we spent all the time talking on the phone these days.)

But it was only a few more days before Mouse gave me the proof I didn't want. We went to Victor's flat for lunch the next Saturday, to celebrate the end of Mouse's exam retakes. She'd been out on Friday night (not with the previous week's boyfriend; he was history) and she was still on her clubbing high.

'Neek-Norkova! We went to the Planetarium, and then we went out of town in a Mercedes 600! These guys took us to a gaming club! It was so cool! You know what they say: it's not what you know, it's who you know! They said I was the most beautiful girl there! And they spent hundreds of dollars! On everything: *shampanskoye, kokainchik, geroinchik!*'

'Oh, Mouse,' I sighed, but she was off again, glinting and chirruping, lost.

I took her outside to the landing, and said everything I could think of to discourage her. But I fumbled. While my mouth was forming pious platitudes – 'It's ugly to inject' and 'Taking drugs fuddles your mind' and 'Drug-takers lose the trust of everyone they love' – I was remembering all the times I'd dabbled with this and that myself and come to no harm. Mouse was almost grown-up, anyway; perhaps it wasn't for me to tell her how to live her life.

It didn't make any difference. Mouse wasn't listening. 'Oh Norkova, what do you know? You're old,' she said pityingly. 'I know what I'm doing. I'm OK.'

'She might be just making it up to sound cool,' I said later, clutching at straws.

'I don't think so,' Nick said.

'No, I don't either.'

So I asked Lena if she thought Mouse might have been taking drugs. She pulled a half-humorous, half-outraged face. She didn't believe it.

'Well . . . it would make sense,' I said despondently. 'It's worth bearing in mind.'

It was only a few more days before Lena and Victor got proof they did believe: a shrink who told them Mouse was probably taking drugs. She was gated.

I phoned, and she wept incoherently. 'I'm sorry. I'm sorry. I'll never do it again. Please can I live with you in Moscow? I've got to get away. Living at home is doing my head in.'

Briefly I thought how much less lonely life in my flat would be if someone else was there. But I knew that was only a fantasy. 'I couldn't, Mousie,' I said with regret. 'I'm always off on trips, and you'd be by yourself all the time, and there'd be no one to buy food for you. You'd be lonely, and I'd worry about what you were up to.'

The next time I came to stay, there were no pictures of Mouse anywhere. The flat was strangely neat and quiet.

'Where's Mouse?' I asked.

Victor answered sadly, 'Gone.'

I looked for her in every group of white-faced teenagers hanging about in doorways, but never saw her. There were occasional Mouse sightings. Someone saw her in a bar. Someone else heard she was living in a flat with a man. She kept in touch with her parents through an uncle, but she didn't come home. 'She's turned Lena's hair grey with worry,' Victor said. 'She's lost to us.'

CHAPTER ELEVEN

Getting Away

The news stories about the New Russian elite's outrageous excesses and monstrous ego clashes didn't seem funny any more. When TV carried a light item about the billionaire prime minister (the man our drivers called 'the chief mafioso') boldly going hunting at the wrong time of year, and ignoring the regulations that applied to everyone else by shooting a mother bear suckling her two cubs in the middle of the breeding season, I couldn't find it in me to chuckle knowingly at his wild and wicked ways. I just felt sorry for the dead bears. As summer ground on into autumn and the miserable pre-winter season of wet boots, freezing winds and sleet in the darkness that Russians call *slyakot*, I didn't have the heart to get out of Moscow and go travelling any more. I sat in the office at night, and watched the world go by on the news wires.

One November evening, when the printers were chattering, the bright TV in the corner of the room was showing pictures of some disaster somewhere, and I was looking out of the window at the yellow windows opposite and wet snow beating down on the highway, the phone rang. Our fixer was tied up with his resistance machine in the hallway. I picked it up.

A polite, cagey, southern-accented voice: 'Correspondent Bennett, Vanora, to the telephone, please.'

'It's me,' I said.

'Perhaps you don't remember me? I am the aide of Magomed Khachilayev. We met when you were in Dagestan. He welcomed you into his home and gave you an interview. I treated you to coffee.'

'Of course I remember. How are you?' I said with more warmth than I felt. I did vaguely remember him: thin and polite, hunched in the lobby, talking on his mobile, while builders worked on sandstone arches outside. But I didn't especially want to carry on knowing him.

Nadyr-Shah and his sidekicks in Moscow had taken to phoning me too. Nadyr-Shah was always leaving gruff, bossy messages these days telling me to get in touch, or to report something, or to be somewhere. I felt I'd seen enough of the brothers, now I'd written my stories about Dagestan. I tried to be unavailable when he called.

'My boss sends his regards. We would like you to come back and visit Dagestan again,' the crackly voice said now.

'Oh how kind. Perhaps next year,' I said, trying to hit the right politely discouraging note. Our fixer was looking inquiringly at me through the internal window. *Dagestan*, I mouthed back through the glass. He went into a silent pantomime of firing a Kalashnikov, shaking his body all over the corridor. I smiled at him and went back to the phone. 'We're very busy writing about the Russian political situation at the moment, as you can imagine, but naturally I'll be looking for every opportunity to visit somewhere as beautiful and interesting as Dagestan . . .'

'My boss would very much like to see you.'

The fixer was stabbing an imaginary enemy now, with an imaginary dagger, trying to catch my eye and make me laugh.

'My boss read your article, translated and reprinted in the *Southern Russian Angling Times*.'

'Oh good, I hope he enjoyed it,' I said. Oh God, I thought wearily. I was always promising to send people I interviewed copies of stories, and I was always forgetting. The post in Russia was so bad that it hardly seemed worth trying. But sometimes they got offended. I'd probably forgotten to send Magomed a copy. He was probably cross.

'He would like you to come to Makhachkala immediately and explain yourself.'

What? My face must have changed. The fixer stopped miming being in his death throes from a dagger wound, got up, dusted himself off and started hovering solicitously next to me in the newsroom.

'But, but . . .' I spluttered, flustered, thinking back three or four months to when I'd written the piece, trying to remember whether I'd written anything rude about Magomed. It seemed unlikely: anything controversial would have been checked by a lawyer and carefully pasteurised and homogenised for the reader's breakfast-table pleasure. I didn't think there'd been any questions. I knew I'd quoted Magomed somewhere, briefly, but the story had been about smugglers. He must have been looking very hard to even find his name. 'I'm sorry, I don't understand, explain what? What didn't he like? There was nothing in it that was meant to offend.'

'My boss is very displeased that the article made him out to be some sort of mafioso.'

This call was getting right out of hand. Sympathetically, the fixer opened his drawer and offered me one of his energy-giving chocolate slugs. I held the receiver away from my ear. The voice at the other end of the phone was getting louder and shriller.

'We gave you hospitality! We gave you caviar! We welcomed you as a guest! And you repaid our generosity by accusing my boss of being some kind of mafioso!'

'Oh nononono, I most certainly did not do that,' I babbled back, feeling cold inside. I didn't know much about the brothers, but I knew for sure I didn't want to be their enemy. 'Of course I didn't.'

'The article made him out to be some sort of mafioso. My boss has instructed me to tell you to come to Dagestan and explain yourself. In the next few days,' the voice repeated sternly. I couldn't think what to do to stop him repeating those phrases. He didn't want to get into a detailed discussion. He was clearly only obeying orders.

I took a deep breath, and made my voice as calm and persuasive as I could, trying not to notice that my palms felt clammy and my heart was racing. 'If your boss read anything untoward, I think there must have been a translation problem,' I said. 'I don't know the *Southern Russian Angling Times*, but they probably don't have enough money to pay for my paper's very expensive syndication service. Don't you think they probably translated the story themselves, on the cheap, and got it wrong?'

The fixer looked up from his chocolate slug and gave me a silent thumbs-up.

The voice went quiet. It was a reasonable enough argument.

'You must come to Dagestan in the next few days and explain

yourself,' he said again, but there was less conviction about the phrase this time.

'Please tell your boss that I think there must be a translation problem,' I answered, more confidently.

We went back and forth for another few minutes, but I sensed he was weakening. I leaned over and helped myself to a chocolate slug. I needed the energy.

Finally, he gave in.

'You must send us a copy of your original article, in English. Our professional translators will examine it to see whether the translation my boss read was correct.'

'Of course,' I said, breathing out for the first time in what felt like hours, jotting down an address in wobbly writing. 'I will be delighted.'

But he wasn't letting me off that easily.

'If our professional translators find that the insult was in the original English, you will have to come to Dagestan to explain yourself to my boss. Or else representatives of my boss will visit you in Moscow to discuss the problem further.'

I felt cold again. 'There won't be a problem, I assure you,' I said cravenly.

'Don't forget,' the voice said, and rang off.

'Scary,' our fixer said understandingly, giving me a cup of steaming tea. 'You'd better keep out of their way for a bit.'

'Of course I didn't accuse him of anything. But I did poke a bit of fun at him,' I said, miserably wishing I hadn't.

'Don't worry, you haven't done anything wrong. What do they expect from a foreign journalist, praise? And don't send anything. Those southern mafiosi are dumb. He'll forget all about it in a couple of days. If they call again, we'll say you've left.' He clutched his heart, cheering up enough to feel the imaginary dagger twist again, and started writhing against the table top. 'Mind you,' he grunted, 'I'd check under my car for bombs for a while if I were you.'

'Be serious. It's not much fun to feel hunted,' I said, feeling sorry for myself.

He raised himself from his deathbed, and picked a stray Tass report off his back. 'Well, what can you expect when you hang out with bad guys?' he said. 'You know what they say. Live by the gun, die by the gun.'

The messages piled up, menacing yellow Post-it notes on my desk. There were more every time I went to the office. 'They'll give up soon,' our fixer said. 'I keep telling them you've been urgently called home, and we don't know when you'll be back.'

It was always dark. It never quite snowed. My paranoia level was shooting up. I even caught myself wondering seriously whether to check under my car after work.

People asked me out, but wherever I went I seemed to end up having dinner with beautiful international bankers making the ritual gesture of enjoying the high life by dipping into a giant bowl of caviar. Their numbers were multiplying by the minute because of the economic boom since the election. Their shares in Russian firms were skyrocketing, and so were their holdings in short-term government debt, which earned them fifty per cent a year. Everyone in the dollar bubble was piling merrily in, making up syndicates, setting up funds. Except me. I was so far removed from the celebratory atmosphere that I was even saying no to the caviar.

So I was relieved when my Russian doctor friend Larissa Deville came to stay with me after her latest aid agency job in some remote corner. It was something normal to think about.

If saints had a sense of humour, I'd have said there was something a bit saintly about Larissa. She'd had one of those lives that might have seemed tragic if it belonged to someone else – all partings and sorrows and improvisations. She had no money, no permanent home, no partner, and lived off a series of short-term work contacts in countries at the ends of the earth. On the phone, her voice had a dark, slightly tragic tinge. But when you met her face to face, what you noticed was the amused lift of the eyebrows that brought her withered ballerina's face to life. She was as neat and serene and self-possessed as a Jellicle cat. She had friends everywhere instead of possessions. Things made her uncomfortable. She was always giving them away.

My flat was already full of her kind gestures: a scrubbing mitten made from straw that we'd bought at a collective farm shop after a happy day in the country; a travel iron and a little tin mug from the time when my household goods had got lost on the way to Moscow; a paperback about a painter I loved. Over the years, she'd also found me a plain silver ring from the south, with the jagged Caucasian flame pattern you often saw on local carpets, and a felt cap from Central Asia for the sauna. I kept all her presents.

Larissa listened carefully now while I poured out my woes. 'No, it's not nice to feel hunted,' she agreed. 'Not if you just want to be an ordinary sort of fish, nibbling on a nice bit of plankton and keeping out of the fishermen's way. Like me.'

I laughed at the idea of being a fish, but I was already beginning to feel better.

'And Russia's such a cruel country, especially now, with everyone out to make a quick killing, and no one counting the cost,' she went on, shaking her head. Suddenly she stopped. 'Oh God, I don't know whether you're still going to like my present.'

She'd brought the smallest possible amount of caviar, in an export jar.

'I can't tell you how surprised I was to see it on sale,' she said, still pleased with her find. 'I found it at the fish shop by Clean Ponds metro, when I went to talk to the agency about a posting for next year. I remembered you liked it. It wasn't expensive at all, and they even swore blind that it was legal.'

We took the jar to Galya's. Galya was a big rambunctious female who sang in a religious choir and whose much older artist husband, Alexei Kolli, had died not long before. When Larissa was a young medical student, he'd painted her portrait; artists had been painting her cheekbones ever since. His picture of a young beauty with enormous eyes still hung on his little studio wall, with dozens of other paintings and sketches and wry cartoons. Galya hadn't wanted to throw away her husband's work. They showed me. 'She's far more beautiful now, of course,' Galya said robustly. Then we sat in the cluttered, filthy, friendly kitchen, where you could hardly tell which were the real shelves full of dusty bottles and which were the *trompe l'oeil* ones Alexei had once painted for fun, and Larissa told us about her surreal holiday.

She'd gone with a friend to a Buddhist region near a dying industrial town. That summer, this remote spot had suddenly been descended on by every crackpot seeker after higher truth and gullible New Age philosopher in the country. Word had got around that it was at the centre of a unique electromagnetic field in the shape of a spiral, which could cure illness and energise the healthy. So the tourists were flocking there in their thousands, making for two hills in an otherwise dead flat landscape: the Hill of Love on the left, and the Hill of Wisdom on the right. There, every evening, they soaked up the electro-magnetic charges that they thought were strongest at sunset. Some of them contorted their bodies into elaborate Yoga poses as the shadows lengthened; some did throat-singing; some painted their bodies in gold spirals.

'And the funny thing is, it's only a few kilometres away from Magnitogorsk, which is still a great lump of a town full of black factory chimneys where everyone used to die of cancer from the pollution – it's a bit cleaner these days, but then that's only because the factories have gone bust and stopped working,' Larissa went on. 'I left my friend up the hill with the throat singers (there's only so much craziness you can take) and went to buy some eggs from the peasants in the nearest village. Much cheaper than the filthy takeaway stuff people were selling the God-tourists; much healthier, too. I found a little old lady and her little old husband, and once I'd bought some food from them they started chatting in their nice peasant way, all slow and unworldly and bewildered. And do you know what they said? "We don't understand it. Half of Russia is here. We've never seen so many people in our lives and they all say they've found the secret of eternal life here. But we're still dying." '

We were all laughing now. Larissa delved in her bag again and found more food: a bottle of wine from the Caucasus, and a small plastic bag full of Korean spicy carrot salad, and another deli container of fish-in-a-fur-coat salad, sliced herring topped off with beetroot, potato, mayonnaise and grated egg. I thought we were going to have a picnic at Galya's, but the two of them had a better idea. We went to the sauna.

I can't think of anything more comforting than a Russian *banya*. You've got there from a street where it's harsh and dark, and you've got rotten leaves in your boots, and the almost-snow has taken a layer off your face, and you've negotiated drunks and the litter piling up behind the garish stalls along the pavement around the metro. You leave it all behind in the outer area, hire towels and wraps and flowery flip-flops, and pad through into a warm, steamy, peaceful place of showers and marble slabs and water buckets and plunge pools. In the *banya*, it doesn't matter whether you're rich, poor, big or small, overworked or under-employed, idle, lost, lonely, or harassed. The *banya* is the great leveller. A *banya* is always full of women of all ages: young and smooth-skinned, with curves going all the right ways, or old and inverted, with sagging bits and scarred bits and knobbly bits on view, or somewhere in the middle, with tummies pulled carefully in and faces above clearly hoping for the best. It's a crowd of naked and near-naked bodies and calm, self-absorbed faces: people bent forward scraping rough skin off their feet, or bending over backwards to scrub their spines with loofahs, or meditatively swishing leafy birch twigs against their hands. And everyone is happy.

The piney inner sanctum, where the hot coals are, is dark and red and as solemn as church. You work out how much you can endure, and decide where to sit accordingly: the higher up, the more searing the heat. Veterans protect their hair under white felt cones; the rest wrap towels round their heads. Whichever way you look, all you can see is the other shadowy human forms all around you, heads thrown back in contemplation of their pain, skins prickling and melting and bubbling up into a sweat. A self-appointed someone ladles water on to the coals; the meditative silence is punctuated, every few minutes, by the question, 'More steam?' and a hiss of urgent responses. Just when you think you can't stand any more, the door opens, and the white light of the outer room pours back in. The bodies draw themselves up, yawning, stretching, and supple, for the freezing jump into the water and the obligatory scream. And the next shift troops in.

Hours later, we took our pink and purified selves out to the little plushy room where we'd left our clothes. Larissa unpacked the picnic on the table. She'd even somehow got her hands on three wine glasses. We grazed and gossiped, mostly about whether Larissa should answer the lonely-hearts ad I'd seen in *Private Eye*, from a man whose wife had left him and who wanted someone to help him run his retirement business, a holiday village, in south-western France. 'I might, too,' she laughed. 'I'm not getting any younger, and it would be nice to live in France again.'

'You damn well do it,' Galya ordered. 'A rich Englishman, with a silly polite smile on his face all day long, never heard of vodka; that's better than a poke in the eye with a sharp stick, isn't it? You hurry up, or you'll find *I've* written to tell him I'm moving in. You'll get there and find me already by the swimming pool. It'd be too late for you then. There'd be no messing about with other women once *I* was in charge. I'd keep that old Englishman Englishmanovich on a short leash!'

There was only a teaspoon of caviar each. We licked the spoon clean. 'Ah,' Galya said, concentrating tipsily on making sure hers was the biggest spoonful. 'This is how feasts used to be in the good old days of stagnation, before the world went mad. A nice bit of caviar, a nice bit of wine, not too much of anything (except good company); not a worry in the world.'

She lifted her glass in a toast. We all joined in. It was easy to guess what she was going to say. 'Things were better before,' we chorused. '*Ranshe bylo luchshe.*'

Larissa's week in Moscow was all like that: a trip to a place where azart hadn't taken over. Whenever I wasn't working, we'd go out and enjoy one of the modest pleasures that had always been there but that I'd almost forgotten about. We went to art galleries. We went to the peaceful, rundown Donskoi monastery, and looked at the outbuilding where Larissa's granny had lived when Larissa was a baby, soon after she'd had to leave central Russia because her husband had been arrested for being a rich *kulak*. We went to the Conservatoire for concerts, and looked at the music students scurrying under the pink and yellow arches all around with their violin cases. We sat up one night in another artist friend's studio, laughing over his stories about trying to sell pictures in Paris. We went for wet walks in the park where they'd put all the old Soviet statuary, and paid our not very serious respects to Iron Felix Dzerzhinsky, the first head of the Soviet secret police, and Lenin, and Marx. We paid a few roubles for a sedate lunch under the golden chandeliers at the House of Scientists, a former palace. And we went off at five o'clock one morning to Galya's dacha, three hours out of Moscow by metro and *elektrichka* (suburban train) and bus, and squelched across the sticky black-earth fields, and breathed the clean air, and watched crows swoop down off the naked trees, like pears dropping, like ink blots.

At the office, I was relieved to see that the phone calls from Dagestan had stopped.

* * *

'I wish you didn't have to go,' I said sadly as Larissa packed more presents into her little bag, ready to visit her student son in Marseilles. 'It's been fun in your Russia this week. No New Russians to worry about. No New Dagestanis.'

She nodded. She knew. 'You've really had enough of them, haven't you?' she asked. She was sitting by my bookcase, flicking through some big glossy volume I didn't remember I had. 'Do you ever think about going home?'

'Oh, home, where's that? I've been here so long now I wouldn't know what to do in England,' I answered lightly. 'Perhaps I'll have to wait till you marry your Englishman in France, and come and live there with you and be your gardener. If Galya hasn't got there first, that is.'

She laughed. We both knew that wasn't going to happen.

But Larissa did nudge me towards a place where I might feel at home: a Russia of the past, somewhere that hadn't existed since the days when jewelled Fabergé eggs were more of a status symbol than sturgeon eggs. She didn't mean to. It just happened. It was waiting right there in the book she was looking at.

CHAPTER TWELVE

A Different Kind
of Egg

I watched Larissa from the balcony, a small figure with a lift in her step, until she'd got past the grimy cars and benches and gossiping babushkas and teenagers playing football and disappeared through the towering Stalin arch at the end of the courtyard.

Then I sat down on the sofa, where she'd been sitting. I didn't have a plan for the rest of the afternoon. I picked up the book she'd been flicking through.

I remembered it now. It was an oldish book about Fabergé eggs, full of colour plates of the elaborate, glittering trinkets that the last Tsar's jeweller used to sell. I'd spotted it on a visit to my mother's house in London a few months before (it was one of the many dusty books in the house that must once have belonged to my father's parents or grandparents, and that no one read any more). There was a rumour at the time that a new Fabergé shop for rich New Russians was going to open in Moscow. Thinking that the book might come in handy if I ever had to write about a Fabergé revival, I'd brought it back to

Moscow – and promptly forgotten all about it.

So I turned a few pages now. I noticed that someone had written 'p. 37' three times in wavering old-person pencil handwriting on page 37. It reminded me of my grandmother's wobbly writing. It probably was my grandmother's wobbly writing. I hadn't thought of her for years, but the writing brought her back in a rush – tall and skinny, with a cigarette and a sweet smile under her grey waves, wearing shabby tweed in the middle of summer, feeding us stale Florentines and weak tea on the front steps, trying to stop me teasing her incontinent tortoiseshell cat, Miffy. Page 37 had a picture of the Fabergé shop at Morskaya Street in St Petersburg. Underneath it, more wobbly pencil words: 'Wallich lived at Morskaya No. 17.'

I remembered the name Wallich, too. All the first Russian novels I'd read had come from those dusty bookshelves. They all had the name 'Beatrice Wallich' written in faded copperplate on the flyleaf. That was the maiden name of my grandmother's mother. I'd seen her picture, before my father had taken away all the boxes of his family photos and letters: a dark woman in late-Victorian clothes, with hair escaping from a bun, and a kind, soft, half-smile. I'd even been pleased that she'd stocked up with so much Dostoyevsky, and Tolstoy, and Chekhov. But it had never crossed my mind that she might have family living in Russia.

My heart beat faster. I started looking properly through the book, searching for clues.

On page 46, one of the captions under a photomontage of Fabergé gewgaws was underlined. It read: 'Miniature of Catherine the Great, painted by Horace Wallick, an Englishman living in St Petersburg, from Levitsky's portrait. On the evidence of this work, Wallick was appointed a miniaturist to the House.

In the possession of the artist. 1–7/8" × 2–5/16".' On page 114, in a list of employees at the St Petersburg branch of Fabergé, '*Horace Wallick*, an Englishman' was listed as one of ten miniature painters.

I'd never heard of Horace Wallick/h. But (I was working out ages now, counting on my fingers) if he was a youngish adult, working in Russia shortly before 1917, he must have been the same generation as Beatrice. Perhaps he was her brother, or cousin? Perhaps he'd stayed in Russia? In St Petersburg? And perhaps I might find, after all these years here myself, that I had family of my own in my favourite city?

The book's real treasure was at the very back, where there was a two-page chronology of the rise and fall of the House of Fabergé, showing how the Revolution destroyed the business and what became of the people who worked there. In the same uncertain handwriting, the year 1918, when the firm was finally shut down by the Bolsheviks, had been ringed. Another pencil note was written down the left-hand margin, next to the ringed year. 'Wallich and wife get off from YALTA (this word was written in capitals, and in Russian letters) in British one of small Chan. Isles fleet –? Princess Ina or Ena – to Malta and thus to "peace and plenty". Then after waiting some weeks brought by 13,000 tonner to Southampton and London.'

I flew to the phone. My fingers were trembling as I dialled Victor and Lena's number, and I could hear my voice go squeaky with excitement as I started gabbling my story. 'I've just found out I've got an ancestor who lived in St Petersburg! Right through the Revolution! And worked at Fabergé! Painting miniatures! And had a wife there! And escaped to England in 1918! Isn't that brilliant? He might have known your grandparents! He might have shopped in your shops! I want to find out everything about him! I want to know what he looked like and where he went to church and who he was married to and what his flat was like and who his friends were! Will you help me? How do we begin?'

Victor oohed and ahhed appreciatively. 'We always knew you belonged in Piter anyway,' he said gallantly. 'This only proves it.' But he didn't know how to find out any more, and I could hear he didn't really think it was worth trying: 'I suppose there are libraries and archives, but you'd be lucky to find a bureaucrat willing to let you look without crossing their palms. Anyway, I don't know what information you can hope for after seventy years of Communism. Communism broke all our links with what went before. You remember that English saying, "the past is a foreign country", don't you? It may or may not be true in England. It certainly is here.'

I thought he was being defeatist. He was probably right, but my blood was up. I was surprised how much I wanted to find a real connection between myself and Russia; I was surprised at how much I wanted to reclaim my lost family. 'I'll find a way,' I said defiantly.

For the rest of that winter, my last in Russia, I looked for Horace Wallich in every quiet in-between moment. He became my hobby; I became as obsessive as anyone with an embarrassingly nerdish hobby. While almost everyone I knew in the dollar bubble was obsessing over the higher and higher profits they were making from investing in Russia (you could get something like 150 per cent return on short-term debt paper by the spring of 1998) I was ancestor-hunting.

I tried everything. Someone said the Mormons kept enormous computer archives of souls they wanted to save, with microfiches of lots of Eastern European records of dead people who'd never heard of the Mormons; I looked online, but found nothing.

Someone else said the Gentry Association, a bogus-sounding Moscow organisation for the Soviet descendants of former aristocrats, who now wanted to be known again as counts and princes, might help. They had an ancestor-hunting department, and Fabergé was a Tsarist firm. So I went to see them, and was charmed to find that they had very ordinary post-Soviet offices: desks full of red plastic telephones, clutter and bad photocopies; people who were all too visibly Soviet-trained doctors and lawyers and administrators sitting at them or nipping out to have a smoke by the standard-issue ashtray on a metal stalk in the corridor. Only the hopeful nameplates on the doors, with Prince this and Grand Duke that, suggested something different; only the secretaries who bustled in, interrupting in abrupt Soviet style but calling the men at the desks 'Your Excellency'.

Dukes or dustmen, they didn't know anything about my ancestor, or think there was anything I could find out. The deputy director of the heraldry department let me down gently. 'The thing is,' he said, 'that the archive network in Russia is very far from perfect. Sometimes there are no catalogues, no alphabetical lists or even inventories of the documents in an archive. So the tiny paper that may solve the mystery may be there, but you'll never know it is lying somewhere waiting for you, because it isn't listed in any books or catalogues. It's physically impossible to go through the tons of historical documents stored in all the archives in this country. The only rule is that the further back you go in time, the less traditional methods of research will help you.'

I tried the archive in St Petersburg anyway, a yellow palace on the English Embankment, just by the statue of Peter the Great, with a snake writhing between his horse's hooves, that Leningraders call the Bronze Horseman. The archive was supposed to be open to the public – an achievement of New Russia. But I wasn't surprised when a soldier guarding the front door tried to stop me entering. I waved an important-looking letter at him, with a red and very official stamp (I'd written it myself, asking all readers to offer me every possible assistance in my work). It baffled him enough to let me up the marble steps to the Information Bureau. But my journey ended there. Two sinister-looking bureaucrats said it was quite impossible for me to enter the archive – overcrowded! Overworked! And a foreigner! – but said they could do the research on my behalf for a modest fee. They relieved me of $50, which was supposed to cover a month's research, shouted at me for not knowing my ancestor's religion for sure, and scurried back to their sanctum. The very next day, they wrote saying their month of research had turned up no records of my ancestor's existence.

Finally, I tried researching an article on Fabergé, to see if I could find an expert who knew something about Horace Wallich. There was a story just waiting to be written, as it happened: the usual modern Russian story of two rival groups, each claiming to be the true inheritor of the great man (and of his property). The first lot had American backing and had put on a Fabergé exhibition the previous summer; the second lot had the backing of a present-day Fabergé descendant living in Switzerland. The first lot wanted the mayor of St Petersburg to give them Fabergé's old shop premises on Bolshaya Morskaya Street. The second lot thought the first lot were only after an expensive city-centre property, and wanted to stop them. City politics had dragged the dispute out for years: the first mayor had wanted to give away the shop to the first lot, but hadn't been able to move out the telephone switching station at the back of the premises; then he'd lost an election to a new mayor who didn't want to do anything the first mayor wanted; and now the first mayor was in hiding, in Paris, trying to avoid trial for corruption, and the whole question of the Fabergé shop had been shelved. More importantly, the first lot didn't know anything about Horace Wallich.

The second lot did.

Valentin Skurlov, an amateur Fabergé fan who worked in the marketing department of the St Petersburg Jewellers' Trust, had come across the name Wallich a couple of times during his endless, painstaking years of research into the House of Fabergé. He'd been poring over every piece of Fabergé documentation he could find, in every library in St Petersburg, ever since he first went to work for the Trust in 1985 and got a special pass into the archives. No one could possibly know more than Skurlov.

A Goras Volik had got into trouble with the police over a problem with his passport in 1910, when he first registered as a St Petersburg resident. The police form gave his occupation as 'painter'. Then there were two listings in the Petersburg directory, one for Goras and one for Goratsy Vallikh, miniaturist. He hadn't lived at 17 Bolshaya Morskaya Street (that was where the Fabergé shop was). The address given in the All Petersburg directory was a flat on Bolshaya Konyushennaya Street, which ran from the Winter Palace's enormous stables back to Nevsky Prospekt.

'It was clearly just a rented flat,' Skurlov said. 'And I've looked for other mentions of him, but there isn't much. It's hard to track down all the foreigners who worked at Fabergé, with their difficult foreign names that were always being transliterated different ways. And your Vallikh didn't have his own workshop; he wasn't permanently attached to any of the established ones. There were about sixty miniaturists, at different times, but I only have full biographies of ten of them. I don't know what his life was like. I only wish there was more I could tell you.'

We were hanging around in the doorway of the Jewellers' Trust, watched by a suspicious guard. I wasn't allowed into the tall, scruffy block because I was a foreigner. (Soviet-style rebuffs were getting more and more common these days.) But neither of us minded the gusts of wind blowing in from today. We were in another time. That one detail had brought my Horace Wallich to life. I could imagine him cringing apologetically in front of some bossy Tsarist policeman, trying to explain away whatever detail had been left off his *dokumenty*, not yet knowing how to bribe himself out of trouble. And Skurlov was happy to find someone almost as obsessed as he was to talk about Fabergé with. By the time we finally parted, darkness was falling, St Petersburg-style: sleet, ice in the wind, bite in the puddles. I hardly noticed.

There probably weren't going to be any more facts, but I went to see the building where Horace Wallich had rented his flat. It was a big pinkish-brown turn-of-the-century apartment block, with bay windows, touches of wrought iron over the entrance and a decorative strip of Neptunes and jellyfish running above the ground floor. It would have been new in 1910. There was no way of knowing which of the many staircases leading up from the dirty inner courtyard was his.

Even if I couldn't know for sure, I could make good guesses about his day-to-day life. He would have bought his groceries on Nevsky, at the end of the road. He might have shopped at the posh Yeliseyevsky's, with its art nouveau styling and chandeliers, for caviar and champagne for special occasions. He would have gone to church in one of the nearby Lutheran churches. There was a green Lutheran church almost directly opposite (now being restored after decades as a poultry farm); there was a yellow Lutheran church around the corner on Nevsky (being restored after decades as a municipal swimming pool – it was where Natasha and Mouse had learned to swim).

I walked his walk to work: along his wide street's central strip of grass, where the horses from the Imperial stables at the far end of the road presumably exercised; right into Nevsky just by the semi-circular Kazan Cathedral; left at the wrought-iron hump bridge; along the crumbling palaces lining the Moika canal for a few hundred yards; right again into Bolshaya Morskaya. It's a sad enough street today, all litter and fading posters. But there's still a jeweller's at what was once the Fabergé shop.

A vague clue about why Horace Wallich might have gone to Russia came when a friend in London found his name for me in the 1881 census. He was eleven then, and living with two older schoolboy brothers and an elderly father (a retired Indian Army doctor from Bengal), in Norwood, south London. It sounded an eccentric household: there was a Bengali law student lodging with them, an elderly lunatic lady in the attic who was the father's patient, and a clutch of stolid-sounding servants from Kent. The boys had all been born in wealthy Kensington; the family must have fallen on hard times since. Most of the neighbours listed on the same page sounded poorer and less educated: a carpenter called Cornelius Binstead from Hampshire; a Lady Housekeeper. But there was one other out-of-place group of exiles, with exotic birthplaces and the Wallichs' vague air of being down on their luck. A Russian family lived next door, at 5 Springfield Road, with a governess, cook and nurse. The 39-year-old mother, Isabelle Wiensienska (a Polish-sounding name, but Poland was part of the Russian Empire in those days), had clearly spent her life on the move. She had a seventeen-year-old schoolboy son, born in Gravesend, and four daughters. The fifteen-year-old, Isabella, had also been born in Gravesend; Henrietta, the four-year-old, and one-year-old Irene in Brussels. The Wiensienska daughter closest in age to Horace Wallich – ten-year-old Wera – had been born in St Petersburg. It was sheer guesswork, but I began to imagine the two children playing in each other's suburban gardens, and a small Horace spellbound by Wera's and her mother's soulful voices, their icons, their glittering trinkets and nostalgia for palaces and snow.

I had no way of knowing what had happened between then and the moment, twenty-nine years later, when a forty-year-old Horace Wallich reached St Petersburg (though I liked to think he might have married Wera). But I did build up a picture of what the eight Russian years that followed might have been like, a montage of scraps, anecdote and conjecture that began with Valentin Skurlov's stories about working at Fabergé's.

By the time Horace Wallich turned up in Russia, Skurlov told me, Fabergé was the best job in town for anyone in decorative arts. The modest business begun half a century before by a Swiss immigrant called Gustave Fabergé had turned into a soaraway success under his two sons, Carl and Agathon (who died in 1895); Carl was the official court jeweller to the Tsars. There were branches of Fabergé in St Petersburg, Moscow, Kiev, Odessa, Nizhny Novgorod, and London. Fabergé's fame had spread as far as the King of Siam's court.

There was so much work, in fact, that Carl Fabergé farmed it out to a series of semi-independent workshops, each of which dealt with a mountain of orders for gold and silver artefacts, and jewellery. Each workshop used the latest techniques and the most elegantly antique of styles to make modern mechanical articles; cigarette cases and toilet cases, clocks, inkwells, ashtrays, and buttons for electric doorbells gradually took the place of snuff boxes. Each workshop had about fifty apprentices; each also employed about fifty masters of one craft or another. There were probably about five hundred people working in the various Fabergé establishments at any one time.

Those who were closest to the heart of the business lived at the workshops or over the shop on Bolshaya Morskaya, a solid granite-fronted premises with bulging stonework, a five-minute walk from the Winter Palace, a five-minute walk from the shops and restaurants of Nevsky Prospekt. Other employees rented flats on the boulevards and canals of the town centre. Carl Fabergé was a kindly boss. He paid his many foreign specialists three times as much as other jewellers were offering (one English employee called Ernest Dzhones received 170 roubles a month); Fabergé had their flats properly decorated, and made sure they were warmly welcomed into their new country.

Fabergé himself lived in a flat over the shop, and his cheery bearded face could be seen every day, popping in and out of the workshops, tweaking at designs, and talking, not always politely, to the clients. The jeweller didn't suffer fools gladly.

Once, after the New Year celebrations, he was visited by a foppish prince who took great pride in his stars and ribbons. The prince started talking about the New Year's awards, just so he could boast that he had been awarded the order of the White Eagle. 'Imagine, I have no idea what for,' he said, clearly expecting Fabergé to shower him with congratulations and praise for his merits. The jeweller only smiled and replied, 'Indeed, your Highness, I too have no idea what for.'

Another of Fabergé's clients, a lady of the high aristocracy not known for her intelligence, came to the shop several weeks before Easter and began to annoy the old gentleman by asking whether he had invented anything new in the way of Easter eggs. It was a sore point in the workshops; jewelled Easter eggs were the most popular Fabergé item, there were only so many ways you could decorate an egg, and everyone who worked there was heartily tired of thinking up new variations. Carelessly, and with the most innocent expression, Fabergé told the lady that square eggs would be ready in a fortnight. Some bystanders smiled; others were embarrassed. The lady herself seemed to have understood nothing, and in due course arrived at the shop to make the purchases. The old man explained to her, with a serious expression, that he had really hoped to make the square eggs, but had not succeeded.

Fabergé was absent-minded, too, and always in so much of a hurry that he often forgot the details of the orders he'd just taken. He would then interrogate all his staff, looking for the person who had been nearest when he had talked to the client, and wonder aloud how a person who had been so near could remember nothing. Once when the prayer 'Our Father' had to be engraved on the back of an icon, he carefully inscribed the lettering of the first two words, followed by 'and so forth'. Instead of the full text of the prayer, the engraver obediently carved the words 'Our Father and so forth'. 'Well well,' remarked Fabergé, 'our priests should have hit upon the same idea to make their services shorter.'

It sounds cosy enough, but that doesn't mean everyone was perfectly happy. The apprentices grumbled that their workshop masters didn't pay them properly; the foreigners grumbled that the Russian craftsmen were so shiftless and disorganised that they produced less than half what a Westerner could in the same time. And, of course, everyone grumbled about the clients.

For a long time the main clients had been the Imperial family and their courtiers. From the 1890s, when Russia had a late industrial revolution, they were joined by a new financial and commercial aristocracy, the spendthrift New Russians of the day. The royal family were the most infuriating of the clients. The most typical feature of Imperial commissions was urgency: everything had to be done quickly, as though by the wave of a magic wand, and the design often had to be completed in a few hours, usually at night. This was because orders were held up at various court departments before reaching the shop, and the Fabergé craftsmen then had to rescue the officials from the consequences of their incompetence.

Nicholas II made no claims to artistic taste, but his wife, the Tsarina, was a different proposition: her combination of a rudimentary notion of art and curiously middle-class stinginess often put Fabergé into tragic-comic situations. She would accompany her orders with her own sketches and set the cost of the article in advance. Since it was impossible both technically and artistically to make the articles according to her sketches, all kinds of tricks had to be invented to explain the inevitable changes – a misunderstanding on the part of the master, or the loss of the sketch. But there was no point in offending the most important client in Russia, and Fabergé only ever charged her the price she had dictated in advance.

Every afternoon, between four and five o'clock, the great and the good of St Petersburg poured into the shop, especially during Holy Week, when they all wanted to buy traditional Easter eggs and to look at the special Imperial eggs, miracles of glitter and clockwork, that the Tsar would give the Empress and Dowager Empress.

The Imperial eggs for the Empresses took almost a year to make. Work began right after Easter and went on to Holy Week the next spring. The last Tsar's father, Alexander III, began the tradition back in 1885 with an annual Easter gift to his wife; Nicholas II doubled the workload with gifts to both his mother and his new wife after he married in 1895. If we include the two eggs that were nearly, but not quite, finished when Nicholas abdicated in 1917, shortly before Easter, that makes fifty-six Imperial Easter eggs in all. They were an annual torment. As each Easter approached, the workshop masters fussed over their creations day and night, too scared to leave their benches for fear that, at the last moment, the fragile treasures might break or fall.

War brought a hint of unease into this settled life, but nothing worse. At first, when St Petersburg's German name was patriotically Russified to Petrograd, Fabergé feared that war would reduce demand for his luxury goods. It didn't. Instead, state orders for military equipment brought banknotes flooding into the economy, a hysterical live-for-today feeling into smart Petrograd life, and a whole new class of *nouveaux riches* to the shops with money to burn. After a few months of stagnation, the House of Fabergé did better than ever.

Carl Fabergé offered in 1914 to turn his workshops over to making equipment for Russian soldiers. It took the bloated, inefficient Department of War a year to reply. But by 1915 the Moscow factory was re-equipped and a new workshop for war goods opened in St Petersburg. As well as Easter eggs and tiaras, Fabergé started producing syringes and grenades.

He probably felt pleased with his patriotic gesture. He should have worried more.

Even at the beginning of 1917, before the revolutions began, the poets and artists of Petrograd remembered it as having been a frightening place to live. The German armies were winning. The streets were full of unhappy crowds. Refugees from the conquered western provinces were streaming into town. Of the locals, most were women; more and more of the men were wounded. Silent, threatening processions of the poor trooped down Nevsky, waving banners demanding bread. Teenage thugs sat smoking under the Bronze Horseman. A curfew was imposed from eight in the evening (though it didn't stop the prostitutes).

Nothing stopped the Petrograd glitterati pouring into the Imperial Alexandriinsky Theatre on the night of 25 February for the premiere of *Masquerade*, a melodrama about love and death, in a production that had been five years in rehearsal and cost hundreds of thousands of desperately scarce gold roubles. The city was eerily empty, but the square between Nevsky and the theatre was packed with row after row of black cars. The performance sold out. There were grand dukes in the royal box. A rapturous audience gave the cast a standing ovation; bouquets heaped up on stage; to applause, the actor playing the doomed hero was solemnly presented with a gift from the Tsar, a gold cigarette case with an eagle picked out in diamonds.

The play ended, ominously, with the doom-laden clang of a bell from an Orthodox memorial service. Even during rehearsals, the actors had been joking that this selfish display of wealth represented the 'sunset of the empire'. Later, one critic, quoted in Solomon Volkov's *St Petersburg, A Cultural History*, would look back and savage 'this artistically perverted, brazenly corrupting, meaninglessly frenzied luxury . . . so close, in the same city, next to those starving for bread. What were we going to do afterwards, go to Lucullus to eat nightingales' tongues, and let the hungry bastards howl, seeking bread and freedom?'

What the poet Anna Akhmatova – Petrograd's most beautiful woman, willowy and hawk-nosed and aloof – remembered most about the evening was the trouble she had getting home afterwards. There were shots on Nevsky. Horsemen with bared swords attacked passers-by. Machine guns were set up on rooftops and in attics. She had no car, and taxis didn't want to take her to her home on the other side of town. The drivers were embarrassed to say why, but they were afraid of being killed.

A few days later, the Tsar abdicated. The February revolution began nine months of wild street oratory, indecision, chaos and unrest. No one knew how it would all end. But Fabergé's, the symbol of the monstrously frivolous old order, was doomed.

Just before the October Revolution, which finally brought a Soviet government led by Lenin to power, a posse of Bolsheviks 'requisitioned', or robbed, Fabergé's safe. He had six million roubles there, some of it his own, some of it the property of his clients. With the money went Fabergé's rock-solid reputation.

Once in power, the Soviets passed their first odd, idealistic laws. They abolished the two weeks that would ordinarily follow 31 January 1918, making the next day 15 February instead of 1 February, and bringing Russian time, which had lagged two weeks behind the West's until then, bang up to date. They did away with all the old-fashioned glitches in Russian spelling and killed off a couple of useless letters, turning the written language into a logical modern construct. And, in January 1918, they decreed that jewellery in the People's Russia could be made of nothing fancier than low-quality nine-carat gold. Even before Fabergé's was formally shut down by the commissars, shortly afterwards, the firm was dead on its feet.

Events in the next couple of months moved with the manic speed of old film reels. The Germans were still coming. There was looting and shooting. Someone took a pot-shot at Lenin. He ordered alcohol stores to be destroyed. Anna Akhmatova saw huge brown frozen chunks of stinking cognac on the street.

In March 1918, Lenin and his men fled to Moscow in a sealed train and announced that hostile Petrograd was no longer the capital of their Soviet Russia. From Moscow, the new capital, they also announced peace with Germany.

Peace saved Petrograd from occupation. Volkov's poetical account of the city's decline tells how the richer citizens ventured back out to the cafés, hopefully discussing the rumour that a secret clause in the peace treaty would leave the city free and self-governing.

It was a false hope. There was no secret clause, and losing its status as the capital was a disaster for Petrograd. Without the

Imperial machinery that had given birth to it and sustained it for two centuries, the city began to die.

Factories stopped working. The sky became pitilessly, cloudlessly blue. Food stopped coming from the provinces. People tore apart fallen horses and ate dogs and cats and rats. Pipes froze. Furniture and books had to be used for firewood.

The Bolsheviks spent what money they had on extravagant gestures of People's Art. The avant-garde critic Victor Shklovsky wrote triumphantly that Petrograd 'heated itself with its own fire, burned everyone who attacked it. Potatoes and carrots were bought like flowers; poems and tomorrow were sacred.' His hero, the leftist poet Vladimir Mayakovsky, wrote enthusiastic 'Orders On the Army Of Art':

> *Wipe the old from your heart.*
> *The streets are our brushes.*
> *The squares our palettes.*

Palace Square (which was now called something else) was festooned with giant propaganda posters. So were the Hermitage, the Admiralty, and the Academy of Sciences. The soaring Alexander Column in the middle of Palace Square was enclosed by a giant red and orange Cubist-style rostrum, whose jagged planes looked like flames; it seemed to be blowing the column into the sky.

But anyone not drunk on ideology was terrified to see the past die. Anna Akhmatova wrote:

All the old Petersburg signs were still in place, but behind them, there was nothing but dusk, gloom, and gaping emptiness. Typhus, hunger, executions, dark apartments, damp logs, people swollen beyond recognition. You could pick a bouquet of wild flowers at the Gostiny Dvor [market]. The famous Petersburg wooden pavements were rotting. It still smelled of chocolate from the cellar windows of Kraft's. The cemeteries were torn up.

Akhmatova and her precise, scholarly, serious friend and poetic colleague Osip Mandelstam were in love with the orderly classical world and had never wanted revolution. Yet in some of Mandelstam's notes there was a tinge of reluctant admiration for the sheer beauty of the apocalypse.

Grass on St Petersburg streets – the first runners of a virgin forest, which will cover the place of modern cities. This bright, tender green, amazing in its freshness, belongs to the new animate nature. Truly Petersburg is the most avant-garde city in the world. The race of modernity is not measured by the existence of subway or skyscraper, but by merry grass breaking through the urban stones.

. . . Nothing is impossible. Like a dying man's room open to everything, the door of the old world is now wide open to the crowd. Suddenly everything has become common property. Go and take. Everything is accessible: all the labyrinths, all the secret places, all the hidden passages.

After Fabergé's closed down, the bewildered foreign artists and craftsmen who had worked for the Tsar crept away, one by one, from a city that was eating itself.

They set off through the civil war between Red and White

armies that was breaking out all around them, trying to find a safe way back through the war zones all over the rest of Europe to home countries they hardly remembered.

They weren't the only ones to be scared away from starving Petrograd. In 1915 the city had two and a half million inhabitants. On 2 June 1918, two and a half months after it stopped being the capital, there were fewer than one and a half million people left. By the summer of 1920, only 799,000 residents were still there.

The best way out, towards the end of 1918, was south-west. One of the territories that the Bolsheviks had surrendered to the Germans as the price of peace was Ukraine. For a few months, at least, a puppet government favoured by Germany held sway there. The railway from Moscow to the Ukrainian capital, Kiev, was still open. Anyone who could somehow get their hands on false Ukrainian papers might be able to wangle a corner on one of the packed trains leaving for Kiev. The journey took ten days.

From Kiev, it was easy to carry on south to the Jewish seaside city of Odessa and then, by ship, to the resort of Yalta on the Crimean peninsula. The Crimea was filling up with White refugees, including the Tsar's mother, the Dowager Empress. Yalta was a sensible place from which to follow the civil war. The nearest White armies, commanded by General Denikin and supported by British and French troops, were doing well nearby. It still seemed unlikely then the Bolsheviks would win; if they did, the refugees could hope for evacuation over the Black Sea by Allied ships.

This is the route that Horace Wallich took, before he finally left Yalta for Malta on the *Princess Ena*.

It is exactly the same route that Prince Dmitri Obolensky's family took, at the same time, and that Dmitry Obolensky – son of the prince, and a distinguished British academic – later described in his memoirs.

The Obolenskys waited in Yalta, and watched the war, for six months. Suddenly, the Bolsheviks broke through, capturing Kiev and Odessa and moving towards nearby Simferopol. On 9 April 1919, the aristocratic refugees of Yalta, who could expect little mercy from the Reds after openly collaborating with the Whites, were hastily evacuated on British and French ships.

The grandest nobility, led by the Dowager Empress (who was the sister of the Queen of England), set sail on *HMS Marlborough*. In the evening, the infant Dmitri and his mother were given places on a big British transport ship travelling with the *Marlborough*, the *Princess Ena*. They set off through heavy seas for Sevastopol, where Dmitri's father joined the family. On the night of 10 April the ships left Russia forever.

It was a melancholy departure.

'A British sloop embarked about 400 of the Imperial Guard, mostly officers, who had collected at Yalta, for transport to Sevastopol. On sailing, the sloop steamed slowly round the *Marlborough* to allow those on board to salute the Empress Marie and obtain a last sight of her,' a British observer, Sir Francis Pridham, wrote later.

Gathered on our quarter-deck were a number of our distinguished passengers, including the Empress and the Grand Duke Nicholas. The Empress, a little lone figure, stood sadly apart from the others near the ensign staff, flying, of course, the White Ensign, while the voices of the Imperial Guard singing the Russian Imperial Anthem drifted across the water to her in last salute. None other than that beautiful old tune, rendered in such a manner, could have so poignantly reflected the sadness of that moment. The memory of those deep Russian voices, unaccompanied, but in perfect harmony, which few but Russians can achieve, has surely never faded from the minds of those who were privileged to witness this touching scene. Until long after the sloop had passed there was silence. No one approached the Empress, while she remained standing, gazing sadly after those who, leaving her to pass into exile, were bound for what seemed likely to be a forlorn mission.

The *Princess Ena* crossed the Black Sea and anchored at the island of Halki, home of a Greek Orthodox seminary. The Crimea refugees were moved to Constantinople. From there they sailed to the safety of Malta on the British merchant vessel *SS Bermuda*, arriving a few days after *HMS Marlborough* on 24 April. That wasn't the end of the Obolenskys' travels. Six weeks later, they set off again, this time for Rome, Paris, and eventually England, where they lived for a few months in the Kentish town of Southborough. There, Dimitri's father joined another White army, that of General Yudenich, which the British were equipping to try and take back Petrograd. It was ten years before the family finally settled in Paris.

Horace Wallich must have watched the Imperial Guard's final salute to the Dowager Empress too, and shared a deck with the Obolenskys (and many more of his former clients) for the next fortnight. It was probably fanciful to think that he went on travelling with them, landing at Southborough – not Southampton, as the note in my book suggested – a few months later, or that he would have hung around the optimistic White

Russian officers there as they made their hopeless plans for a comeback. But it pleased me to think that he might have done.

The other Fabergé exiles never forgot the glamour and swagger of their time in Russia. Franz Birbaum, one of Fabergé's most respected colleagues, still felt lost years after he got back to Switzerland. 'And still I am an exile in my own country,' he wrote lugubriously in 1921. 'This does happen sometimes.'

I'd found out pretty much everything about the tumultuous events that had shaped Horace Wallich's life, but the central narrative was still missing.

All I could be sure of was that Horace Wallich's time in Russia, in the eight years leading up to Communism, almost exactly mirrored my own seven years there, which had started as Communism collapsed.

Yet I knew nothing about the man himself: what he looked like, who his wife was, how he financed his escape, or what became of him after Russia. I assumed he was still alive in the 1950s, when my Fabergé catalogue had been published, because of the photo caption under the miniature: 'in the possession of the artist'. (And where was the miniature now?) But I'd run out of trails to follow.

I took it as a cautionary tale: Horace Wallich had spent so long living in the shadow of other people's wealth, power, ambition and azart – imitating them with a few mouthfuls of caviar and a glass or two of champagne and dreaming that he was really one of them – that in the end his own small life had been completely blotted out. If I didn't want the same thing to happen to me, I thought, I should stop chasing dreams in Russia and go home. The idea didn't fill me with wild joy; it was just, obviously, the sensible thing to do. I put away my notes, and started looking for work in London.

Valentin Skurlov had one more Fabergé story. He said he knew how to find the last Easter egg made for an Empress.

By the time the February revolution swept away the Russian royal family, Fabergé had been working on the two Empresses' eggs for Easter 1917 for ten months. They were nearly ready. What became of the eggs afterwards was one of the Revolution's many mysteries. Fabergé's associate, Franz Birbaum, wrote only that 'someone whom I do not know proposed that they should be finished and sold to him, but the firm did not accept the offer'.

But, eight decades later, someone in modern Moscow was trying to sell one of those 1917 eggs, and Skurlov had got wind of it.

The egg was to have been made of angels, wrapped around a cloudy glass sphere with a clock set in it. A hidden mechanism would make the angels fly apart, revealing the clock.

'It's been stripped, of course: the angels have gone. All that's left are the clouds and the glass sphere and the base,' Skurlov said, his eyes full of dreams.

He gave me the business card of a jeweller colleague of his in Moscow – Alexander Nikolayevich Ivanov, from the Russian Treasures antique shop.

'Ivanov knows about the person selling the egg,' he went on. 'I have an idea. You could go and see Ivanov. He might help you find out more.'

It would be a wonderful story, the kind any journalist dreams of Skurlov had already told me that Imperial eggs fetched between five and ten million dollars at auction; what would be the value of an egg with a history as impossibly romantic as this? I could already imagine the headlines. Eagerly, I pocketed the phone number.

The doubts only began halfway back to Moscow, as I lay awake in the night train listening to the silence. Uneasily, I remembered something else Skurlov had once said: that there were four or five fakes for every genuine Fabergé object still in existence, and that Fabergé jewels were the most forged valuables in the world. Even if this egg was genuine, I didn't know enough to know how to tell. And phoning Ivanov, and angling to be allowed near the mystery owner might mean devoting months more to a new group of wily New Russians, trying to spot every sharp manoeuvre and power sales trick that buyer and seller might be trying on each other, and keeping a cool head as get-rich-quick dreams flew in all directions.

Even thinking about it made me feel tired. By dawn, when I got off the train, I knew I wasn't going to bother calling. I put the card away, and felt relieved.

A few weeks later I went to London to be interviewed for a job I was nearly sure I would get. Afterwards, I took my father out to dinner.

We were both a little nervous. We didn't meet, or talk, all that often, and we had to plan the things we might say to each other. It was as though the whole of my life since growing up had been just a fantasy, and I was a tongue-tied teenager again. A smiling waiter ducked under the fisherman's nets draped all over the heavily themed south London restaurant we were eating in, and took our order. Then we were on our own.

After a couple of bursts of near-conversation – 'Holiday good?' 'Good, good'; 'Moscow OK?' 'Fine, fine' – I was relieved to remember that I had a far better ice-breaking subject: Horace Wallich.

'You'll never believe this,' I began, smiling a bit too much, leaning forward a bit too eagerly. I wanted him to be astonished and impressed. 'But I've discovered that we've got an ancestor who lived in Russia before the Revolution. Isn't that an amazing coincidence? I've been finding out all about him. He worked at Fabergé's, in St Petersburg, and he painted miniatures . . .'

I paused. My father didn't look astonished at all. In fact, a big smile was spreading across his face.

'You must mean Uncle Horace,' he said.

Uncle Horace.

Uncle Horace?

I didn't know what to say. After a while, I realised my mouth was opening and shutting, in complete silence. 'You mean you actually knew him?' I finally stuttered. 'Horace Wallich?'

It had never crossed my mind to ask my father. It had never for a moment crossed my mind that what I was looking for might have been here in London all along.

'Oh yes,' my father was saying, looking happy and school-boyish, and I could suddenly see he was as relieved as I was to have something proper to talk about. 'Of course I knew him. He was my old ma's uncle, really; I just called him that. He used to come and see us after the war, at the house. He lived in an old people's home in Richmond by then, and he used to escape every now and then and get on the bus and come for tea – and borrow a fiver from my ma.

'He borrowed a fiver every single time. He was very poor, and he smoked very expensive cigarettes. Balkan Sobranies, the black ones with the gold filters, you know? With a cigarette holder, and white gloves with a button – but they were always a bit grubby.'

My father was drawing pictures on the paper napkins, eager to show me Uncle Horace's face, concentrating on getting a good likeness.

'He looked a bit mournful . . . I got the impression that Russia hadn't treated him very kindly . . . he was short, maybe five foot five, and he looked shorter, sort of hunched up, and his feet were too big, and he shuffled more than walked . . . and his nose always had a drip at the end, as if he had a cold . . .'

Uncle Horace didn't have a wife by the time my father knew him. He'd done odds and ends of jobs from time to time, but never managed to keep them. One time a nephew had got him a job at the V&A, restoring antique chairs; but Uncle Horace had scraped the veneer right off with a paint scraper, and been fired.

And he was a sharp-tongued old soul. He'd dropped by one day while

my teenage father was practising a hard new piece on the flute, raised an eyebrow and said, 'Ah yes, I see you favour the atonal school of music.'

'But he always brought pictures of the Tsar's treasures with him to show me,' my father finished up, and his voice was tinged with an old affection. 'Glittery things: boxes and baubles. I thought he used to guard them. I didn't know he made them.'

I was looking at my father's sketches, still shocked that it had all been so easy in the end, still not knowing whether to be pleased or angry about the story ending like this. 'All those years I've been doing Russian, and living in Russia – I'd have loved to know about Wallich . . . Horace . . . Uncle Horace . . . but you never even mentioned him,' I said, fidgeting with the pictures. 'Why didn't you tell me?'

A lot of emotions I couldn't quite name flitted across his face. Among them I thought I detected evasiveness, interest, and sadness. But what he said in the end was disarmingly simple. 'I didn't think anyone would be interested. No one ever asked.'

It was true. I never had. Our eyes met for the first time in the evening, and I burst out laughing. It was just beginning to dawn on me that I might enjoy coming home.

CHAPTER THIRTEEN

Farewell to Dagestan

I got a job offer in London as the hot Russian summer began. I had a couple of months to wind up my life in Moscow: find removals firms, say goodbye to friends.

There was a carnival atmosphere in Moscow in the summer of 1998. The joyful near-hysteria (or was it suppressed panic?) of people with spare investment cash grew more intense as the yields on short-term debt went up to nearly two hundred per cent. Yet more people piled in, even though sometimes you now also met doubters at the skittish, feverish, dollar-bubble parties, wondering how long the government could afford to make these huge payouts just to go on getting dollars, wondering when the crash might come. I'd never bought any Russian debt. I smiled and passed on.

The only thing I really had a hankering to do before leaving, strangely enough, was to make one last trip to Dagestan. There was someone there I wanted to talk to more: a skinny, quiet, middle-aged typesetter at the boy journalists' paper, who had once been a caviar thief but had given it all up to become a poet. The boys had taken me to see him one night, but it had been a bad time to meet. His wife was about to emigrate to America. All there was in their flat was bare boards and piles of suitcases. I'd promised to go back, but then got too nervous of the Khachilayevs to try.

But it was only a question of time before the Khachilayevs, like anyone else in the grip of azart, began to self-destruct. By late summer, they were lying low.

In May, they led a violent, confused uprising in Makhachkala, which went wrong.

Nadyr-Shah Khachilayev and a posse of at least fifty armed bodyguards were driving back into town, after a trip to the Chechen border, in the early hours of 21 May. Not far from Nadyr's house, local militiamen plucked up the courage to stop the armoured cavalcade's only car with Chechen plates and order the driver out. Instead of showing them his papers, the driver sprayed them with bullets. He killed one policeman and seriously wounded six more.

Nadyr and the bodyguards retreated to his mansion. As dawn broke, crowds gathered; assault rifles and grenade launchers were smuggled in. Police ringed the house and ordered Nadyr's men to surrender by ten in the morning. Nadyr ignored the order. Instead, he and hundreds of supporters broke out through the police cordon, rushed to the central square yelling 'Allahu Akbar!' and occupied Government House.

The Khachilayevs' men broke windows. They ransacked rooms. They took hostages. They beat up the guards and threw them out into the street. They blew open every safe in the building and took the money inside. Finally they lowered the republican flag, and raised a green Islamic one in its place.

Russian troops and border guards sealed off the roads into Makhachkala to stop any more Khachilayev supporters getting into town. The mayor denounced the Khachilayevs' men as 'rebels and criminals', and put his own armed posse on guard across the square from Government House.

It seemed explosive, but by nightfall tempers were cooling and boredom setting in. A deal was struck. Everyone went quietly home. The Khachilayevs were too rich to make an example of. (Later, Nadyr lost his seat in the Russian parliament, and the brothers were tried and detained; but they were quickly amnestied.)

The brothers got into more trouble just a month later, in June 1998.

This time, one of three candidates for the local presidency accused the brothers of kidnapping him to prevent his election. Sixty-year-old Ali Aliyev, a fiery and persuasive intellectual whose glory days had been back in the perestroika era, had wanted power now so he could crack down on Dagestan's corrupt trades in vodka and caviar. He accused the Khachilayevs of trying to persuade him not to run, and, when that didn't work, using violence to make sure he wasn't in parliament at the time of the vote. He said the brothers gave him poison in a shot of vodka the night before the elections. Then they drove him to a half-built house on the edge of Makhachkala. He woke up the next morning with his wrists manacled to a radiator and his head covered in blood. By the time he got free and made it back to the parliament building, the vote had taken place and the incumbent president re-elected.

That seemed even more explosive. But the Dagestani Supreme Court threw out Aliyev's case. Nervously, the Dagestani government denied that there could be any link between the Khachilayev brothers and what happened to Aliyev.

In August, there was another murderous drive-by shooting in Makhachkala. This time Nadyr-Shah's rival, the Mufti of Dagestan, died.

The Mufti had made plenty of enemies by denouncing the Wahhabis, especially now that three little Wahhabi-run villages in the mountains had declared an Islamic republic. Nadyr was also publicly against the Wahhabis, even though a rumour was doing the rounds that it was the Khachilayevs who were secretly supplying the Wahhabis with their guns.

Much more trouble was in store for the brothers in the future. It would be another few months before Nadyr-Shah was reported fighting with the Wahhabis and their Chechen allies, against Russian troops, in the separatist Islamist villages. It would be another two years after that before his brother Magomed was killed in a murky shoot-out with his bodyguards. Two years after that, in 2002, Nadyr-Shah was arrested and interrogated in connection with another terrorist bomb in Kaspiisk, which went off during the Russian Victory Day holiday on 9 May and killed seven Russian soldiers. His house was found to be stuffed with weapons and explosives. He insisted he was innocent. He went on hunger strike. As usual, he was freed within days.

But even in August 1998 I thought the brothers had too much else to worry about to worry about me. The coast was clear. I phoned the typesetter and made a date.

* * *

It is evening, on my last trip south. I am sitting in a white-walled room with Sergei Bodagovsky, the former grand master of caviar poachers, who spent his youth stealing four tons of caviar. By 1982, when he was convicted by a Soviet court, he had made an illegal profit of half a million roubles. It was the equivalent, in those days, of the average Soviet wage for four hundred years.

Sergei keeps one grainy black and white photo of those times, on cracked Soviet paper. There's sunlight in it, and a dark wild boy with a beaky nose is standing on a beach, by a wooden boat, grinning. He is wearing ragged cut-offs and nothing else. He has a cigarette in his mouth and a knife in one hand. Hanging from the other is a huge sturgeon.

The swagger has gone now. Sergei was twenty-eight when he was arrested. His friend Rudolf was tried too and condemned to death: a bullet in the brain. Sergei got off relatively lightly with a fifteen-year sentence in the camps.

'When they read out the verdict,' he tells me, 'everyone in court gasped in horror.'

He is sitting on the bed in his sister's shabby flat in Makhachkala, a careworn and fastidious man of forty-four, a little stooped and thin for his clothes, his voice filtered through bluish cigarette smoke. But the photo still makes him grin.

'Me, I'd been expecting execution,' he says. 'So all I could do was heave a sigh of relief.'

So much caviar, I say. Why did you take the risk?

'Power,' he answers. 'And money. In those days, I thought money was everything.'

Plenty of people think that way today in Dagestan. It is the poorest region in Russia. But from Sergei's window you can see the Mercedes and mansions of 'Santa Barbara' district, with its fantasy homes in the style of Walt Disney, its arched windows, ornamental waterfalls, jacuzzis, ten-foot-high garden walls and overwrought ironwork. No one yet knows who owns most of these houses, or who will move in and become the Khachilayevs' neighbours. But everyone knows that they will soon be the homes of the men who are making crooked fortunes today.

The rules were different when Sergei started stealing caviar, back in Soviet days when money meant very little and naked power almost everything.

When caviar was still a perk of Soviet power, in little blue and yellow and red glass jars for top people, it wasn't meant for the likes of Sergei. His family was nowhere near the top. His father was an ordinary worker who mended telephones and his mother was a typesetter. Sergei went to technical college, not university, and had a conviction for brawling during military service. By his twenties he was married with two daughters to support.

He started work for a fish factory in Astrakhan in the middle of the 1960s. It paid 100 roubles a month, enough for bread and sausage but not much more.

He would steer his fifty-foot boat along the Caspian and up the Volga, picking up sturgeon caught by fishermen from collective farms. The fish was weighed and a fixed state price paid before the boat took the carcasses back to the factory.

Sergei loved the muscle and freedom of life on the water: sun-roughened skin, the click of bony sevruga snouts against metal as he hauled them on to the scales, and the wind that nearly knocked him down when he opened the throttle. He liked meals carved straight from the fish. He liked breakfasting on caviar.

He spent the hot nights of his first summer on his bunk,

reading. He listened to waves rippling against the side. He listened to the wooden planks creak and settle. And he listened to the rowing boats drawing quietly alongside in the darkness.

'They were coming and going all night. You couldn't get a wink of sleep. It was all footsteps, voices, whispers . . .' It was the fishermen returning to sell more fish and eggs, but this time privately, illegally, and for much more money.

The next year, Sergei was promoted to inspector – or fish buyer. 'At first, I never thought I'd steal,' he says now. 'I was a child of the sixties, and I didn't think it would be so easy to be dishonest. But then I saw that everyone was at it, and I decided to go for it while I had the chance. It was beautiful there, a wonderful life, but I didn't want to spend all my days in rags, you know? I needed to feed the kids and dress properly and have something left over.'

In a way he had no choice. An inspector needed to be on good terms with the police, the fishermen and the mean, hard-drinking types from the slums around the fish farms. That meant bending the law, softening people up with drinks and bribes.

But there was more to it. Sergei also found he liked stealing.

Whenever a team of fishermen came to him with their catch, he would hurry just one of them to his cabin to do the paperwork. They'd have a shot of vodka, and another, and then Sergei would lean forward and whisper, 'Now, Vanya (or Petya, or Lyosha) . . .' Down in the half-dark, he'd strike a deal to buy half the fish privately, at ten times the state price, and give the fisherman an official receipt for the other half Everyone was happy. Vast quantities of fish would come on board, and Sergei would stay up all night with his two-man crew, harvesting the caviar. They stored it in milk churns, sunk underwater on lines and buoys. They filled four churns a night.

Under cover of darkness, or at dawn before anyone else was up, Sergei would sell the caviar from a little rowboat with an outboard motor. He'd chug out to the cruise liners sailing down the Volga, with their banquets and noisy bands echoing across the water. 'Do you need caviar?' he would shout up at the watchman. He charged half the state price.

'They always said yes. I could sell as much as my conscience let me,' he says. 'They'd put the brakes on, and we'd do our deal. Then we'd draw up enough caviar from the water to supply our client. Everyone was at it, but no one sold as much as us. Most people sold on a smaller scale. But as my friend Rudolf said: "What's the difference? They'll shoot you whether you take one ton or four." So we took four.'

Rudolf, sixteen years older than Sergei, was an exotic charmer. He'd been a chef; he'd been in a band; he gambled, danced, told wonderful stories, could drive any car and could shoot straight at any target even when drunk. Impulsive and flamboyant, he was the king of thieves. Sergei's eyes cloud at the memory. 'He had an artistic nature, he was an individual and an adventurer. He had to make his presence felt, refused to act as a slave. So he made enemies. I couldn't afford that luxury; I tried not to be on bad terms with anyone. But that's how he was. It's probably what did for him in the end.'

Those were wild days. Sergei was making more than 30,000 roubles a year, and spending it on extravagant food and champagne. Rudolf bought two houses, three cars, a gun and some Tsarist roubles. They invested in bogus graduation certificates from grand Soviet universities, paying 3,000 roubles each for officially stamped fake papers that might one day admit them to the Soviet upper class. Sergei left his wife; there was too much high living to be done. He and Rudolf were entertaining the Astrakhan elite who were now their clients, the police and politicians. Moscow was one thousand miles north, and the local Party people felt safe with their grimy new friends. Sergei and Rudolf went to their dachas. They shared drink, jokes and women.

But one former colleague, a fisherman called Boris, felt left out and resentful. When he was caught by a local inspection team with a ton of illegally bought fish, he thought that Sergei and Rudolf must have informed on him So he informed on them in retaliation. He wrote to Brezhnev's interior minister, denouncing his ex-partners. It was well known in Astrakhan that the authorities had a system for intercepting such letters, picking them out of the mail at the post office. So Boris got his letter posted in Moscow. It arrived safely. To the terror of the town bosses, a commission of government inspectors came down from Moscow to investigate.

The local politicians had everything to lose if they were named in Moscow as clients of the caviar thieves. They tiptoed away from the scandal, leaving Sergei and Rudolf – the outsiders – exposed.

According to Sergei, Rudolf used to drop in to the police station as if it was home. 'Everyone there was his friend. He was so light-hearted and good-natured, and the guys there would spend evenings and weekends with him and eat the caviar he brought them. So when they said the police chief wanted to see him, he got in his car and scooted right over. He waltzed in swinging his keyring on his finger, breezy as ever. 'Hi, guys, what's new?' he said. But they kept quiet. They were too scared to answer. And when he went into the police chief's office, there were six strangers sitting there. They had an arrest warrant, and a search warrant, and handcuffs.'

Three months later, Boris the letter-writer was re-arrested.

'I was still free,' says Sergei. 'I was trying to help. I was going to the prison, talking to the governor, trying to work out answers to these questions with him. He was another of our friends who'd just drop in to see us whenever he felt like it. But the thing was, everyone was scared now because these Muscovites were around.'

In prison, Boris carried on naming names. Sergei was arrested.

The day they came for him was warm, with a hot wind. Sergei was on his boat, alongside a rickety jetty with other boats tied to it. There were groups of fishermen standing around, drinking, talking or sweating as they lugged their fish towards Sergei's boat. Some had ropes in their hands, or knives that glittered in the sunset.

Sergei was in his cabin with a few bottles of champagne on ice. He'd been drinking, and he was in an evil temper. He saw clearly that he'd been wrong to equate money, which had temporarily bought him freedom and friends in high places, with real power. His Party acquaintances were closing ranks. He knew what to expect.

When the fleet of official black Volga cars drew up to arrest him – the police, the District Party Committee, the City Party Committee, and the Regional Party Committee – he was ready. As his ex-friends trotted nervously down the jetty in their suits, Sergei came out on deck.

'Will you have a drink?' he asked. No one answered. He

paced up and down, in and out of his cabin. No one dared approach him. 'Suit yourselves, I'm having one,' he said.

He poured himself a glass of champagne. The men in suits streamed after him.

'Seryog,' they wheedled. 'Come with us.'

'What for? I don't want to go anywhere with you. I'm going home, or perhaps I'll throw myself off here into the depths.'

Sergei smiles at the thought. 'I kept them waiting for four hours; oh, I was vicious and despairing that day. I'd have stabbed them if I'd had a knife. I suddenly saw them, those cops and Party people, for what they really were. I didn't like them at all. They weren't enforcing laws that were fair, just ones that protected them at everyone else's expense. They were legal criminals. I was drunk, but I didn't want to lose my freedom. I was twenty-eight, and I loved that freedom and the robber's life. I wanted sea wind in my hair. But in the end there was no choice. I gave myself up.'

The case took two years to come to court. The whole city knew that bosses were implicated but would not be named. During interrogation, Sergei saw he would be shot unless he cooperated. He gave up his hidden bank books and pleaded guilty.

But Rudolf refused. When the trial opened he looked defiantly at the prosecutor – a man named Nikolai Chishiyev, who'd been at his house more times than he could remember in the days of caviar and champagne and girls. Rudolf told the courtroom: 'I will plead guilty only if the following people are put in the dock too.' In the hush that followed he listed forty of Astrakhan's most prominent bosses.

This was the most dangerous of Soviet crimes: shaking the established order, exposing the hypocrisies of the authorities to the public gaze. The judge ordered Rudolf's words to be struck out.

'When they read out Rudolf's sentence,' Sergei says. 'they started with the small stuff and worked up. It was fifteen years for this, fourteen years for that. They were reading them out for two hours. Then they got to the last charge: stealing especially valuable state property. And the sentence was *rasstrel* – execution.

'Rudolf didn't react. He'd been taking notes of the whole trial and he was still writing. A cop came up with handcuffs and barked his name. "I'm listening," Rudolf said. "Handcuffs," the cop said, and clinked them.

'The hall was packed, and Rudolf said calmly, "Are you taking me to be shot *right now*?" He looked at the judge. No one expected a question like that. People react differently to the death sentence, hysterics, fainting, whatever. But he was talking clearly, and he embarrassed the judge, who muttered, "No."

' "OK, then, just wait while I finish writing," Rudolf said. And he went on writing. And when he'd finished, he beckoned the cop over, and they put the handcuffs on, and he went to the cells with his head held high. Oh, he was a cool customer.'

Sergei's first days in prison were all discipline and pride: press-ups before reveille, silent hours at the stinking workshop, stoicism at the indignity of sharing a hot cell with a hundred others. He divorced his wife. Not yet thirty, he tried to suppress the thought that he would not leave Smolensk Penitentiary until he was forty-three. He read.

He borrowed journals from the prison library and became absorbed in the political changes happening in Russia. The new politics offered him a kind of self-justification. He learned to argue that his theft had been benign, a Robin-Hood redistribution of wealth from Party to people. He had paid more for caviar than the state offered, and sold for less than the state demanded. This was a crime under Communism, but undercutting a competitor by taking a smaller profit margin would be seen as good business under capitalism. With hindsight, he cast himself as a 'fighter' against an unjust Soviet regime.

He also started writing poetry.

'I began to feel I had something to say. I'd always known I could sing a bit, and play the guitar, but when I started reading the people in those journals, I wanted to write my own last word on life in verse too. I'd never written a line before, but I felt I could. So I read less at night, but I wrote. I'd deliberately stay awake to be in that state just before sleep, when your body's relaxed but your brain's awake, when you can catch thoughts. And the lines just ran out. Life turned into thought and writing and sleep. I'd write till five, but I'd get up refreshed, with my soul singing.'

The poems changed everything. When his mother and sister next visited, Sergei gave them some of his writing. His sister passed the manuscripts to a local newspaper, *Young Dagestan*. It published them without knowing the author was in jail.

Publication caused a furore. It was 1991, and Sergei's bitter verse perfectly matched the public mood on the eve of the Soviet collapse. Fan mail arrived in heaps. The National Poet of Dagestan telephoned, demanding an introduction. When Sergei's sister confessed that the poems were written by her brother, eight years into a fifteen-year jail sentence, Sergei became a prisoner of conscience. Every scrap of his work, however raw and self-pitying, was published and praised.

A public campaign took off, led by a Moscow group working to release 'economic criminals'. Letters were written to the new president of Russia, Boris Yeltsin, as he moved into the Kremlin. Yeltsin signed Sergei's pardon in August 1992.

Sergei didn't believe it when they shook him awake and told him to go to the governor. 'Let me sleep,' he said. 'I was up late last night.' But by four that afternoon he was leaving prison with a second-hand suit and the train fare home.

No one told his family that he'd been released five years early. When he walked into his mother's kitchen, on her sixtieth birthday, she stared at him and fainted.

Soon after Sergei got out of jail, a married doctor called Lyuda was so entranced by his poems that she left her husband and three children to live with him. They married. They have a baby son.

When I first met them in 1997, Lyuda had found a way to emigrate to America with her elderly Jewish father and the baby. Sergei wanted to go too, but he couldn't: the US embassy had refused him a visa because of his criminal record.

Sergei was philosophical. After they had gone, he moved across town to his sister's flat. His mother and sister share a pull-out bed in the TV room. Sergei has the small bedroom at the end of the corridor. There is nothing in it but a single bed, a table, a tape recorder and Lyuda's letters and photos from Houston.

Sergei is treated with exaggerated respect in Makhachkala, as someone who suffered unjustly and escaped by a miracle. He enjoys his reputation; back at the Smolensk Penitentiary, he says with a little grin, most of the prisoners have started writing poetry in the hope that they too will get their sentences cut in half.

But he's a monkish oddity in a place and time where money and power, the things he once wanted so much, are uppermost in people's minds.

Sergei is no longer interested. He has published a book of prison verse, but he gives the copies away. He dresses modestly. He only does his typesetting job at the local paper so he can buy food. He often forgets to eat.

Mostly he sings. He's found his voice, and is recording an album of his poems set to music. He plans to name it after the last words of warders to prisoners: 'Get your things and go.'

In the evenings, when the wind blows, he sits in his white-walled room, playing his half-finished tape and trying to think how to join his family in a country where no one will understand anything of his life.

It's hard to imagine today's Sergei bashing a female sturgeon on the head, slitting her open with a knife, washing the roe in a bucket of salted water and straining the eggs into a sieve. He looks too gentle, and too frail. But he still talks about it, with a happy, faraway, reminiscent look. 'You can get the caviar ready even before the fish stops flapping. It takes less than ten minutes,' he says, then adds proudly, 'And *I* could do it in two minutes and twenty seconds.'

He doesn't fish any more, though he still knows both how to gut a sturgeon and how to gentle one by stroking its head. He has eaten the rarest of delicacies, Tsar's Caviar, the pale eggs of albino sturgeon. He talks with love about the fish – the rhythm of their spring migrations down the Volga, the big beluga under the ice in February, Caspian roach when the river rises in March, then bream, pike, wild carp, herring and finally the smaller sevruga and osyotr sturgeon. And he talks with sorrow about the war on the sea today.

'Everyone's massacring the fish: ministers, lowlifes and Azerbaijanis in big boats, all racing to make the biggest profit. No one lets the sturgeon mature or reproduce. No one stops to think that this greed is robbing our children and grandchildren of our greatest treasure. There's never been anything like this — people trawling in military boats through a sea so festooned with nets that the fish don't know how to escape. Soon those fish will exist only in our memories.'

Before I left, I asked Sergei if he'd come to the market and help me choose some good caviar. I thought I might get presents to take back to London. But he shook his head.

'Oh no,' he said. 'I never go near the market or the sea any more. Every now and then I eat a very tiny bit of fish, so as not to lose the taste for it altogether. But caviar makes me sick to my soul.'

I thought he was right. I left empty-handed, but with my head held high.

CHAPTER FIFTEEN

Home

By the time I got on the London plane, Moscow was in hysterical crisis again. Too many greedy people had bought get-rich-quick debt. At the end of August, the government stopped paying for it. The rouble crashed. The people who had kept their money in dollars under the mattress were gloating. But queues of anxious customers waited at the banks for savings that were never coming back. There were three prime ministers in as many weeks. The foreigners were almost all leaving, and people were talking again about a winter of hunger and cold.

'This is exactly how it was when you first came to Russia, isn't it?' Victor said, fangy and ironic as ever. 'Seven years of progress, but here we are back in the same bloody awful situation. You're well out of it. Go home. Don't come back (except to see us). Have a normal life.'

I took his advice. I got happily married, had two children, bought a house in a suburb of London and learned to talk about the weather.

Every now and then, friends come to visit from Russia. Victor has just been from St Petersburg, with delicious, simple presents from Lena – cheeselets, jam, darling doves and salt cucumbers –

and the good news that Mouse is back home at last and starting college. More often, people come from Moscow, and, if they're from the swashbuckling classes, they bring smuggled caviar. Now that I lead a blameless, bourgeois English life, I can hardly wait to taste it again. I know that every spoonful will taste of azart, the manic mood in the Russian soul, and jolt me back for a few mad moments into gazing at the moon and believing anything can happen.

Someone has promised me caviar for my next birthday. I plan to spend the day in my mother's garden, among the sprays of roses behind her house, sharing the caviar out between her, my husband, my little boys and myself, and dreaming dangerous dreams.